THE FOOTSTEPS OF ST PAUL

TRAVELING IN A TRACK BOAT.

FRONTISPIECE.

Footsteps St. Paul. p. 369.

CARTERS, NEW YORK.

THE

FOOTSTEPS OF ST. PAUL

BY THE AUTHOR OF

"MORNING AND NIGHT WATCHES," "THE WORDS OF JESUS," "THE MIND OF JESUS," "FAMILY PRAYERS," "THE GREAT JOURNEY," "WOODCUTTER OF LEBANON,"

ETC., ETC.

NEW YORK:
ROBERT CARTER & BROTHERS,
No. 530 BROADWAY.

1866.

"Should any one ask me to name the man who, of all others, has been the greatest benefactor of our race, I should say, without hesitation, the *Apostle Paul.* His name is the type of human activity the most endless, and at the same time the most useful that history has cared to preserve."—*Monod.*

"May we not believe, in a sense higher than Chrysostom ever dreamt of, that the pulses of that mighty heart are still the pulses of this world's life—still beat in these latter ages with greater force than ever."—*Stanley's Essays on the Apostolical Age.*

PREFACE.

In venturing, in the following pages, to occupy ground which has been so often and so well traversed, it is perhaps superfluous to disclaim any great attempt at originality. The complaint of Chrysostom is now no longer, or *should* no longer, be true, that St Paul is not known by Christians as he ought to be. Much interesting light has been recently thrown by a mass of able authors on the history and character of the Great Apostle; and good service it was thought might be done by translating into a simpler form what had been so admirably supplied for more advanced and thoughtful minds. All the more valuable Commentaries, as was to be expected, are copiously interspersed with learned and valuable disquisitions on questions of great moment, and important in themselves, but which are little fitted to interest and instruct younger students. The writer has endeavoured, therefore, in a course of reading on the Life of St Paul, to cull from "treasures new and old" what would be serviceable to the latter class of readers.

He has to acknowledge his obligations to the following among other works:—Howson and Conybeare's "Life and Epistles of St Paul" (London, 1852), especially in the opening chapters; the less known but able work of Mr Lewin, "Life and Epistles of St Paul" (1851), frequent references to which will attest the amount of obligation; Cave's "Lives of the Apostles" (1676); Stanley's "Sermons and Essays on the Apostolical Age" (1847); Neander's "Planting of the Christian Church;" Olshausen on the Acts of the Apostles; Stackhouse's "History of the Bible" (1764); Benson's "Planting of the Christian Religion" (1750); Barnes on the Acts; Horne's "Introduction;" Blunt's "Sermons on St Paul;" Suetonius' "Lives of the Cæsars;" Josephus' "Wars and Antiquities;" Kitto's "Bible Cyclopædia." Besides these, many books of travel, such as Kinneir's "Travels in Asia Minor" (1818), Beaufort's "Karamania" (1817), Eustace's "Classical Tour in Italy" (Paris, 1837), &c. &c.

While following, however, in the wake of these great explorers, and not ashamed to profit by the lights they have hung out astern, it is hoped there will be found sufficient, in what follows, of independent research and thought, to redeem it from the unattractive character of a mere compilation.

Another reason may be mentioned for giving these pages a permanent form. Amid the vast, the perplexing multiplicity of "Religious books," and "Books for the Young," of all kinds, in the present day, the writer has felt, by experience, the want of a class of volumes suitable for youths (say from ten to seventeen years of age), which would tend, by combining historical and biographical interest with religious instruction, to attract them to a more careful and devout study of the Word of God. What nobler model could be selected in this respect for the youthful mind—what history more replete with stirring interest and noble spiritual lessons, than the Life of "the Scholar of Gamaliel?" It has been truthfully said, that "no romance has ever been written so interesting as the Acts of the Apostles." It is a sort of inspired *Picture Gallery* of stirring scenes and events. The centre portrait, on which the eye rests, or rather the prominent figure reproduced in all the others, is the Great Apostle of the Gentiles. Since it is for youthful readers this volume is mainly designed, the endeavour has been made to sustain throughout, the pictorial and descriptive character of the narrative, which forms not the least charm in the pages of Messrs Howson and Conybeare. The writer will be happy should the perusal of what he has written, lead, at a more advanced stage, to the study of a work in which learning and eloquence have been so successfully brought to bear on the greatest of biographies.

One other sentence to a Preface which has already outrun its due proportions. The author made use of the substance of these notes at a weekly meeting in a rural parish; and the interest manifested in hearing them has formed an additional inducement to commit them in their present shape to the press. The auxiliary of a large map the reader cannot enjoy, in which he was able to trace the "Footsteps of St Paul;" but it is hoped that this want will be in no small measure compensated by the series of wood engravings illustrative of scenes and incidents in these "oft journeyings."

December 1854.

*** When the whole of these pages were written, and one half were finally revised, the writer obtained the last volume of (alas! now) the late Dr Kitto's "Scripture Readings"—the "Apostles and Early Church"—in the preface to which, he finds that esteemed and lamented author acknowledges similar obligations to many of those English works to which he has been so largely indebted.

Although the same ground has, in some respects, been trodden, yet his object—to write a *simple consecutive* history of St Paul—has sufficiently prevented collision; and any similarities that may occur, must only award to a less skilful hand the credit of discrimination in what gleaning was best from those ample storehouses to which both have been led.

CONTENTS.

CHAPTER I.

The Youth.

"Sweetly wild! sweetly wild!
Were the scenes that charm'd me when a child.
Rocks—grey rocks, with their tracery dark,
Leaping rills, like the diamond spark,
Torrent voices thundering by,
When the pride of the vernal floods swell'd high.
* * * * *
It was sweet to sit till the sun laid down
At the gate of the west his golden crown.
Sweetly wild! sweetly wild!
Were the scenes that charm'd me when a child."

MRS SIGOURNEY

If you look at the map of Asia, you will see, to the north-west of Palestine, washed by the blue waters of the Mediterranean, the country of Asia Minor. In the south-east corner of it, running parallel with the coast, are the Alps of that region—the high mountain range of the Taurus. As the snow which covers their summits is melted by the sun's heat, many rivulets flow down to water and refresh the thirsty plains below. A stream, larger than the rest, is seen to dash its way, first through the rocks and valleys of the upper regions, and then to wind its dark and sluggish*

* The name of the river now is "Kara Su," or "Black water," and it must have greatly changed its course, as it is now more than a mile from the modern Tarsoos.

course through the rich level country bordering on the sea.

The name of the river is the Cydnus, and of the province Cilicia. You may try to form a picture to yourselves of the animated scenes on its banks at the time of which I am going to write. Women coming down to fetch water, with veils over their faces, and pitchers on their heads; shepherds playing on their reeds, with their flocks of goats and sheep browsing around them. Now and then, bands or caravans of merchants from distant parts, with camels bearing spices and wools, are glad to pause at mid-day, under the shade of the palm-trees which cast their beautiful reflection in the stream, and there get refreshment ere they pursue their journey.

Following this river in its course from the mountains, you come to the walls of the large town of TARSUS, which, at the same period, formed the capital or chief city of the country. It was beautifully situated among luxuriant gardens; the houses were ranged in the form of a half-circle on either side of the river, giving it something of the shape of the wings of a bird. If you had gone inside its walls, you would have seen a great variety of faces and dress, and heard spoken many different languages. Sometimes you would meet with native Cilicians; at other times you could not mistake the features of Jews, or Greek merchants, or haughty Romans. Like the greater portion of the known world, Cilicia and Tarsus had fallen into the hands of the Emperor Cæsar. Roman soldiers would be seen now and then pacing up and down its streets; Roman ships were sailing up the Cydnus into its harbour, and with Roman names and signs painted on them, filling its docks. It enjoyed privileges, however, peculiar to several Roman towns. It was one of those cities which was called *Libera* or *free*. It was ruled by its own magistrates, and had its own laws, just as is the case with some modern cities on the continent of Europe, such as Frankfort-on-the-Maine, Hamburg, Lubeck, Bremen, and others. These, for special reasons, while remaining under the protection of Prussia and Austria, have an independent government of their own, as Tarsus had under the broad shadow of imperial Rome.

In other and more important respects, Tarsus was "no mean city." One of the three great universities, or seats of learning, in the world, at that time, was within its gates; those of Athens and Alexandria being the other two. Many of the young men trained at the Tarsus schools were found afterwards at Rome, tutors in the highest families of the state, and even in the palace of the emperor on the Palatine. Indeed, at this very time, a philosopher named Nestor, who had been tutor to Marcellus, the nephew of Augustus, was ruler of the city.

Along the banks of the Cydnus there was a lawn of grass, with shady trees similar to our modern parks. Aged philosophers and learned men, with their long beards, might be seen walking up and down engaged in deep thought or earnest discussion; while youths of the university, at their holiday hours, were busy practising those athletic games which were so famous among the Greeks. I daresay the young Tarsians would have among themselves their own trials of strength—running, leaping, wrestling, boxing. They would have their own mimic crowns of olive or laurel to put on the brow of youthful victors; and doubtless would often talk about the day when they would be able to go to Corinth, and take part in its well-known contests.*

It was in a house in this Cilician city that "Saul of Tarsus" was born. People go to a great distance to visit the birthplaces of famous men. There are spots on the earth's surface which will be ever memorable as being the scenes of the childhood of Cæsar and Alexander, Luther and Melancthon, Howard and Wilberforce. We shall find afterwards, that the little reed-thatched cottage, where Romulus the founder of Rome was born, was preserved sacred and untouched among the splendid palaces on the Palatine. What an interest must gather around the birthplace of one who, in the highest spiritual sense, was hero, scholar, philanthropist, all in one,—the greatest of those "great men" who have left their "footprints on the sands of time!"

I remember looking down several years ago in Switzerland on the little rill flowing out of that vast wall of ice, "the Rhone glacier." What interest was connected with it as the commencement of that giant river which sweeps past the walls of Lyons and Avignon, and waters the most fertile provinces of France! From Tarsus and its snow-capped Taurus, we watch the first tiny rill of a more glorious river, "the streams whereof," in every land and under every clime, have "made glad the city of God."

I cannot tell you the exact year in which Saul's birth took place. It was, however, at a most memorable era of the world's history. When he was lying

* See Strabo, the geographer, who lived in the same age of which we write.—Book xiv., w. . ii.

an infant in his cradle in Tarsus, there were other little children training up by God in other places for great duties and great services.* On the banks of a solitary lake in the land of Judea, there were a number of youths about that same time going out day after day with their fathers fishing in their boats, or helping them to mend their nets on the beach. These were afterwards to become the apostles of Christianity. There was a little child who was recently born in the old city of Hebron, a son of a priest, who was ere long to appear as a great preacher to prepare the way of the Lord, saying, "Repent, for the kingdom of heaven is at hand;" and more interesting and solemn still, while Saul was an infant boy at Tarsus, there was a wondrous Being in an infant's form growing up at Nazareth,—it was the holy child Jesus, the promised Messiah! Little did the proud world know the worth that was contained in these two distant homes—two helpless children unknown to one another; but the one was the Son of the eternal God, the Redeemer of mankind; the other, His greatest minister and apostle.

As regards even the political history of the world, the period of Saul's birth was an eventful one. Augustus, the greatest of the Roman emperors, was on the throne of the Cæsars; his vast dominion extended over a large portion of the human race; the wealth of his capital was unbounded; its temples were filled with the spoils of conquered nations; the ruins of vast buildings, aqueducts, arches, bridges, and harbours, remain to this day, to tell the grandeur of what was called by the poets "the golden age." Alas! it was but a painted glory; like the whited sepulchres of the

* Howson and Conybeare, vol. i. p. 63.

prophets, "within was full of corruption and wickedness.' God seemed to read mankind a lesson what a poor world this would be, with all the power and wealth of Rome, and all the learning and wisdom of Greece, if it had not the gospel of Jesus to make men holy and happy. "The world by wisdom," the boasted wisdom of this its greatest and wisest epoch, "knew not God;" the religion of Rome, such as it was, had become a mere form; the palaces of the nobles were filled with vice and crime; the simple morals of her common people were gone; and thousands of slaves from her conquered provinces were pining in the hardest drudgery. It was at this mournful period, when the grossest spiritual gloom had settled over the nations, that the great Sun of Righteousness, and His brightest attendant star, arose.

You would doubtless like to know all about Paul's parents—what his father's trade was, and whether he was a rich man or a poor man. We are not told. Most probably he was neither the one nor the other, but a respectable merchant or trader, engaged like other Jews in traffic with the cities on the coast of the Mediterranean. We may conclude, however, that he could not have been in straitened circumstances, from his being able to bestow on his son an education at Jerusalem. In this respect, young Saul was placed in a more favourable position than other three apostolic men who lived 1500 years after him, and who, both in their mission and character, most nearly resembled him of any since his time. We read that "the Reformer Zuingle issued from the cabin of a shepherd of the Alps; Melancthon, the theologian of the Reformation, from the shop of an armourer; and Luther from the hut of a poor miner."* This last (the great German Reformer) is perhaps the individual who, of all others, is most worthy to be placed side by side with the Apostle of the Gentiles, and we shall have more than once occasion to compare them together.

With regard to Saul's father, we know, from the letters his son afterwards wrote, that he was very strict in his religion. Though he had changed his native country, he had not changed his creed. He still remained a strict *Pharisee,* and brought up his little boy as such. You know that the Pharisees were the most rigid of all the sects among the Jews. They wore long dresses, and used long prayers; they fasted, and made a great show about religion; they loved to be seen of men, and to get the praise of men more than the praise of God. Many of them, however, I believe, were good people—tried to *be* good and to *do* good, and brought up their children in the way of truth. I would be inclined to think that Saul's father was of this number. He tells us afterwards that "he served God from his *forefathers.*" This would seem to imply that not only his father but his grandfather, and farther back still, were strict Pharisees, serving the God of Israel in their synagogue, in the midst of that Gentile city. We are led to infer, too, that one of these ancestors of his had been a brave man, and was rewarded for his courage; for they had received in some way the honour of Roman citizens, which Paul himself inherited, and which we shall afterwards find proved on many occasions very serviceable to him. It has been a question with many how this citizenship was

* D'Aubigné's *Reformation* book ii. chap. i.

obtained. I have just told you that the great houses and palaces at Rome were supplied with numerous slaves, and these we know, moreover, were principally obtained from the coasts of Asia Minor. It is possible that Saul's father or grandfather may have been in this way purchased, during their youth, by some Roman. Their master may further have taken a fancy to them, and as a reward, perhaps, of good conduct, have bestowed upon one or other their freedom. I by no means venture to say that this is the accurate explanation. I merely state it as one of the more likely of the suppositions which learned writers have made regarding the possession of this family privilege.

We have spoken of Saul's father — who was his mother? Most children who, on growing up to manhood, have become good and great, have owed very much to their mothers. And it would have been interesting to know who Saul's was. But there is nothing in any place said about her. Perhaps she may have been taken early away from him, and he left in his infancy a motherless little orphan; or, perhaps the tears may have fallen fast from her eyes when she heard, in future years, that her son had deserted his sect and his creed, and become a disciple of Jesus; or who can tell (may we not speak of the barely possible hope?) that, before he became "Paul the aged," he was allowed to sit by his mother's dying pillow, and point her sinking eye to the "Lamb of God, who taketh away the sin of the world?"

He had, at least, one sister.* We may picture to ourselves in thought the two little ones in their early years, seated on their father's, or, it may be, their

* Acts xxiii. 16.

mother's-knee, hearing from their lips about all the wondrous deeds of their ancestors. Sometimes their young minds would be turned to the story of Moses in the ark of bulrushes, and the awful plagues of Egypt; at other times, to the passage through the Red Sea, and how Pharaoh and his hosts were drowned in its waves. At others, they would love to listen to the tale of the wanderings of their fathers in the desert—the arrival in Canaan—and the glories of David and Solomon. We may imagine them hushed to sleep, night after night, with some of the sweet songs of Zion which the great Psalmist King had played upon his harp, or the poor captives had sung by the rivers of Babylon. The Jews were strictly enjoined by Moses, in the 6th and 11th chapters of Deuteronomy, to teach their children the law of God. Five was the age when they generally began to read the law. We have every reason to think that Saul's parents were not slow either in obeying the divine command, or following the usual practice of their countrymen, making their little boy "from a child to know the Holy Scriptures," which were afterwards (in a way they never dreamt of) to "make him wise unto salvation."

Our young readers, then, may imagine "little Saul" in his Hebrew home. Many a league separated him from the city of Jerusalem; but he was not the less brought up "an Hebrew of the Hebrews." As was the custom with Jewish children, he had been "circumcised the eighth day" after his birth, and then received the name of *Saul.* You will not wonder at this being a favourite name in the tribe of Benjamin, to which he belonged, when you remember that the first king whom the Jewish people chose was "Saul the Benjamite." Some indeed have thought he was called "Saul," because the Hebrew word for *Saul* literally means "*the desired*," or "*prayed for*," and that he was named so from being the first-born child of his parents, and given to them in answer to prayer.* Be this as it may, let us think of him in his infancy, a little boy playing, perhaps, as Timothy did, around the feet of another "grandmother Lois and mother Eunice," and they delighting to watch the progress of his mind as his infant lips began the first attempts at speech. What *did* he speak? What was his language? We have reason to believe, from what is told us in the Acts of the Apostles, that he was taught to speak both in Greek and in Hebrew. The Greek was probably the tongue he was *most* in the habit of using. It was very much then what French is now, the language known more than any other among the nations of Europe. It is worth observing, that when at any time he refers in after life to the Old Testament, he quotes the Septuagint,† or Greek version of it, and not the Hebrew. But at the same time, he was far from ignorant of Hebrew—the language of his fathers. Though Greek was chiefly spoken in Tarsus, the Jews there never forgot to teach their children their native tongue. They generally had many friends and kinsfolk in Palestine who came from time to time to visit them (Paul, for instance, had himself a nephew at Jerusalem‡), and with these they could converse only in Hebrew.

It was the practice always among the Jews to in-

* Neander's *Planting of the Christian Church*, p. 80.

† This is the oldest translation of the Old Testament. It was so called from its having been translated by 70 learned men.

‡ Acts xxiii. 16.

struct their sons in early youth in some trade. This was not the case among the very poor only, but with those of a better class. It was a common proverb among them—"If a man does not teach his son a trade, he teaches him to steal;" and we know that several learned Rabbis, whose writings have come down to us, were brought up with the knowledge of some common business. "We have an instance of a great and eminent critic who was a carpenter, another an iron-founder, with many similar examples."* The custom was a wise and prudent one. It was to prevent them ever falling into idleness, and to enable them, if they ever were in straits, to have the means of earning their bread. Saul's father chose for him a very natural occupation. He taught him, or sent him to learn, to make "*tents*." This would seem to have been a favourite trade in Cilicia; indeed the material of which these tents were made was called *Cilicium*, from the name of the province. The goat was an animal that was common there, as in many other parts of the East, and from its hair, which was long and beautiful, these tents were constructed. Occasionally it would seem that they were made of the hides as well as the hair; and hence an old father of the Church, in speaking of Saul's occupation, calls him sometimes a tent-stitcher, and sometimes a worker in leather.† We shall, by and by, find how fortunate it was that the young Jew of Tarsus had thus early learned this useful trade. It relieved him, for many years of his after life, from a state of poverty and dependence. Many a midnight hour found him hard at work at his web of goats' hair, for he "laboured night and day, that he might be

* Blunt's *Sermons on St Paul.*

† See Olshausen on Acts.

chargeable to no man."* I may just add, that this hair-cloth, which was a thick stuff like *felt*, seems to have had the property, if not of keeping out wet, at all events of not rotting soon under the influence of damp or moisture. It served very much the purposes which our modern *gutta percha* and oilcloth do. It was employed in making coats and coverings for those who were much exposed to the variable weather in these mountain districts. Sailors used it, too, for bad weather at sea, and when we come, long after this, to describe Paul tossed for fourteen days and nights, amid black skies and rain-torrents, we may think of the sailors and crew around him, plying the pumps and reefing the sails with their Cilician hair-coats on.

Very possibly this manufacture formed the greater part of the merchandise of his father in the market towns around; and it is striking to hear from travellers who have visited these countries in our own times, that at present, during harvest, the rich corn fields may be seen dotted with the very same goats'-hair tents, the peasants and reapers living in them till the harvest work is over.†

We may imagine, then, the young apostle, when he was the age of many of my readers, spending his happy boyhood in his Tarsus home. We are apt always to think of Paul as the grown-up man—an apostle—not perhaps advanced in life, but still with the marks of hard toil, and "the care of all the churches" on his furrowed brow; but we must remember he had once a boyhood like ourselves, his boyish amusements, and occupations, and pleasures.

* 1 Thess. i. 9. † Beaufort's *Karamania*, p. 233.

The youth of the Reformer Luther, which we have already spoken of in connexion with his, was formed amid much less beautiful scenery. The banks of the Wipper, and the plains of Mansfield in Saxony, were poor and tame compared with the snowy cliffs of the Taurus range, and the verdant banks of the Cydnus. Still more cheerless, in other respects, was the infancy of the young apostle of Germany. He tells us, that often he had to follow his father and mother to the forest to gather bundles of sticks, which they afterwards carried on their backs to the village and sold, to relieve them from their extreme poverty. Even at school he met with anything but kindness. His master beat him fifteen times successively in one day!

We are led to think of a sunnier morning of life in connexion with Saul. We love to follow him in thought in his boyish rambles amid the beautiful scenery in the midst of which his childhood was cast. We can imagine him gazing often and again on the noble hills which rose like wall above wall behind the city, their white tops sparkling in the rays of the sun. He and his sister would love to watch, from the flat roof of their house, the deep shadows chasing one another across the mountain sides, or, perhaps, on a longer holiday, they would go and climb part of their craggy slopes, and look down on the lovely plains beneath. Often, I daresay, they would like to wander up by the banks of the Cydnus, as you see them in the picture at the beginning of this chapter, to watch the leap of the waterfall a mile north from the town, which grew very large after the melting of the snows in the mountains.*

* "The extreme coldness of this celebrated river is said to have occa-

We may think at other times of the Jewish boy, in company with his hardier playmates, going, on those greater holidays when all work in the city and schools was stopped, to the gymnasium to witness the runners and wrestlers in the athletic games. We cannot wonder if we should come afterwards, in reading some of Paul's writings, to find these contests which his childhood had looked upon lingering in his memory. Or, to change the scene, we may imagine him, during the day, in some Jewish school near the Sanhedrim; the circle of black-eyed scholars, with their white cloaks, seated on the ground (as was the custom) round about their Jewish teacher, learning them to read and to write, and getting by heart portions of their sacred law.

We read of Martin Luther, when he was of a similar age, probably a little younger, that a young man of Mansfield, called Nicholas Emler, was in the habit of taking him to the house of George Emilius, and returned to fetch him thence. It would, in all likelihood, be the same with young Saul. A slave or servant would be employed to conduct him to school and wait to bring him safe home again; according to his own beautiful comparison, when he speaks, in one of his epistles, of "the law" being like "the *slave* who takes us to the school of Christ."* Once more, we may picture him, at other times, perhaps at night, when the day's duties were past, seated by a blazing fire at his father's

sioned the death of Frederick Barbarossa, and to have proved nearly fatal to Alexander. We found the water undoubtedly cold, but not more so than that of the other rivers which carry down the melted snow of Mount Taurus, and we bathed in it without feeling any pernicious effects."—Beaufort, p. 266.

* Gal. iii. 24. See Conybeare and Howson, vol. i. p. 54.

feet, giving his help to complete some goats'-hair tents they were wishful to have finished, either in good time for harvest, or in order that they might be able to leave as soon as possible, according to the universal custom, for their abode in the mountains, to escape the burning heat of the summer plains.

There would probably be several other schools in Tarsus, but they were Gentile ones. Saul would be brought up, not perhaps with a determined hatred to the youth attending these, as many young Israelites were, but at least with no friendly feeling. As it is with the Jews to this day all over the world, the children of Abraham would dwell in Tarsus "alone," and not be "reckoned" among the rest of the citizens. The young apostle would get what other religious knowledge he possessed from the reading of the law, Sabbath after Sabbath, in the synagogue; and with reference to his expectations regarding the Saviour promised to his fathers, he must have been taught, like others, to look for some great temporal sovereign who would drive the Romans out of Judea, and make it once more a glorious kingdom, as in the days of David and Solomon. Little did he think, at that very moment, the Messiah was toiling unknown and unnoticed as a carpenter in a workshop of Nazareth.

CHAPTER II.

The Scholar.

Fair boy! the wand'rings of thy way
  It is not mine to trace,
Through buoyant youth's exulting day
  Or manhood's bolder race.

What discipline thy heart may need,
  What clouds may veil thy sun,
The eye of God alone can read,
  And let His will be done.

The historian of the Reformation, in speaking of the boyhood of Luther, tells us that his father had, in a little time, saved as much money by hard labour as enabled him to erect two furnaces at his native Mansfield; and from the profits arising from his new trade, he began to think of a better education for his boy. "He wished to make his son a man of learning; the boy's remarkable aptness and persevering industry inspired John (the honest miner) with lively hopes. When Martin, therefore, in 1497, had attained the age of fourteen, he resolved to part with him, and send him to Magdeburg to the school of the Franciscans. His mother was obliged to consent, and Martin prepared to quit his father's house." *

Such a time had now arrived for young Saul of Tarsus. He had got what education a Jewish school in the city of his birth could afford. He might doubtless have carried on his studies much further in the celebrated Tarsus university; but his father would probably, for the reason given at the close of last chapter, be averse to his boy mixing with Gentile youths. He might be afraid, lest in a heathen seminary any influence might be used to abate his love and reverence for the faith of his ancestors; he therefore determined to send him away for some years to complete his education, probably sharing in the ambition of the humble miner of Germany to make him a distinguished scholar; or rather, what to a Jew was the highest of all honours, that he should become a scribe or doctor of the law.

I daresay some of my young readers may remember with what sorrowful feelings they found themselves for the first time going far away from the happy scenes of their infancy to a strange place, and among strange faces and friends. I doubt not Saul, who, when he was an older man, chided those who would "make him weep, and break his heart,"† had his own mingled thoughts in going from that happy mountain home where the morning of life had been spent. But there were joyous feelings also at the prospect of this long journey; he was going not so much away *from* home as *to* home; for although he never had seen it, Jerusalem was always a happy "homeword" to every Jew. From their earliest childhood they were taught to feel

* D'Aubigné's *History*, book ii. † Acts xxi. 13.

it as such The gladdest day of their lives was that on which they were able to say, "Our feet shall stand within thy gates, O Jerusalem!" Every thought about Palestine, its hills, valleys, cities, villages, were holy thoughts. Often would the Jews of Asia Minor, as they returned year after year from the feasts, pause at Saul's father's dwelling, and lodge for the night, before crossing the heights of Mount Taurus to their own homes. While seated there, we may well believe the young listener would often and again have heard them speak of the glories of Zion and the temple. When his school-days at Tarsus, therefore, were about to be concluded, we may imagine, in such an ardent mind as his, with what feelings he would hear his father telling him—"I am going ere long to take you to see all the glorious things spoken of the city of God!"

It must have been when he was between the age of eleven and fourteen that Saul set out to his new abode. We cannot suppose it likely that one so young would be allowed to go *alone*. His father would himself most probably be too glad to have the opportunity of visiting the city of his people, and would delight to be the first to point out the wonders of the land of promise to his dear boy.* Neither is it likely, when they were so near the sea, that they would attempt the long journey by land. If you look again to the map, you will see how easily they could sail by vessel. We may imagine the Hebrew youth bidding an affectionate farewell to his old friends at Tarsus; his little sister, it may be, accompanying him to the ship in the docks, and, with a tear in her eye, following him, after the anchor was weighed, till he was lost from her sight amid the other

* Howson and Conybeare, vol. i. p. 56.

vessels that crowded the harbour. We may imagine him sailing slowly down the river, which, near the town, was still and motionless; some hardy Phœnician captain at the helm, perhaps, struck with the sharp and intelligent features of the Jewish boy, delighting to give him his first ideas of a seafaring life. We may suppose him wandering on the deck until the sun has set behind the mountains of his childhood. They have now reached the mouth of the Cydnus, twelve miles below Tarsus. Here the river swells out, before joining the sea, into a large basin or lake, which by art had been made into docks, and was called the port of Tarsus.* By and by, they have passed the promontory which encloses it, and the silvery moon has risen on the great wilderness of waters all around.

Another day finds them gliding along the waves of the Mediterranean. Its surface may have been the calm, deep blue for which it is remarkable, with an unclouded sky looking down into it. Or the young voyager may have had the words of the Psalmist of Israel often in his mind—"They that go down to the sea in ships, that do business in great waters; these see the works of the Lord, and His wonders in the deep. For He commandeth, and raiseth the stormy wind, which lifteth up the waves thereof. They mount up to the heaven, they go down again to the depths. . . . They reel to and fro, and stagger like a drunken man, and are at their wit's end. . . . He maketh the storm a calm, so that the waves thereof are still."†

"See!" we may imagine his father saying to him, as he points his eye to something in the far east, "seest thou yonder white mountain peaks like our own

* Strabo, quoted by Lewin. † Ps. cvii. 23–29.

Taurus?—these are the heights of Lebanon;" and the boy's thoughts wander up and down the hazy steeps, till he imagines he sees them clothed with dark cedars, and then he remembers he is sailing on the very waters by which Solomon got these giants of the forest floated on rafts for the building of the temple. No scene in the holy land can have undergone so little change since the days of Saul as the appearance of this "goodly mountain." The picture given, therefore, by a recent writer, of the view of Lebanon from the sea, describes with accuracy what the eye of the youth of Tarsus then gazed on. "At sea the mountain rises before the spectator as a whole, and the eye can pass leisurely from its snowy peaks to the rich gardens at its bottom. The spectator never wearies in gazing on the goodly prospect before him. The undulating line of its promontories and bays extends for many a mile along the coast. On the mountain itself terrace rises above terrace, displaying at once the industry of the inhabitants, and the fertility of the mountain. Villages, with their flat-roofed houses, are seen sweetly placed amidst groves of vines and mulberries, or plantations of sugar-cane, oranges, and lemons."*

But they have passed Lebanon—its heights are receding in the distance, and by and by they come to a bold mountain, with rocky front jutting out into the sea. "This," his father would again say, "is Mount Carmel,—yonder is where our father Elijah stood. From this very sea he brought up his barrels of salt water to pour into his dug trenches, and from yonder top the smoke of his sacrifice ascended to heaven!" Shepherds, who were attracted to Carmel by the "ex-

* See Wylie's *Modern Judea*, p. 70.

cellency" of its pastures, may have been looking down at the moment from its heights of pine and olive on the lonely vessel that was now sailing by its base. Little did they know the value of the youngest member of that crew, or the influence that one life in its manhood was yet to exercise on the world. As little did the young voyager himself foresee with what different feelings he would make the *same* voyage in after times! He was now full of boyish glee—a bright world before him! Forty years later, a care-worn missionary, his back marked with scourging, and his hands hardened with toil, would be seen, as he bounded over these same waves, lifting up his dimmed eye, not to Carmel nor to Lebanon, but to the "everlasting hills," from whence alone came his aid.

A few hours more, and the sails are lowered. With a joyous heart, Saul sees the land coming nearer and nearer; they are within sound of Jewish voices on the shore; and entering among many vessels into a spacious harbour, they find themselves safely moored, probably in the newly-built town of Cesarea, one of the last and greatest of the works of Herod. The Hebrew boy is treading the sacred soil of Judea.*

Soon he commences the remaining land journey. We need not pause to describe it,—the more so as the last of its many interesting scenes casts all the others into the shade. We may think of the two travellers standing on the eastern slope of a gentle eminence, where for the first time the glories of Jerusalem open before them.—What three-topped hill is this, its

* We need not say that, in describing Saul's journey, only a *probable* account of his route, and the incidents that took place in it, can be given. In this we have followed Howson and Conybeare in their interesting narration—pp. 57, 58

sides partially clothed with wood, rising immediately behind the city? It is the green Mount of Olives—the same mountain across which old King David went weeping and bare-foot, and which was ere long to be trodden (if it had not been trodden already) by Holier footsteps. What stately roof is that, which seems like a sheet of solid gold glittering in the sun, with pillars and porticoes all round about it? It is Solomon's famous temple, with the holy of holies,—where the God of Israel dwelt in visible glory! Perhaps at the moment Saul saw it, the smoke of the morning or evening sacrifice was ascending. And what is that, towering high on the right, nearer where they are standing—a noble pile of building, with ranges of pillars, and surrounded with lovely gardens? It is the royal palace—the same in which David and Solomon once lived—where the latter erected his house of the forest of Lebanon, and which King Herod had now rebuilt in more than its former splendour. Soon the western gateway is passed, and the feet of the young Cilician boy are standing within "the joy of the whole earth"—"the city of the Great King."

Without pausing to describe more particularly the sacred spot which Saul was now for several years to make his home, let us at once accompany him to the place where most of his time was to be spent. It was at a celebrated school in Jerusalem. There were several of these within the city famous for their learning. But one of the chief (if not *the* very chief) was that of Hillel, which dated its origin about sixty years before the birth of Christ. Hillel, the founder, is supposed to be the father of old Simeon, who took the child Jesus in his arms in the temple, and blessed him.

The grandson of Hillel, and probably the son of Simeon, was a very learned and eminent Rabbi of the name of Gamaliel. To shew in what esteem his learning was held by the Jews, we are told that they designated him "the beauty of the law." We know from the Acts of the Apostles that "he was had in reputation of all the people."* We have reason to believe he was a candid, upright, honourable man—amiable in himself, and beloved by all who were acquainted with him. There is a tradition which says that he was afterwards converted to Christianity by the preaching of Peter and John; but this does not seem likely. Indeed, it is to be feared he lived and died a zealous Pharisee. Had it been otherwise, we could not well credit what is said in the Targum, that another learned pupil, named Onkelos, spent seventy pounds of incense at his tomb, out of respect for his memory.

Such was Saul's teacher. We may follow the pupil to the school, where, morning after morning, he was found "at the feet of Gamaliel," along with a group of other ardent students like himself. Among his other school-fellows was very possibly Barnabas, who was, in future years, his travelling companion and fellow-labourer; also, the sons of Gamaliel, Jesus and Simon—the former of whom became high priest. The learned teacher, with his quick eye and long flowing beard, is seated in the centre. At one time he instructs them in Greek, at another in Hebrew; more seldom, perhaps, in Latin. By far the greater portion of their time is devoted to the well-used scroll he has by him, out of which he teaches the Jewish law. He explains its precepts and promises, its ceremonies, pro-

* Acts v. 34.

phecies, and types; although the Rabbi, with all his wisdom, had his own eyes blinded to the greatest of the truths he was trying to unfold.

It was fortunate Saul had a liberal instructor like Gamaliel, who did not object to impart to his scholars a knowledge of the Greek language. Many others in Jerusalem, at that time, would on no account have done so. In the case of Saul, it formed a very important part of his training for the great work of his future life, in preaching to the Gentiles. Greek, as I have already said, was then understood and spoken in many countries of the Roman empire; and we find him afterwards, when, on different occasions, he addresses Athenians, Corinthians, and Cretans, making quotations to them from their own poets, shewing that he must have been familiar with their writings. We can trace, also, in his future epistles and letters, the peculiar way in which he had been trained by Gamaliel to argue. When we think of such Jewish schools, we must not imagine them similar to our own, or our own colleges, where the master or professor only is the examinator. The Jewish doctor encouraged the youths under him to question and cross-question one another—he himself, too, being asked by them in turn about anything they did not understand. It was a school for *debate*, for, in this way, the Jews considered the minds of their youth to be best trained for sharpness and acuteness. A question was started, objections were raised to it, and then these objections were answered. If you look to the Epistle to the Romans, you will see more than one example of how Paul used this form of debate or dialogue for the defence and explanation of Christian doctrine. "What advantage, then, hath the Jew, and what profit is there of circumcision?" * "What shall we say, then? Shall we continue in sin, that grace may abound?" †

We have good reason to imagine that the young Tarsus stranger, as well as his companions in the school of Hillel, loved their master, and listened with attention and reverence to his instructions. The quick mind of Saul grew more in love every day with the law and the religion of his fathers. As he himself tells us, "I made progress in the Jews' religion above many my equals (those of the same age and standing with me) in my own nation, being more exceedingly zealous of the traditions of my fathers." ‡ The thorough study of the ancient Scriptures in such schools accounts for the readiness he shews in his after life in quoting passages from the Old Testament. Writers have noted no less than eighty-eight quotations, one half of which seem to have been from memory. I doubt not the eye of the old Rabbi, as he surveyed the little countenances that surrounded him, often fell with peculiar hope upon that of the Cilician youth. Perhaps he expected that, when his own head was laid in the grave, the young Tarsian would take his place as a great Jewish doctor. But "God's thoughts are not as man's thoughts." That studious boy was training for a nobler use!

The thought may occur—did Saul at this time, when he was in Jerusalem, never meet any of those with whom he was afterwards to be joined in such sacred bonds? Did he never see any of the young fishermen of Galilee, when they came with their fathers and friends to attend the great annual feasts? Did he

* Romans iii. 1.
† Rom. vi. 1. See also Rom iii. 9, iv. 1, ix. 14; Lewin, vol. i. p. 11.
‡ Gal. i. 14.

never see the young Baptist, before his voice was heard in the deserts of Jordan? or, more than all, did he never see the blessed Saviour—"the holy child Jesus"—as he came, year after year, with Joseph and Mary, and mingled in the crowds at the temple? Most probably he *did* see one or all; but if so, they were unknown to one another. It has been thought by some, that Gamaliel was more than probably one of the doctors in the temple whom Jesus, when he was twelve years of age, astonished by asking questions. If this be the case, possibly Saul may have been there in company with his teacher, and heard the tender voice of one who was afterwards to claim him as his most "chosen vessel."* But, be this as it may, the occasion passed by; and we shall end this chapter by leaving our readers to imagine the future apostle, seated, year after year, at the feet of his instructor, having his head stored with learning, and his faculties ripened and matured, for great duties and great services, which at the time he little dreamt of.

What a bright future must have seemed to his companions, and perhaps to himself, to be opening before him! God had given him, as his inheritance, the greatest of all wealth—the wealth of intellect—the riches of a cultivated mind. He was active, bold, eloquent, virtuous, learned. He gives every promise of future greatness. The army of Titus is, in a few brief years, to be with their battering-rams at the gates of Jerusalem; and if we were asked to point out one in the whole nation of Israel, who gives best promise of acting the hero in that terrible conflict—heading the ranks of his desponding countrymen, and keep

* Acts ix. 15.

ing back, for a while at least, the Roman eagles from their prey—we should, without doubt, point to that quick-eyed youth who has battle-fields marked out for him, nobler far than Roman valour ever contested. A conquest is to be his, greater than the world's greatest victors. Meanwhile, he is learning lessons of bitterest hatred to that truth which he was afterwards to proclaim with a giant's voice. He was now taught to boast of nothing, save the traditions of his fathers—the pride of his birth—the distinction of his sect—the glory of his nation. We know not if Gamaliel lived to read in a letter, sent by this boy of Tarsus, in after years, to some poor Christians, "*God forbid that I should **glory***, SAVE IN THE CROSS OF THE LORD JESUS CHRIST!"

CHAPTER III

The Persecutor.

"Foremost and nearest to His throne,
By perfect robes of triumph known,
And likest Him in look and tone—
The holy Stephen kneels."

Christian Year.

We must now pass over a considerable number of years. The period of Saul's boyhood was over, and he was entering on manhood at the age of thirty or upwards. He had probably, many years before this, left Gamaliel's school at Jerusalem, and was once more at Tarsus, pursuing in private, or in the schools there, different branches of knowledge. We may take for granted, that, before leaving the Holy City, he had received the lowest "*degree*" of learning, which was known among the Jews by the term "*Rab;*" and perhaps, too, from being so distinguished among his fellow-students, he may have received the next highest title, viz., that of "*Rabbi.*" There was only one higher than these, which was reserved for seven individuals who had attained to a great age, as well as to great learning, such as Gamaliel; it was called "*Rabbah*" or

"*Rabban*." This, also, the young Tarsian scholar might, with confidence, have looked forward to, had he not learned, ere long, to "count all these titles of earthly wisdom as *loss*," for the excellency of a higher "knowledge."

If we have dismissed in silence twenty years of his life, it is not because these years have no interest to us. They were, indeed, the most eventful time in all the 6000 years of this world's history. The Saviour of mankind had lived in them. He had lived his holy life, and died, on Calvary's cross, his bitter death. A new dispensation had been ushered in upon the earth —"old things had passed away, and all things were made new."

We may imagine the future apostle, then at the age of thirty or upwards, once more at his native Tarsus. He never makes mention, in any of his writings, of the public ministry of Christ, or of his miracles and discourses. It is not probable, therefore, that he had continued to reside at Jerusalem after finishing his education. Had he done so, it is reasonable to think he would often have spoken, like John, of what "he had *heard*, and seen with his *eyes*, and looked upon"—the mighty works and the holy words of Him who "spake as never man spake."* If we are correct in supposing that he had once more gone to his native city, many changes, doubtless, had occurred since we last found him there, while yet a boy, climbing the heights of Mount Taurus, or watching the foam as it dashed over the falls of the Cydnus. His sister had now grown to be a

* We follow in this the view adopted by most, although there are other opinions advanced by learned writers as to the reason of Paul's silence on this subject.

woman, and was probably married—the mother of one we shall find afterwards mentioned towards the close of the apostle's life. The quiet of his home, too, must have been disturbed, during his absence, by civil war. A Roman historian tells us that Piso, a former governor of Syria, made an attempt to conquer the country for himself—that, for this purpose, he gathered the warlike chiefs of Mount Taurus together, and pitched his hostile camp at the town of Celenderis, not far from the mouth of the Cydnus.* We have reason to believe, however, that, before the return of Gamaliel's pupil, all was quiet again.

Let us leave him for a little under his father's roof, busily carrying on his studies in Greek and Hebrew—or, from time to time, making use of his learning in the synagogue—while we glance at the position and prospect of that Church called "Christian," of which he was ere long to be the great apostle.

The Lord Jesus Christ had risen from the grave, and appeared again and again to his disciples. He had taken them up, after forty days, to the top of the Mount of Olives, and, while talking with them "concerning the kingdom," and pronouncing a parting blessing, "a cloud received him out of their sight." The sorrowing eleven were left alone, and returned with sad hearts to Jerusalem. There was no time to be lost. While it was their dear Lord and Master's last request to preach his Gospel to "every creature," they were to "*begin at Jerusalem.*" They assembled, first of all, in a small upper room. There were but 120 of them. There they began with what all the great and important duties of life should be begun and ended—

* Tacitus

prayer to God to help them in their great work, and then they proceeded to proclaim the name and religion of the risen Saviour. Their first sermon was a never-to-be-forgotten one. Peter preached it, and 3000 Jews were converted to the new faith. Many of these had come from far distant parts of the world, to attend the great feast of Pentecost, and, when the festival was finished, they returned back to their several homes, and told all the wondrous things they had seen and heard.

The different sects in Jerusalem were alarmed at the progress the "Nazarenes" (as they called them in mockery) were making. They resolved, if they could, to crush the infant Church. The Sadducees had now the greatest influence. To their party the high priest belonged. And as the apostles of Jesus dwelt, in their discourses, more especially on His resurrection, this sect were more violent in their opposition than any others; for you are aware that the Sadducees denied altogether the doctrine of a resurrection. They saw that, in young Saul of Tarsus, with his energy, and zeal, and learning, they had one in every way qualified to carry out their purposes of vengeance against the followers of Jesus. He was willing enough to listen to the call. His proud spirit could not for a moment believe that that meek "Man of sorrows"—whose only birthright seemed poverty—who had lately expired, like a common felon, on the cross, could be the Messiah whom he and his fathers had looked for. Would the great Shiloh, of whom the patriarch Jacob spake—the "Prince of Peace," of whom Isaiah sung—have none but twelve peasants of Galilee for his companions, and make these the teachers of the world?

No, no; the manger of Bethlehem, the carpenter's shop at Nazareth, the cross of Calvary, the fishermen disciples—all shocked the pride of the young Pharisee. The very thought of a Messiah so lowly seemed an insult to God and to the whole Jewish nation. He had thought, at first, that the new religion of this "one Jesus" would soon be forgotten—that, after this death of shame and humiliation, all his other followers would, like his apostles, have forsaken him and fled. But when he saw the sect growing daily in strength, he resolved to do God service, by entering with his whole soul on the work of persecution.

There was a holy man who rose into note at this time among the disciples of Jesus; his name was Stephen, one of the seven deacons of the infant Church, chosen to take charge of the money collected for the relief of the poor. He is described by Jerome, and some of the early fathers, as a person of great learning and eloquence. In Scripture he is spoken of as "a man full of faith and of the Holy Ghost." He was bold in the cause of his crucified but now exalted Lord. He went day after day into the synagogue, disputing with the learned men and doctors, and trying to shew them, from their own Old Testament scriptures, that Jesus was the true Messiah. We are told (in Acts vi. 9, 10) that among these synagogues into which he entered was that of "*the Cilicians;*" and we have reason to believe, that among those whom this "devout man" addressed, was one who had again left his native Tarsus and come up to Jerusalem.

It is more than likely that the "young man Saul"* (who is now again brought before our notice) often

* Acts vii. 58.

and again disputed with Stephen; that all the powers of argument he had learned so well under Gamaliel's teaching were put in force; but that he, like the other Jews, "were not able to resist the wisdom and spirit" with which the holy deacon spake.* Their malice was excited, and they resolved to have him condemned. How can they best succeed? False witnesses are hired to convict him of speaking blasphemous words against the law and the temple, "against Moses, and against God." No charge could more certainly rouse the passions of the Jews against the accused than this. "What! this Nazarene to assert that all we love as most sacred is to be destroyed!—the *law*, which our great father Moses received from God himself on Sinai, to be abolished!—the great temple of Solomon, the wonder and glory of the world, whither for ages on ages 'the tribes have gone up, even the tribes of the Lord, unto the testimony of Israel,' was all its magnificence now to pass away!—were they to see no more their high priests in their splendid robes!—the smoke of their morning and evening sacrifices!—to hear no more the music of the timbrel, and harp, and stringed instruments at their sacred feasts, or the silver trumpet of jubilee pealing over the land! It is the height of blasphemy! No sentence can be too severe, no death too terrible for such a scoffer as this." These, doubtless, would be the feelings alike of Pharisees and Sadducees; and we can readily calculate what the result will be when Stephen is dragged before the Sanhedrim—the great Jewish court of law—to answer to the charges thus preferred against him.

A great meeting is called of this tribunal. The

* Acts vi. 10.

place in which they were wont to assemble was a hall called "*Gazith*," or the "*stone chamber*," situated close by the wall of the temple, with the rocky side of Mount Moriah immediately beneath. Before this time, indeed, the Jews were forbidden to meet here. They had religious scruples about Gentiles crossing the sacred enclosures; and the Romans, not unreasonably, dreaded lest the holding of assemblies, in a place *they* were not permitted to enter, might become a dangerous privilege.* In the present instance, however, the prohibition had been winked at, and the "stone chamber" was the place of meeting.

Our young readers may fancy to themselves the scene. The president of the assembly, the high priest (Theophilus the Sadducee, one of the sons of Annas) occupies a raised seat at the upper end of the room; other seventy-one members are ranged in a half-circle around him, consisting of the heads of the twenty-four courses of priests, twenty-four elders, and twenty-four scribes. Stephen stands in front of his judges; but he is not afraid—his God and Saviour is with him. Indeed, at that moment, while the eye of Saul, along with the others, is fixed with rage on the prisoner, the young Tarsian sees what he never afterwards could forget—a bright heavenly light or glory resting on the face of Stephen, as if the flame of truth in his inner soul was seen reflected on his countenance. Saul looks on the faces of the judges; he sees them, as his own was, flashing with fire and indignation; but the eye of the first martyr is directed up to heaven; with him, all is peace!

The great charge, as we have said, brought against

* Lewin.

him was, that he had foretold the destruction of the temple, and "the change of the customs which Moses had formerly delivered to them." * The president hears the false witnesses first; after they state their charges, he turns towards Stephen and puts the usual question, whether he pleads "guilty, or not guilty." "*Are these things so?*" The prisoner, unmoved, with a calm and clear voice enters on his defence. He begins by minutely rehearsing the leading events in the history of their nation, from the calling of Abraham and the Exodus from Egypt, to the building of the temple during the reign of Solomon; he declares that he was no enemy to the Old Testament rites—these he loved in common with all Jews; but, at the same time, shewed that Moses himself had spoken of a time when *his* law would be displaced by a better dispensation, quoting the very words of the great lawgiver—" A Prophet shall the Lord your God raise up unto you of your brethren like unto me; *Him shall ye hear.*" † He charged his hearers with trusting too much to outward privileges, and sinfully resisting the grace and Holy Spirit of God, as their fathers did. The whole assembly are roused into fury! Like wild beasts springing upon their prey, "they gnashed upon him with their teeth." ‡ As their rage, however, increases, so also does his calm composure; a holier brightness gathers over his countenance. We cannot wonder at it; for we are told that then "he looked up into heaven, and saw the glory of God, and Jesus standing at the right hand of God." § He looked far above the cruel assembly gathered in the earthly Jerusalem. He was gazing upon "the gene

* Acts vi. 14. † Acts vii. 37.
‡ Acts vii. 54. § Acts vii. 55.

ral assembly and church of the first-born in heaven." The veil of the skies had been drawn aside. He saw holy angels smiling upon him; and, better than all, that blessed Saviour he had probably last seen expiring in agony on the cross, "*standing* on the right hand of God." As an early father says, "not '*seated*,' but '*standing*,' as if he rose from his glorious throne to welcome his first apostle and martyr."

Beautifully does a Christian poet say—

"Well might you guess what vision bright
Was present to his raptured sight,
Even as reflected streams of light
Their solar source betray;

"The glory which our God surrounds,
The Son of man—th' atoning wounds—
He sees them all,—and earth's dull bounds
Are melting fast away."

But he can expect no mercy from the hands of men; they saw no such bright heavenly vision! The seventy-two are all against him. "They cried with a loud voice, and stopped their ears, and ran upon him with one accord." In that loud voice there mingled, doubtless, the shout of the young rabbi of Tarsus. If there was one event in his life more than another Saul afterwards bitterly wept over, surely it was that mad rush he made on an innocent and holy saint, and when he helped to urge him, unresisting along, from the place of trial to the place of death. It was contrary to the Jewish law to commit murder inside the walls of the city; they must therefore for some moments repress their rage till they are outside the sacred enclosures. They drag their victim through the gate, which still bears his name, and by which, in ages long after, the brave and victorious Godfrey of Bouillon conducted his armies with loud acclamations in entering Jerusalem.

Soon they reach the scene of violence. It is supposed to be a lonely spot, low down in the valley of Jehoshaphat, not far off from where Stephen's Saviour had suffered far more terrible agonies in the garden of Gethsemane.* The brook Kedron is murmuring in his ear. He could not fail to remember that Jesus too listened to its sound in that darkest night the world ever saw. What a "mixed multitude," we may imagine, are present! There are the idle mob from the city, who are ever hanging on, ready to take part in any tumult, and to be witnesses of savage deeds. There are priests and scribes, by their words and gestures stirring up the passions of the rabble, and hurrying them to execute with all speed the act of cruelty. While, lurking in the crowd, afraid to utter a word which might bring down on themselves similar vengeance, are the trembling disciples of the same Master whose cross Stephen so meekly bears. Who is to begin the bloody work? A number of stones lying in the channel of the Kedron, or that have fallen from the rocky ridges of Jehoshaphat, are the weapons of death. According to the Jewish law, it is the witnesses in the trial who must cast the first. And these seem resolved to effect their purpose thoroughly; for their upper loose garments are cast aside, that their arms may be able to dash the stones with sufficient force. There is one close by, who is ready enough to assist. They lay down their coats at his feet to take charge of them. It is a young man, described by early writers as being "short in stature, of a fair complexion, and with expressive eyes." His name is *Saul!* The dreadful tragedy is soon over—stone after stone is

* See the picture at the beginning of the chapter.

hurled upon that bruised and tortured body. The green turf is dyed with the first martyr's blood. But he utters not one revengeful word—a new spirit has been introduced into the world. Like his Lord before him, he prays with his dying lips for his murderers, and then "falls asleep."

"With such a Friend and Witness near,
No form of death could make him fear;
Calm amid showers of stones he kneels,
And only for his murderers feels!" *

That prayer was heard for *one* at least of those who were in that crowd.—There is a cave or grotto still pointed out in the valley of Jehoshaphat, where it is said the murderers dragged the mangled body of the martyr when life was extinct.†

"The shades of evening closed around that guilty city, which had that day added another sin to her catalogue of crimes, and maintained her ancient character as a murderer of God's messengers. The multitude had dispersed to their homes. The priests were recounting with joy the events of the day, and the disciples were weeping in secret the loss of one so honoured and beloved. But everywhere was heard the name of one who had stood prominent in these fearful scenes. Among the groups who lingered at the corners of the streets, and talked over these transactions—at the fireside, where Jewish mothers heard with glistening eyes of this new triumph of their faith—in that mourning assembly, where the Nazarenes blended their tears and prayers, the deeds of the youthful Saul were canvassed with joy on the one hand, and terror on the other. It seemed a sad day for the religion that had lost her eloquent and earnest preacher, and not less bright and

* John Newton. † Maundrell.

promising for that ancient system which had called forth a champion worthy of her happiest times. The rich and poor, the Pharisee and Sadducee, were loud in praise of the rising zealot, and everything seemed to augur for him a career of high distinction. The path was already open for Saul to the most exalted honours which a Jew could receive from the rulers of his people."*

The Bible tells us nothing as to how Saul himself must have really felt at Stephen's death. I doubt not, though he concealed it, there were other feelings that mingled with rage and bigotry, as the dead body lay at his feet, and he heard the sound of the "sore lamentation" made by sorrowing friends over their "loved and lost" one. He must have thought to himself—Can all that peace, and calmness, and prayer, and forgiveness, and love have been that of a hypocrite? Meanwhile, however, we know that he *did* go away from the place a furious zealot as before. Perhaps he thought he saw in that tranquil death only the power of the evil one at work on a naturally pure and holy mind, tempting him to desert the faith of his fathers for a miserable heresy. This would only give him the greater desire to extinguish it, and prevent others from falling into the same snare. But there were thoughts and impressions, notwithstanding, made on his heart, which he never could forget, and which he never *did* forget, when he came afterwards to follow in Stephen's steps, and to pant for Stephen's crown.†

* *The Apostle Paul: a Biography.* 1854.
† See Acts xxii. 1.

CHAPTER IV

The Convert.

"See me, see me—once a rebel,
Vanquish'd at His cross I lie;
Cross! to tame earth's proudest able!
Who was e'er so proud as I?
He convinced me; He subdued me;
He chastised me; He renew'd me.
The nails that nail'd—the spear that slew Him,
Transfix'd my heart, and bound it to Him.
See me, see me—once a rebel,
Vanquish'd at His cross I lie."

"Grace came, omnipotent grace, and the rampart of that great soul fell like the walls of Jericho; the impregnable citadel was carried in an hour, and all its ample magazines were redeemed for the service of the Lord."

THE flames of persecution were now fairly lighted. The Jewish Sanhedrim waxed fiercer than ever in their hatred to the disciples of Jesus. Soon, alas! did the Saviour's words come true, John xvi. 2—"They shall put you out of the synagogues: yea, the time cometh, that whosoever killeth you will think that he doeth God service." We are not, indeed, warranted to suppose that the Sanhedrim were permitted to persecute unto death. Stephen's martyrdom was doubtless an act of treason against the government of the land, and, at other times, would have been dealt with as such. But Pilate had now been deposed, his successor was not yet appointed, and the Jews felt themselves at guilty liberty to commit this cold-blooded murder.

Although it is not probable the repetition of such a violation of law would be allowed, no such interference was made in the case of lesser cruelties.

The "young man Saul," now advancing to manhood, is elected one of the council; and he seems to exceed all the others in the amount of his rage and fury against the followers of Jesus. "He made havoc of the Church," seizing not only on *men*, and making them the objects of his cruelty, but women also were bound in chains and put in prison. Sometimes he was not even satisfied with this, but had individuals ready to whip and scourge them. By making them thus suffer torture, he tried to induce them to blaspheme the name of Jesus.

Think, in this happy and favoured age and country of ours, what all these poor Christians must have been suffering then in Jerusalem! The old and infirm—the Simeons and Annas—who had had the evening of their days gladdened by that bright Gospel Sun which others had only seen afar off—think of their tottering frames borne down with heavy irons, their hoary locks in vain appealing for mercy! Think of the daughters of Jerusalem—the wives and mothers who once had wept for the Lord they so loved, when they saw Him carrying his cross—now called to weep and carry that cross for themselves—their helpless children torn from them because they would not deny the name of Him who was dearer than the dearest on earth! In connexion with these dreadful doings, the cruelty of the Rabbi of Tarsus was known hundreds of miles off. "How much evil he had done to the saints of God at Jerusalem!" * Little was he aware, at the time, how literally true

* Acts ix. 13.

the saying of his future Lord and Master would be in his case—"With what measure ye mete, it shall be measured to you again!" He had taken part in "stoning," "scourging," "imprisoning." In all the three, he himself was yet to "bear, in his own body, the marks of the Lord Jesus!"

I do not think, however, that we can argue from this, as many have done, that Saul was naturally of a savage and cruel nature. He was a true and sincere worshipper of God, and a person of correct life. He tells us himself that "as touching the righteousness of the law, he was blameless." It was a blind and erroneous zeal, in what he supposed was the cause of truth, which led him to such acts of oppression. He thought all the time he was "doing God service," and that the more he shewed his hatred to Jesus and his people, God would love him the more. His own words are striking —"I verily thought I *ought*"—(it was a false sense of duty)—"to do many things contrary to the name of Jesus of Nazareth." * Besides, the principles of toleration prized and acted on in our happy country were not known in his time, or at least never manifested. We may be struck indeed at the *amount* and *bitterness* of his persecuting zeal; we read that he was "*breathing out* threatenings and slaughter" (with all the ferocity of a *wild beast*, as the word means). This may at first sight seem strange, if what we have a little ago said be true, that he was impressed with Stephen's holy death. But alas! this is often one out of many ways that people take to resist conviction, and thereby to silence the voice of conscience. Just as the sun, shining upon a stagnant pool, draws

* Acts xxvi. 9

forth from it only noxious vapours, so the holy radiance on the countenance of the martyr seemed but to extract stronger feelings of hatred from the proud heart of the persecutor. As a writer has well said, "The arrow of conviction, when it fails to bring the sinner bleeding to Christ, saying, 'What must I do to be saved?' seldom fails to exasperate his natural enmity so as to rouse his violent opposition to Christ and his cause; insomuch that, when at any time we see a man breathing out violence and threatenings against the ministers or people of God, we are ready to think that at one time that sinner must have had an arrow sticking fast in his conscience, and that he is uneasy and restless and wretched within, in consequence of its rankling and festering sore."* These dreadful scenes and cruelties in which Saul now engaged, were like scorpion-stings afterwards to his warm and tender heart. They pained and lacerated him more than the thongs of the gaoler, or the rough irons that bound him—"I am the least of the apostles," he says, "that am not meet to be called an apostle, *because I persecuted the Church of God.*"† "Beyond measure I persecuted the Church and wasted it."‡

Till now the Gospel had been principally, if not altogether, preached in the city of Jerusalem; but these mournful cruelties were beginning to scatter the disciples among the neighbouring provinces of Judea, and even among the countries beyond. Philip, Stephen's old companion and friend, was preaching and working miracles in Samaria, and Peter and John shortly after followed him there on the same errand. Thus the rage of the persecutors was overruled by Divine Pro-

* Buchanan *On the Holy Spirit*, p. 291 † 1 Cor. xv. 9. ‡ Gal. i. 13.

vidence for the spread of the glad tidings of salvation in other lands. The martyrdom of Stephen was like the fall of the forest tree, which, as it comes with a crash to the ground, scatters its seeds on every side.

These seeds, however, are not to be allowed long to rest in peace. The Christians who had taken refuge in other lands are to be hunted out by this fierce zealot as well as when they were within the walls of Jerusalem. Where is he to begin his new warfare? what spot does he fix upon first, in order to spring upon his unoffending prey?

There was a city far north of Palestine, Damascus, the capital of Syria, where many of the poor saints had taken refuge, and where many more, by their preaching and influence, had become disciples of the Lord Jesus. Saul could of himself exercise no authority at a distance; but he received from Theophilus, the high priest in Jerusalem, letters to the Jewish synagogues in Damascus, in order that he might seize hold of all the converts he could find there—"any of this way" (as he in words of bitter contempt expresses it), whether they were men or women, and bring them bound to the prisons in Jerusalem.

You have heard of the Crusaders of the middle ages, who went to Palestine to fight for the Holy Sepulchre, and how manfully they endured every kind of hardship and suffering in what they thought was a holy enterprise. You have heard of the poor wretched Hindus in India travelling on their knees for hundreds of miles, under a burning sun, to the temples of their idol deities, thinking thus to obtain their favour. Never, we believe, did Pilgrim, or Crusader, or Hindu, set out with a more honest conviction that he was "doing God service," than did Saul of Tarsus at this time to the Syrian capital.

To explain this "authority from the high priest," it must be borne in mind that the Roman emperors, though ever jealous about giving their own power to others, had (since the reign of Julius Cæsar) invested the Jewish high priest, as head of the Sanhedrim, with full authority over all Israelites who might be living in foreign cities,—at least to the extent of "excommunication, scourging, and imprisonment." When they wished to enforce any of these, "a mandate" was sent by the hands of a special messenger (as was the case now with Saul) to the synagogue of the city where the Jews resided, whom they wished to punish.*

What a journey was this! how much hung upon it! and yet the Bible throws no light upon the journey itself —as to what route the future apostle took, or who were with him. There were several ways by which he could reach Damascus; but as it is more than likely that by this time the Roman roads were made through Judea,† we may suppose that Saul, mounted on horseback and surrounded with his companions, proceeded out of the north-western gate of Jerusalem, taking the great paved road, whose remains are traced at the present day, similar to the paved highways we shall afterwards come to speak of in Italy, and other countries.‡

It has been attempted to give a precise date to this memorable journey—about November A. D. 37, a few months after Stephen's martyrdom. It may help to

* Lewin.

† For a description of the different routes from Jerusalem to Damascus, see Conybeare and Howson. We have adopted the one selected by them as most probable.

‡ *Biblical Researches*, vol. iii. p. 77.

assist our impression of the incidents connected with it, to assume the date to be the correct one. The usual time which modern companies take to travel between Jerusalem and Damascus is a week—the distance being 136 miles. On the supposition that Saul and his companions were a mounted band, they would do it sooner; but it would seem, from his own description, that the party in this respect very nearly resembled caravans in the present day, some being mounted, and some on foot.* Ascending the ridge, on the left of which are the tombs of the Judges, they would wend their way across a hill which was to become more memorable, some years later, as that where the Roman standards were first planted by Titus when he came against Jerusalem. The temple has now sunk from the view of the travellers, and the road lies, with many devious windings, through a mountainous district, till they come to Ramah of Benjamin. Two cities of a similar name open upon them right and left. The former, Gibeah of Saul, could not be without interest to the young Pharisee, who proudly bore the name of Israel's first king. Here was the monarch's birthplace. They could follow in thought his brave son in his midnight exploit, with his armour-bearer, when he left his father's tent under the pomegranate tree in Gibeah, and by the morning the Philistines were fleeing in disorder over the plain. The city, towards the right, had recollections equally interesting. It was over the walls of Gibeon that, at the command of Joshua, the sun stood still in the heavens. Here, under David and Solomon, the tabernacle had for many years been set up, and the latter monarch, on ascending the throne,

* Lewin.

offered up his thousand-burnt-offerings. They hasten onwards through a rocky country, occasionally relieved by gentle slopes or artificial terraces, where the melon and cucumber are found cultivated along with patches of grain. The eye of the inquisitor is doubtless intent on the great object of his journey; he may have little inclination to gaze on the various spots of renown which are crossing his path; but surely he could not pass Bethel without a solemn pause and many hallowed remembrances. Was this the spot he had so often read of in his Tarsus home, where father Jacob had taken the stones of the place for his pillow, and saw the ladder stretching down from heaven to earth—the angels of God travelling up and down upon it? The impressive typical meaning of that vision was to young Saul yet sealed. He had yet to know the glory of that mediatorial work which connected earth with heaven—the sinner with God. Who can tell but these same angels that hovered over the weary patriarch 1700 years before, had now "charge given them to encamp" around another erring fugitive! If there be "joy in heaven among the angels of God over *every* sinner that repenteth," what must that joy be when they can bear tidings to the throne that there is one weeping at the cross like *Saul of Tarsus!*

But they pursue their way. Shiloh was the last place of note they passed before entering the hills of Samaria. Here they could not fail to think of the touching story of old Eli and the youthful Samuel; but there was nothing in the town itself to attract attention. Ever since the "Ark of God" had been taken from it by the Philistines, Shiloh had sunk into insignificance. Perhaps, from some height here, the young

Benjamite may have got a glimpse of the blue mountains bounding the horizon on the north; they are the heights of Gilboa. On yonder mountain side, the stately king, whose birthplace he had recently passed, fell, when "the archers hit him, and he was sore wounded of the archers." He might see, or fancy he saw, the direction by which the messenger hurried along to Ziklag with the crown and bracelet of the fallen monarch, carrying the heavy tidings to David that "the beauty of Israel had been slain upon the high places."

After crossing the hills of Ephraim, we may listen in thought to their horses' hoofs sounding along the winding valley between Ebal and Gerizim, close to Sychar. They may have even possibly paused to refresh themselves at the very fountain—the well of Jacob—where a Samaritan woman had the water of life first pointed out to her.

If we have said in a former chapter that the glories of Lebanon and Carmel must have been much the same in the days of Saul as now, we may say the same of this lovely valley; for while the features of nature in her bold mountains and valleys never can be changed, the old Shechem of Scripture still survives when many other towns and villages of Palestine have been swept away. As Saul rode through its groves and orchards, scenes which have met the eye of recent travellers were those most likely to meet his own. "A beautiful stream would be running through the valley, and a shepherd might be seen seated on its bank, playing a reed-pipe, with his flock feeding quietly around him." "Along the valley he might behold a company of Ishmaelites coming from Gilead, as in the days of

Reuben and Judah, with their camels 'bearing spicery, and balm, and myrrh,' who would gladly have purchased another Joseph of his brethren, and conveyed him as a slave to some Potiphar in Egypt. Upon the hills around, flocks and herds might be feeding as of old; nor, in the simple garb of the shepherds of Samaria, would there be anything to contradict the notions he might entertain of the appearance formerly exhibited by the sons of Jacob." *

Samaria is soon passed, and Galilee is entered. They have reached a lofty ridge from which they look down into the deep basin of the Sea of Tiberias—that spot which had become sacred with the presence and deeds of a Greater than the greatest of apostles. It was there that a mighty Voice had stilled a furious tempest, and rescued a sinking disciple; the same Voice and the same Hand was ere long, by a mightier miracle, to rescue him who now rode unconcerned along its white pebbly beech! Crossing to its other side, they come in view of Capernaum and Bethsaida. Boats might be flitting, as they passed, to and fro in the calm surface of the lake, in which probably Peter, and James, and Andrew, and John, once sat and toiled, and in which Jesus had sat along with them.

After the hills which rose on the eastern side of the lake have been climbed, the view becomes quite altered; the land of mountains and valleys is about to be left behind, and one vast plain, extending for miles on miles, stretches before them. Towards the extreme north, the brow of Hermon, white with snow as if hoary with age, towered far up in the blue sky. It formed the highest point in the range of Mount Leba-

* Stephen's *Travels*, and Clarke's *Travels*, quoted by Wylie.

non—the giant boundary-line of the north of Palestine, and which now lay right between the persecutor and his native Cilicia. The journey presently is over a flat and even country, but wasted, dry, and sterile. A hot burning sun pours its rays down upon their heads, and many a league has to be trodden before their eyes are gladdened with cooling streams or welcome shade. At last, in the far distance, a dotted streak of sparkling white greets their vision, and circling lines, glancing in the sun, seem to mark the presence of a flowing river. It is their longed-for city—the towers and pinnacles of great Damascus.

"The mid-day sun, with fiercest glare,
Broods o'er the hazy twinkling air,
Along the level sand.
The palm-tree's shade unwavering lies,
Just as thy towers, Damascus, rise
To greet you wearied band." *

Damascus, the "head" or capital of Syria, is one of the oldest towns in the world. When the patriarch Abraham lived, Damascus was built. His trusty and faithful servant was "Eliezer of Damascus." In the reign of David and Solomon, it carried on an extensive trade with neighbouring and distant cities. The prophet Ezekiel speaks particularly of its commerce with Tyre — "its wares, emeralds, purple and broidered work, the wine of Helbon, and white wool." While Nineveh can only be dug out of its grave, and the ruins of Babylon can scarcely be found, Damascus remains a great and beautiful city to this day, the wonder of all travellers, with its busy throng of 120,000 inhabitants, its same bright white buildings, its long streets, its busy bazaars, its sparkling fountains, its

* *Christian Year.*

lovely palm-trees and delicious fruits.* It is called by eastern writers, "a pearl surrounded by emeralds." Abana and Pharpar, the rivers which Naaman of old liked "better than all the waters of Israel," and which (united) the ancient geographers knew by the name of "the Golden Stream,"† still come tumbling down from the heights of Lebanon, and wind in graceful curves through the long flat plains, carrying beauty and freshness in their course, more especially around the rich gardens and forests of olive-trees in which the city itself is embosomed.

It is said of an Arabian prince, that when he was on his way to Damascus, and first beheld it, he stopped his horse and refused to go any further, erecting on the spot where its towers first burst upon his view, a monument with the following inscription:—"I expect to enter *one* Paradise, but if I enter this city, I shall be so ravished with its beauties as to lose sight of the Paradise which I hope to enter."

"We were looking down," says a recent traveller, "from an elevation of 1000 feet, upon a vast plain bordered in the distance by blue mountains, and occupied by a rich luxuriant forest of the walnut, the fig, the pomegranate, the plum, the apricot, the citron, the locust, the pear, and the apple, forming a waving grove of more than fifty miles in circuit. . . . Then conceive our sensations to see, grandly rising in the distance, . . . the swelling leaden domes, the gilded crescents, and the marble minarets of Damascus, while in the centre of all, winding toward the city, ran the main stream of the river Barrada."‡

* Among these is the well-known Damson, or *Damascene* plum.

† *Bible Cyclopædia.* ‡ Addison.

Truly we need not be surprised at Naaman thinking more of his own native rivers, the Scripture "streams from Lebanon," than all the waters of Syria; for the former, with their "golden streams," and *never-failing* ones, too (as *Amana* or *Abana* literally means), make Damascus, though on the borders of a desert, one of the loveliest spots on earth; while the rivers of Judea (the Jordan excepted), are small and scanty, and their narrow rocky channels generally dry in the summer.*

It may be further interesting to mention, that Christian missionaries are at this day labouring among the Jewish population of Damascus, which recently amounted to the number of 5000.

But to return. We may imagine the band of horsemen, with the fiery Cilician at their head, nearing the walls of this "eye of the east." The sun of the last day of their journey is brightly shining upon them. They are hopeful that they will, ere long, either be screened from the sultry heat in the house of one of their brethren, or at all events attain the cooling shade of one of the many avenues leading to the city. Soon they are riding along among palm, orange, and citron groves, getting, through some occasional openings, a glimpse of Mount Hermon. Natural and artificial streams are murmuring at their feet. Birds with their lovely plumage are hiding themselves among the branches. Creeping flowers in endless variety and beauty, and especially among these the Damascus (or *Damask*) rose, are diffusing a grateful perfume all around. In the distance, they may see mules and camels approaching the city from other quarters, laden with goods and merchandise, just as at this day cara-

* *Bible Cyclopædia.*

vans are still observed carrying Indian manufactures in great quantities from Bagdad, or from Mecca and Aleppo. The words of a modern writer* may, with little alteration, have described what Saul and his followers beheld—"The rich turbans and flowing robes of respectable merchants, are finely contrasted with the rude sheep-skin covering of the mountaineer, and the dark abba of the wandering Arab."

They are riding along with no thought but that their errand will soon be done. They are thinking of the number of their victims, and how they will best be able to return with them through these burning plains—

> "The leader of that martial crew
> Seems bent some mighty deed to do,
> So steadily he speeds;
> With lips firm closed and fixed eye,
> Like warrior when the fight is nigh,
> So steadily he speeds."

And now they have reached a spot half a mile from Damascus, where, at the present day, there is a village called El-Kochaba (caucabe), or "the star" (brightness), from the marvellous occurrence we are now to relate.†

But what is this! In a moment they are stopped on the way. One of them reels from his horse and falls senseless to the ground. It is mid-day—the sun is right above their heads in the cloudless sky; but a light brighter than even a bright Eastern sun dazzles their eyes. It is a "great light," and it shines "suddenly" upon them. They are all struck for the moment speechless!

The others at least cannot tell why they should tremble so, for they neither "hear any voice nor see any vision." It was different with their chief. The

* See *Biblical Keepsake*. † *Bible Cyclopædia*.

Jew of Tarsus is lying speechless on the earth; but in his ear there sound some strange and thrilling words. He lifts up his eye towards the awful brightness. It is nothing else than the emblem of God's presence—the "shekinah" or "glory," which he had often heard of as dwelling in the tabernacle of old, and in the Holy of holies in the temple. But it is no mere light—no mere vision which he sees. There is a glorious Person also. It is *Jesus of Nazareth* whom he persecuted. He leaves us no doubt, in other places where he speaks of this great event in his history, that it was actually Jesus in his glorified *person* he beheld,—"Have I not seen *the Lord?*"—and, "Last of all *he was seen* of *me* also." And Ananias we shall presently find saying to him, "The Lord, *even Jesus,* who appeared to thee in the way as thou camest." Saul knows Him at once! JESUS addresses him in the Hebrew tongue—the same language in which He had conversed with his twelve disciples. He names him! and in mingled tenderness and rebuke thus speaks, "Saul! Saul! why persecutest thou *me?*" as if He said, "It is not my poor innocent people you are cruel to, but what you do to *them* I feel as if you were doing to *me,*—in hurting *them* you are hurting *me.*" What a gracious, tender word of this gracious Saviour! What a laying bare of his loving heart! What even was Stephen's dying love to this? If we may suppose Saul venturing to reply, and saying, "*When* persecuted I *thee? I* took no part in the awful scenes of Gethsemane and Calvary! I formed not one of the assassin band. I gave thee no traitor's kiss. I weaved for thee no crown of twisted thorns. I plunged no rough iron into thy side. My tongue was not raised to add to thy last agonies, mockery and insult." The reply was ready. "Inasmuch as ye did it unto one of the least of these my brethren, ye did it unto me."* The awe-struck horseman, scarce knowing what he says, replies, "Who art thou, Lord?" The answer comes from the same glorified lips, "I am *Jesus of Nazareth* whom thou persecutest." † "I am that very Jesus whom thou thoughtest to be a despised and crucified malefactor; but *I am the Lord of glory*— 'I am Jesus of *Nazareth*'—the name thou wert in the habit of using in mockery, calling me and my people the *Nazarenes*." The whole current of Saul's thoughts must have been in a moment changed. What! Jesus of Nazareth, whom he had imagined was a mere pretender and impostor—*Jesus*, whom he really supposed to have been crucified as a wicked person, dying between thieves, and laid dead in the grave! Could it be that all this while he had been wrong in thinking him a deceiver—that he had been all this while guiltily "fighting against God?" Yes—he looks up to that awful brightness, and a glance there tells him that he *was* wrong—that that glorious Being is "that same Jesus"—risen, exalted, glorified! It was a silent sermon (but a far more solemn and powerful one than Peter preached to the thousands at Pentecost) on the text, "Him hath God exalted to be a prince and a Saviour." It was the whole Gospel Christ the Son of God is shining above his head in glory brighter than the brightness of the sun! No wonder the awe-struck persecutor lies powerless on the ground, "trembling and astonished." "What!" we may suppose him saying to himself, "Jesus! to whom all power is committed. May he not have come to seal my blaspheming lips for ever? There

* Blunt. † Acts xxii. 8.

surely can be no hope for *me*. I have been rushing with madness against the thick bosses of his buckler. I have been hunting down the innocent sheep of this gracious Shepherd, and in injuring them I have been injuring *Him*. I can surely listen for nothing from his lips but words of sternest rebuke and vengeance!" He listens; but there is no terror or upbraiding in the voice. Jesus proceeds to soothe with words and tones of kindness his agitated spirit.

"It is hard," he says, "for thee to kick against the pricks." Our Lord, when he was on earth, often employed terms taken from common customs to enforce his sayings. He does so here in speaking from heaven. It was the habit in Judea for the man who was at the side of oxen, to have a goad or pointed steel to drive them with. Often these animals would refuse to move; they would kick and grow restive when their master was goading them on. When they did so, he only applied the pointed steel more severely, and they found it was vain to resist. Jesus says the same to Saul,—"It is hard for *thee*." There was fresh discovery here, too, of love. He does not say, "It is hard for *me*;" but, "It is hard for *thee*;" as if he had said, "Poor man, thou art wronging thyself, Saul. It is of no use thy attempting to resist my grace; I have long had great things in store for thee. Thou need'st try no longer to be my enemy; I have marked thee out for a great apostle. It is hard for *thee* to go any longer against my bidding. I have struck thee down a persecutor; I will raise thee up 'a chosen vessel unto me.'" It was even so. He can no longer "fight against God." He sees—he trembles—he believes—he rejoices! That look of mingled reproof and love which smote Peter to the heart, melted a harder still. As he beholds the vision and listens to the words of mercy, he can say, "He loved *me*, and gave himself for *me*." As Benjamin, the youngest of the twelve sons of Jacob, was at last brought to see Joseph in Egypt, so Saul, of Benjamin, the youngest of the twelve apostles, "as one born out of due time," has the *true Joseph* at last revealed to him. He can say, "This is our brother, he talks kindly to us." The same adorable Lord and Saviour further proceeds to tell him, ere he vanishes from his sight, that He is to send him forth to be His minister "to the Gentiles, to open their eyes, and to turn them from darkness unto light, and from the power of Satan unto God." He had just pleaded with him in tenderness and love, now He speaks to him with the authority of his risen and glorified Master—the Sovereign in whose ranks he was now to fight—"Arise, and go into the city." There he was to be told what in future he was "to *be*, to *do*, and to *suffer*."

After a few brief moments of terror, the brightness is past—the voice is hushed. He who fell a bigoted Pharisee, is now an humble and humbled follower of Jesus. A glorious light is shining in his soul; but the dazzling brightness had been too much for his bodily eyes. He rises stone-blind! What a different entrance through the Damascus gate!* The proud horseman is led by the hand as a little child, along the street called "Straight,"† to the house of one named Judas.

* "On the 25th day of January, annually, the Christians in Damascus walk in procession to the scene of the conversion, and read the history of it from the Acts of the Apostles, under the protection of a guard furnished by the Pacha."—*Biblical Keepsake.*

† To the indifferent crowd that thronged the street, there would be little worthy of attention in a blind Jew being conducted along. Yet was there more true interest, more real greatness, and more momentous results con

Interesting and strange spectacle! "Whosoever," says Christ, "shall not receive the kingdom of God as a little child, shall in no wise enter therein." Such a little child had the bold and proud Israelite of Tarsus become—"born again" by "the WORD of GOD which liveth and abideth for ever." He is heard engaged in prayer—prayer, the "cry of the new creature"—that blessed means by which he and all who have trodden his steps, "out of weakness have been made strong, waxed valiant in fight, and turned to flight the armies of the aliens."*

We have been already led more than once to mark points of resemblance or comparison between the early history of Luther and that of Saul. We cannot resist adverting, in passing, to a remarkable similarity in this the great turning point of their two lives. Luther, when in the prime of youthful manhood, was returning one day from his father's house at Mansfield, to resume his labours at the university of Erfurth. All at once a thunder-storm overtook him. The lightning flashed fearfully and vividly around him, and one bolt fell and burst at his side. That road was to him a *Damascus highway!* His troubled conscience was roused from its depths. He threw

nected with this event than with the most gorgeous of Eastern processions or the grandest of Roman triumphs. One cannot help thinking, in contrast with it, of another very different cavalcade which takes place in Damascus year after year in honour of another "Apostle," whose influence on the human race (though an influence of falsehood and delusion) is only second to that of the Apostle Paul. "Every year the standard of the false prophet (Mahomet) is displayed. It is of green silk, with passages from the Koran embroidered in gold, and the camel which bears it is ever after exempted from labour. The Koran itself is also carried by the pilgrims, bound in silk, and borne by a camel richly caparisoned, around which armed Mussulmen are stationed, playing on all kinds of instruments."

* Heb. xi. 34.

himself, like Saul of Tarsus, on his knees. Death, judgment, and eternity, were before him; and with all the terrible thoughts of how unprepared he would be to meet his Judge, he vowed that if it pleased God to rescue him from these "terrors of death," he would leave the world, and give himself entirely to religion. From that hour he was an altered man. The age of miracles and special visions had now indeed gone by. No "Lord Jesus" did appear to him visibly and personally "by the way," as he had done to his other servant; but He whose "voice is the thunder" had spoken to him in language he could never forget. Humbled and trembling, he puts the very same question which the awe-struck persecutor put fifteen centuries before—"Lord, what wouldest thou have me to do?" A great work truly God had in reserve for both these "sons of thunder." Those two quiet spots in Asia and Europe—the one on the way to Damascus, the other on the road to Erfurth, must be memorable to all time.* Meanwhile, we shall leave the elder apostle in the lonely chamber of the "Straight street" of Damascus. The owner of the house, and perhaps some of his companions, beheld with amazement the blinded traveller on his knees, calling again and again in some such words as these, he came afterwards to write, "Jesus! Jesus! Thou Son of God, whose grace I have so long despised! This is a faithful saying, and worthy of all acceptation, that Thou didst come into the world to save sinners, of WHOM I AM THE CHIEF!"

* Rubianus, one of Luther's friends at the University of Erfurth, wrote to him at a later period,—"Divine Providence looked to what thou wast one day to become, when, on thy return from the house of thy parents, fire from heaven made thee, like another Paul, fall to the ground, near the city of Erfurth, and snatching thee from our society, drove thee to enter the sect of Augustine"—D'Aubigné's *History of the Reformation*.

CHAPTER V.

The Fugitive.

"And can I be the very same,
Who lately durst blaspheme Thy name,
And on Thy Gospel tread!
Surely each one who hears my case,
Will praise Thee, and confess Thy grace
Invincible indeed!"

JOHN NEWTON.

"Truly these were three memorable days in the life of Paul; and, if we except the three days spent in the new tomb in Joseph's garden, the most wonderful in the history of the Church and the world."

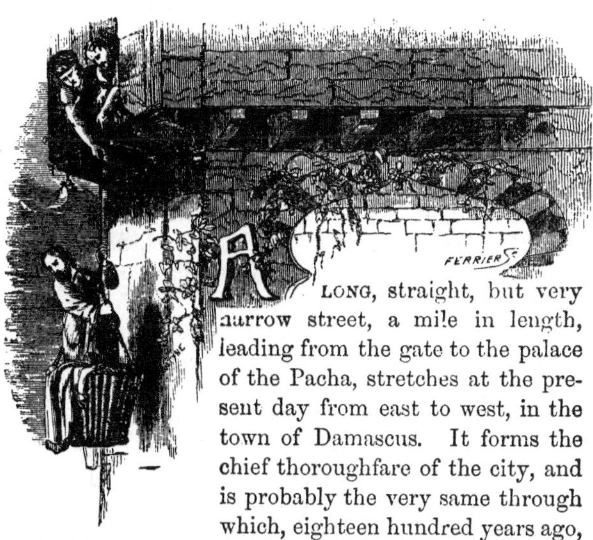

A LONG, straight, but very narrow street, a mile in length, leading from the gate to the palace of the Pacha, stretches at the present day from east to west, in the town of Damascus. It forms the chief thoroughfare of the city, and is probably the very same through which, eighteen hundred years ago, a blind Jew was led along "trembling and astonished." At the east end of it there was a gate, which now bears the name of "Paul's gate;" as it is said that by this he entered the ancient town. Travellers who have recently been in Damascus, describe this gateway as having been at one period an imposing one, consisting of a centre arch for carriages and waggons, and two smaller side ones for foot passengers. The central opening, however, and the lesser one towards the south, are now filled up with stones, forming part of the city wall. At a short distance, on the right, there is still pointed out to the curious stranger, by the monks of Damascus, the "House of Ananias;" and farther on the left, forming a grotto or cellar below the level of the street, is the reputed house of Judas.* When Saul reached the dwelling which had been provided for him, he was in a state of great helplessness. He could take no meat. He ate nothing and drank nothing, and for three days groped in darkness. We cannot think he had any friends to be kind to him. The Christians would be afraid to go near him, for they had heard of his cruelties, and perhaps of the object of his present journey. "*Saul of Tarsus is on his way hither!*"—we may well believe what terror and agony such an announcement would produce in many a bosom and home among the refugee converts at Damascus. They would suspect the vision and the blindness were all a pretence, and that, if they went to his lodging, his companions might be concealed somewhere near, ready to seize them and put them in chains. The Jews, on the other hand, would shun and hate, with a bitter hatred, the man who was now on his knees praying to Jesus, and calling him by the title of God!

How many strange thoughts must have been passing, meanwhile, in Saul's own bosom! He would revert, perhaps, to his Tarsus home. What would his loved father, and sister, and friends think of such a change? and Gamaliel! how could he meet him again as a *Christian?* and, worse than all, he would think of his former cruelties to the poor saints at Jerusalem. He would remember, with bitter tears, the heavenly look of the martyr Stephen—his unearthly forgiveness,

* Rie Wilson's *Travels*

his holy resignation, his triumphant death—and how *he* had helped in that scene of blood! But one thought, rising above all these sore reflections, would comfort his spirit. When no earthly voice was near to cheer him, he would remember those tender tones that were still ringing in his ear, "*Saul! Saul!*" and the last glorious sight his eyes had seen ere they were smitten with blindness. God had seemed purposely to exclude the outer world, that the eye of His dear servant might be taken away from all earthly things, and fixed on his own heart, and on his adorable Redeemer. "Behold! he prayeth!" What! had he never prayed before? Were not the Pharisees *famed* for their many and their long prayers? Can we suppose the young disciple of Gamaliel, who, "after the straitest manner of his religion, lived a Pharisee," was a stranger to prayer? No, not to prayer in its *outward* form. He had repeated *words* often before; but he had never really, till now, uttered the cry of faith. The Jews of his own sect might often point to him as a man of prayer; but God, the "searcher of hearts," says of him for the *first* time, when he sees him in that vaulted chamber, "*Behold!* he prayeth!"

While wrapt in such mingled thoughts as we have supposed, a humble Christian stranger knocked at his chamber door. Saul was prepared for his visit; for God had told him by a dream or vision that one of the name of Ananias would come and lay his hands on him, and restore his sight. Who Ananias was, we are not specially informed. Probably he was one of the scattered sheep whom Saul, like a ravening wolf, had set out from Jerusalem to destroy. He had known, indeed, the object of the persecutor's visit to Damascus.

Very probably "the men" who had come along with Saul, and whom we lose sight of after he was struck to the earth, had not been aware of the wondrous change that had taken place on their leader, and were making publicly known in the city the cruel errand they had come to discharge. But God appeared by a vision to Ananias, and instructed him to go and lay his hands on the blinded Pharisee. "And there was a certain disciple at Damascus, named Ananias; and to him said the Lord in a vision, Ananias. And he said, Behold, I am here, Lord. And the Lord said unto him, Arise, and go into the street which is called Straight, and inquire in the house of Judas for one called Saul, of Tarsus: for, behold, he prayeth, and hath seen in a vision a man named Ananias coming in, and putting his hand on him, that he might receive his sight."* We can hardly wonder at the simple-minded disciple being astonished, and, at first, even afraid to go on so strange a mission. "Then Ananias answered, Lord, I have heard by many of this man, how much evil he hath done to thy saints at Jerusalem: and here he hath authority from the chief priests to bind all that call on thy name."† What! to go to the man who, above all others, was signalized for his cruelties to the people of Christ! But God's wish is enough. "He is not disobedient to the heavenly vision;" and, although we had known nothing else of this kind messenger, we know enough from one word to see the strength of his faith in God's command, and his love to one whose name he was wont to think of only with terror—"BROTHER SAUL!" He is no longer afraid. God has told him that the lion

* Acts ix. 10-12. † Acts ix. 13. 4

has become a lamb—the fierce persecutor a true believer. He goes at once and speaks to him as such. Saul was a bold and courageous man. He was not in the habit of shedding tears; but I think a tear must have rolled down from his rayless eyes as he listened to the first word that a Christian friend ever spoke to him. It was the kindest word that *could* be used. It must have put away all his fears if he had any. "*Brother* Saul, the Lord, even Jesus, that appeared unto thee in the way as thou camest, hath sent me that thou mightest receive thy sight, and be filled with the Holy Ghost." *

Who can tell but this kindly little word may have at the moment sunk firm and deep into the soul of the great apostle, and taught him those large-hearted views and feelings of Christian brotherhood which led him afterwards so often in closing his letters thus to write, "Grace be with all them that love the Lord Jesus Christ in sincerity!" God had owned him as a son, and whenever Ananias knows this, he hastens to own him as a brother. "The Lord, even JESUS." It was the first time he had listened to that name with feelings of unmingled joy. Christ, indeed, had Himself spoken to him, saying, "*I am Jesus.*" But at the moment that comforting word was mingled with many self-accusations. Now it came like a strain of heavenly music. It was the name of one who was henceforward to be better to him than the best of of all earthly friends. "The Lord, even Jesus, hath sent me," not to upbraid thee for thy great guilt, and pierce thy heart afresh with new sorrows, but to tell that he has selected thee as a chosen vessel, to bear to

* Acts ix. 17.

distant nations "the unsearchable riches" of his Gospel.*

What a specimen had Saul here of the love and kindness both of Master and disciple! How specially impressed must he have been with the interest manifested in him by the Lord Jesus! He had been breathing out slaughter against ONE whom he now sees could have struck him dead in a moment, and made him a monument of vengeance! But *that One* not only employs words of love and kindness towards him, but He goes to the street of a city—He selects a particular house in that street, where the new convert is to be lodged—He goes to another disciple, and tells that disciple to see to the safety of the blind Hebrew, and "speak comfortably unto him."

While Saul was thus "called to be an apostle by Jesus Christ," it is worthy of notice that he was baptized into the faith of Christ, not by any *apostle*, or boasted "*successor of the apostles*," but by a humble, lowly, unknown disciple. In these days, when so much is said on the subject of what is called "apostolical succession," and that baptism is no real baptism—no real sacrament, unless administered by the hands of priests who can trace their ordination, in an unbroken line, from the apostles—what can be made of the case of the greatest of all converts, the holiest of saints, the chiefest of apostles? If there had been any such virtue in the administration of the rite, surely the most valued disciple that ever existed in the Christian Church would not have been denied the benefit of it. But just as if for the purpose of shewing that there was no such imaginary charm in the dispensers and dispens-

* Blunt.

ing of the ordinance, and that they who hold the view I refer to, "teach for doctrines the commandments of men," *God himself specially appoints* that his greatest Disciple, Minister, and Missionary, be baptized, not by the hands of Peter, or John, or James, but by the hands of "*one Ananias*," a humble saint whose best "apostolical succession" was his simple faith and brotherly love. How impressively does this tell us, that "neither is he that planteth anything, nor he that watereth, but God that giveth the increase!" As there was nothing in the *administrator*, so there was no virtue in the *element*. It is not the waters of the land of his fathers—not Kedron, or Siloam, or Jordan, which are used in the sacred rite, but one of those countless streams of which we have spoken, that Naaman loved so well. Previous to this, there "had fallen from his eyes as it had been scales," and he had his sight restored to him. He was "a new creature." Thicker scales had fallen from his blinded soul. His whole future history is now to be told in a short verse he himself afterwards wrote,—"I have determined with myself to know nothing else save JESUS CHRIST AND HIM CRUCIFIED." *

He resolves immediately to shew that he is not ashamed of the Gospel. He had come to Damascus in order that he might go into the synagogue to bind men and women, and drag them to suffer death at Jerusalem. He now stands in these same synagogues proclaiming Jesus the only Saviour of sinners! How great must have been their astonishment! "But all that heard him were amazed, and said, Is not this he that destroyed them which called on this name in

* 1 Cor. ii. 2.

Jerusalem, and came hither for that intent, that he might bring them bound unto the chief priests?"* We can well imagine the result. The Jews frown upon him. They are enraged to think that the great champion of their religion is now proclaiming the crucified Nazarene to be *very God.* "But Saul increased the more in strength, and confounded the Jews which dwelt at Damascus, proving that this is very Christ."†

He was directed, at this time, to go for a little season to *Arabia.* Writers are not agreed precisely as to what is meant by this country—whether it refers to some place not very far from Damascus, or whether it was what we more commonly understand by the name Arabia—the desert country near the Red Sea. Among other conjectures, it is supposed Saul may have gone to Aurana, now called Hauran, to the south-east of Damascus. This is a retired and hilly region, where the Arabians are of a peaceful and primitive character, tending herds and flocks, and occupying themselves in the manufacture of goats'-hair tents. If so, we may think of him as possibly returning for a season to his early calling, supporting himself by the work of his hands, and exemplifying in that remote place his own future saying—"Not slothful in business, fervent in spirit, serving the Lord."

It has been thought, and perhaps correctly, that he began now for the first time to suffer from that complaint in his eyes of which we shall speak more hereafter. It was a complaint common in the city and neighbourhood of Damascus during the damps of summer and autumn, and, being generally followed by

* Acts ix. 21. † Acts ix. 22.

fever, compelled those who were subject to it to seek a healthier climate in the uplands. It is not improbable, therefore, that the apostle, suffering in bodily health, and after the severe struggles his mind had undergone, would be glad of a purer and more bracing air than Damascus could afford.

Though this, however, may be so far true, it was by no means the chief reason for his removal from the Syrian city. These Arabian solitudes doubtless listened to many a fervent prayer from his lips. He had received divine intimation of the great warfare in which he was to engage; and not wishing to enter that warfare on his own charges, may we not believe he went thither mainly to receive strength to fit him for his high calling? Although he had for many years studied God's Word, yet how different would its types, and promises, and prophecies appear now? What a *new book* to him in its *Gospel* meaning! We may think of him, therefore, in his retirement, with the holy Scriptures in his hands; the Holy Spirit opening his eyes to behold "wondrous things contained in that law" which he had never before dreamt of, and preparing him, by special gifts and graces, for unfolding it to others. Frequent revelations seem now to have been made to him. God appears to have met him again and again as He did Elijah of old in his lonely cave in the wilderness of Horeb, and made him listen to another "still small voice." He alludes to this on several occasions in the course of his epistles. "But I certify you, brethren, that the gospel which was preached of me is not after man. For I neither received it of man, neither was I taught it, but by the *revelation* of Jesus Christ."* "For *I have received of*

* Gal. i. 11, 12.

the Lord that which also I delivered unto you, That the Lord Jesus, the same night in which he was betrayed, took bread."* "If ye have heard of the dispensation of the grace of God which is given me to you-ward: how that *by revelation* He made known unto me the mystery."† "But when it pleased God, who separated me from my mother's womb, and called me by His grace, *to reveal His Son in me*, that I might preach Him among the heathen; immediately I conferred not with flesh and blood: neither went I up to Jerusalem to them which were apostles before me; but I went into Arabia, and returned again unto Damascus."‡

Wherever, then, this "Arabia" was, to which he refers, although we are told nothing but the fact of his having gone thither, it forms a very interesting period in the life of the "called apostle;" like his blessed Lord before him, retiring into a lonely solitude to prepare, by fasting and prayer, for the great work that was given him to do.

What a change on that fierce and energetic spirit! far away from all the active work of an active life, holding secret fellowship with God alone! He may have felt that no small grace and strength were needed in his new position. He had given up wealth, fame, friends, country, *all*, for a despised Saviour. It must have required much prayer and divine fortitude for Gamaliel's pupil to be willing to endure the loss of all these things, and to get in exchange only poverty, reviling, suffering, and at last death. After a little while he returned to Damascus, and continued there

* 1 Cor. ix. 23 † Eph. iii. 2, 3.
‡ Gal. i. 15-17. Lewin, vol. i. p. 62.

for "three years," or perhaps less, preaching the faith which he once wished to destroy.

What were the Jews about all this time? We cannot think their rage would be abated, or that they would be more inclined to listen with patience to the preaching of one they had learnt to hate as greatly as they once loved him. They doubtless tried first to meet him in argument; but "they could not resist the power and spirit with which he spake." They formed a cruel design "to kill Saul!" Their purpose of murder seemed successfully planned, and they had little doubt of making sure of their prey. The walls around the city were high and well guarded. The ruler, who was a friend to the Jews, assented to the charge they brought against him, and issued a warrant for his apprehension. He gave orders to his soldiers to keep a vigilant guard in case the new Christian teacher would escape; and the Israelites themselves, to make all sure, took their turn of watching him day and night, lest he might elude the vigilance of the soldiers. But a Greater than all was with the object of their rage. The Lord himself is "keeping the city," and His servant within it, and these watchmen "watch in vain." Saul could say, with his great ancestor—"Lord, how are they increased that trouble me! many are they that rise up against me. Many there be which say of my soul, There is no help for him in God. But thou, O Lord, art a shield for me; my glory, and the lifter up of mine head. . . . . I will not be afraid of ten thousands of people, that have set themselves against me round about."* He finds his way probably to one of the houses of his brother Christians, where

* Psalm iii. 1, 2, 3, 6.

doubtless he would be commended in prayer to Him who "bringeth the counsel of the heathen to nought, and maketh the devices of the people of none effect." This house happened to be close by the city wall; probably, like many dwellings in the East, it was built to jut over it, forming what is called a *kiosk*, from which a view is obtained of the open country. The apostle is put into a basket; this is slung from a window by means of a rope, as you see represented in the picture, and gradually lowered to the foot of the wall.

"As I stood with a friend," says a recent traveller, who resided at Damascus, looking at the place referred to, "a couple of men came to the top of the wall with a broad flat basket, full of rubbish, which they emptied over the wall. 'Such a basket,' said my friend, 'the people use here for almost every sort of thing. If they are digging a well, and wish to send a man down into it, they put him into such a basket; and that those who aided Paul's escape should have used a basket for the purpose, was entirely natural according to the present customs of the country. Judging from what is done now, it is the only sort of vehicle of which men would be apt to think under such circumstances.' Pilgrims are admitted into the monastery at Mount Sinai in a similar manner. A rope, with a basket attached to it, is let down from a window or door about thirty feet above the ground. Those who are to ascend, seat themselves one after another in this basket, and are thus drawn up by means of a pulley or windlass turned by those in the convent."*

It may have been at a place which the Jews thought

* Professor Hackett. See 2 Cor. xi. 32, 33.

PAUL ON FOOT.

there was little need of guarding that Saul was let down, or perhaps he was favoured by the darkness of the night. We should rather say the same Saviour, who had "appeared to him on the way," had given His angels charge over him to encamp round about him. He would hear a voice saying in that midnight hour, "Fear not, for I am with thee." Assured of safety, ere long he is beyond the reach of his enemies.

Was there anything cowardly in this midnight escape? On the contrary, I think there was rather something noble in it. Doubtless, if Saul had consulted his own feelings, his natural fortitude and the remains of his natural pride would have said to him, "No! brave it out, and die like Stephen, the glorious death of a martyr!" But he acted in what he did more in accordance with the will of his Lord—that Lord who had left as a special injunction to his disciples, "When they persecute you in one city, flee ye to another." No one who reads the Apostle's life will ever accuse him of timidity. He who could afterwards hear unterrified the growl of Nero's lions, and say, in the prospect of a violent death, "None of these things move me," would not have been afraid now to face "the perils of false brethren;" but he felt that, "to abide in the flesh" was as yet needful for the great work assigned to him. He burned with a holy desire, before finishing his earthly course, to repair those breaches which, while an enemy of the truth, he had made on the walls of the infant Church.

What an eventful night that must have been to him! The once proud horseman, so lately riding along these plains, is now a hated and hunted fugitive! My young readers may imagine him hurrying from his first experience of those "perils of the city" of which he afterwards so touchingly wrote. The night, as we have supposed, may have been a dark one; or perhaps, ere he had gone far, the moon had risen in all its clear eastern splendour, lighting up the hoary summits of the distant Lebanon, and making Abana and Pharpar appear like threads of silver winding along the flat plain. How many thoughts must have crowded upon him, and more especially as the first hills of Palestine reveal themselves in the morning light! He finds himself (now a disciple of *the Nazarene*) looking across in the direction of that village and name (Nazareth) once despised, which he now so loved. Saul had from his boyhood, like all Jews, learned to value and admire the Psalms of David; and we know it was the custom of the Israelites, in going up to Jerusalem to their feasts, to cheer themselves on the way by chanting them in company. Perchance, during this solitary pilgrimage, these formed his "songs in the night." If so, with what new zest must he have sung them! with what new meaning must they have been invested, since he had first learned them at his Tarsus home! The sweet Psalmist of Israel was once, like himself, a lonely, friendless exile, hunted "like a partridge on the mountains." Who can tell but the heavenly musings of the fugitive king may have proved cheering solaces to the spirit of the fugitive Christian? "Why art thou cast down, O my soul? and why art thou disquieted within me? Hope thou in God, for I shall yet praise Him for the light of His countenance." "My heart is fixed, O God! my heart is fixed; I will sing and give praise." "The stone which the builders refused, is become the head-stone of the corner. This is the Lord's doing, and it is marvellous in our eyes."

We need not follow him further in his old and well-known journey. He turned his steps in the direction of Jerusalem, principally, as he tells us himself, "to see Peter." He wished to get acquainted with that great apostle, the companion of his Lord, and the great instrument in the Pentecostal revival, in order to get from him counsel and advice about his future work. It must have been with a trembling step and faltering heart, when the old towers of the holy city once more rose before his view. The glittering pinnacles of the temple and the altar courts—what different feelings does the first glimpse of them now convey, compared with his *first* journey from Tarsus to Jerusalem! Now their glory is all past. He may have seen at the moment the smoke of the sacrifices ascending to heaven. But these were only the shadows—the Substance had come, and with His coming, all the types were done away. These former glories had now in his eyes "no glory, by reason of the glory that excelleth." From the road by which he entered the city, the tiny waters of the Kedron, or at all events the green sward of the valley through which it flowed, must have met his eye. The voice, too, of a brother's blood must have there been sounding mournfully in his ears. How could he meet that dreadful band of murderers who were so lately his bosom friends and companions? What a look of scorn and reproach he must expect to be cast upon him, when he next sees the old master whose instructions he still reveres! How will every Jew hate him! how must every Christian, for a time at least, suspect him! He had left Jerusalem, honoured and caressed—the prayers and blessings of many a father and mother in Israel had followed him—priests and people had spoken of him as a young hero. Now his name would be in every lip as a vile apostate and castaway. All these are very painful thoughts; but he goes manfully on, feeling that "the Lord will stand by him." The words of the Psalmist were, perhaps, often in his lips,—"In God have I put my trust: I will not be afraid what man can do unto me. Thy vows are upon me, O God: I will render praises unto Thee. For Thou hast delivered my soul from death: wilt not Thou deliver my feet from falling, that I may walk before God in the light of the living?"*

Much of what he dreaded does take place. The Jews hate—the Christians are suspicious. He had come to Jerusalem probably supposing that the news of his conversion would have reached long ago, and been well known to them all. We must remember, however, that communications between distant places were neither so frequent, nor so much to be relied on as now; and very possibly the Christian disciples may have heard only floating rumours about the sudden change, and treated it as a very unlikely story. We cannot wonder, therefore, they give him at first a cold reception. "And when Saul was come to Jerusalem, he essayed to join himself to the disciples: but they were all afraid of him, and believed not that he was a disciple."† How cutting to the feelings of the future apostle! How cheerless and chilling an introduction to his future fellow-labourers and friends! One of their number, of whom we shall hear more hereafter, comes and speaks a kinder word for him. Barnabas,

* Psalms lvi. 11–13. † Acts ix. 26.

who proved all that his name implies—"a son of consolation"—takes him by the hand, and told the others "how the Lord had appeared to him by the way, and spoken to him, and how he had preached boldly at Damascus in the name of Jesus." We ought not to place much reliance on mere tradition; but there is a story, beautiful in itself, and not improbable, that has been handed down to us regarding Barnabas and Saul. It is said that, having been schoolfellows and playmates under Gamaliel, Barnabas, who had become a believer at an early date, had often prayed for the conversion of his friend, and pleaded with him personally to no effect: that he met him on this occasion on the streets of Jerusalem, not aware at the time of what had taken place at Damascus. He once more began, as formerly, to plead with him to renounce Judaism, and become a Christian. Saul threw himself weeping at his feet, and told him the joyful news.* Be this as it may, Gospel love cannot any longer be withheld—Peter and James, who alone of the apostles were then present, gave him the right hand of fellowship. From that moment they were brothers. We seem to hear them saying to him, in his own beautiful language, "*Brother!* thou art no more a stranger and a foreigner, but a fellow-citizen with the saints, and of the household of God." It is peculiarly beautiful to see Peter, and very characteristic of him, so ready to welcome Saul, when many of the other disciples were hanging cautiously back. He, doubtless, would remember his own case—how *he*, too, had been a denier of his Lord—basely forsaking Him whom once he had loved, and had been so tenderly loved in return. He must have felt that in this respect

* *Bible Cyclopædia.*

his sin was greater far than that of the Cilician, who "did it ignorantly in unbelief;" and how much more justly, therefore, the brethren might have refused to receive *him* back again as a disciple, and especially as an apostle. But would *he* deny to Saul a welcome, when his forgiving Lord had not denied one to *him?* Saul had abundantly answered that great question of Jesus, which Peter to his dying hour never could forget—"Lovest thou me?" and, conscious of the same love to the same gracious Shepherd from whom they had both wandered, these stray sheep rejoice together in the same fold. Their common Lord had represented Himself as greeting the returning prodigal while he was yet "a great way off." It was befitting, therefore, that when the two brothers met, "they should make merry, and be glad" Saul's going to Jerusalem at this time must, indeed, have required more than ordinary fortitude. It is no easy matter for those with a naturally lofty spirit like him to own that they are wrong, and to find old friends turned against them. Great, too, must have been the courage required to face them in *public*—to stand in the midst of a synagogue where once he could see nothing but smiling faces—now darkened with anger! But he seems to have felt it his duty, in the city where he had done so much harm, "to deny himself, and take up his cross and follow Jesus." His yearning love to his Jewish brethren, of which he afterwards so touchingly speaks, and his earnest desire to remove, if possible, the blindness from their eyes, seems to have greatly prompted him to this early visit to Jerusalem. "I say the truth in Christ, I lie not, (my conscience also bearing me witness in the Holy Ghost), that I have great heaviness and continual sorrow in my heart for my brethren, my kinsmen according to the flesh."* Perhaps, in the first ardour of his new spiritual life, so convinced had he been himself of his own error in rejecting the Saviour, he may have supposed that he would have had little difficulty in winning over to the same belief those with whom he formerly possessed much influence. Alas! he soon found that it is nothing but the grace of God that can melt the hard heart, and open the sealed eyes. Though his old friends and kinsmen, however, thus disowned him, many Christian hearts and homes were open to him. It is not to be wondered at, after what I have said, that the Apostle Peter's house became his dwelling at this time. There he remained for fifteen days. There is nothing told us regarding this fortnight's intercourse between these two great apostles—the fisherman of Galilee, and the pupil of the learned Gamaliel. We can picture to ourselves what their fellowship would be; their talk together, evening after evening, when the day's work was over. Saul would doubtless love to listen to Peter's account of the Saviour's blessed life—the never-to-be-forgotten sayings and doings which he was privileged to hear and to witness. How the fervid soul of the narrator would kindle at the recollection of his Master's many acts of personal kindness and love, and the gracious words which proceeded out of his mouth! Peter, we know, was not afterwards slow to confess and speak of his own failings; may we not suppose he would even narrate with many tears the story of his fall, that he might contrast with it the

* Romans ix. 1–3. See the rendering of these verses in Haldane *On the Romans.*

tender love of Him who so graciously forgave him! He would fondly recall the special message sent by the angel, "Go and tell *Peter;*" and how, when he met face to face the Lord he had denied, he got no harsher rebuke than the thrice-repeated question, "Simon, son of Jonas, lovest thou me?" We may well believe these two holy men, who had each received in different ways such touching proofs of Jesus' love, would pray earnestly together on their bended knees that God would enable them, by their future lives and ministry, to make good the words, "Lord, thou knowest all things; thou knowest that we love Thee." Sometimes their conversation would turn on matters concerning the welfare of the Church, or it may be, after the stormy discussions in the synagogue, other kindred spirits would be assembled along with them in this quiet home, for mutual prayer and encouragement.

It has been reckoned to have been now about the time of the Passover (April, 41). Jerusalem was crowded with Jewish strangers from all parts of the world. Saul himself being by birth one of these Hellenists, or Jews of the dispersion, had probably thought it would be a suitable commencement to his ministerial work to "dispute against the Grecians," and proclaim to them the name of his crucified Master. "He hoped, no doubt, that an enlarged measure of success would attend his ministry in this city, where his previous life, and habits, and education were so universally known, and that the miracle of his conversion would here form an irresistible argument to the truth of his doctrine. Very different, however, are the intentions of God, respecting our future disposal, from the intentions of ourselves and our friends. Saul perhaps expected to spend many years at Jerusalem. The Almighty had appointed that he should remain there *fifteen days!*"*

The Lord Jesus had other work in reserve for him. His special name from this time was to be "*The Apostle of the Gentiles.*" He was to be the great Missionary of the infant Church, as his Lord had declared to Ananias in Damascus—"He is a chosen vessel unto me to bear my name before *the Gentiles*, and *kings*, and the children of Israel." His remaining any longer at Jerusalem at present would be attended with great danger to himself; for, unknown to him, there was already a plot laid for his destruction, and no human means could have prevented the early loss of a life so precious. The Jews at this time, as we learn from history, must have had their fiercest passions roused into action, so as to make them ready for any daring crime. This was owing to a threatened violation of their national and religious feelings by the wicked Roman emperor, Caligula. He had given orders to have his statue erected in the Temple of Jerusalem,—a proposal so abhorrent to the mind of every Israelite, that they resolved to shed the last drop of their blood in resisting it. Fortunately, however, the news of his death by the hand of an assassin reached the Jewish capital during the very time that Saul was living there in the house of Peter.† Their fury, therefore, now finds vent in another channel, against the devoted apostle, and a Higher than any human friend warns him of his danger. One day Saul went up to the temple, in great sadness of spirit at all this violent opposition, to seek comfort and support in prayer. When he was on

* Blunt's *Lectures*, vol. i. p. 89. † Josephus.

his knees, the Lord Jesus again appeared to him in a trance or vision. This memorable occasion he speaks of afterwards, as what he might well "glory in," were he given to boasting. He was caught up into the third heavens, and heard "unspeakable words, which it is not lawful (or possible) for a man to utter.' In that vision Jesus told him expressly to leave Jerusalem, as "they would not receive his testimony." It may be well to quote his own description. "And it came to pass, that, when I was come again to Jerusalem, even while I prayed in the temple, I was in a trance; and saw Him saying unto me, Make haste, and get thee quickly out of Jerusalem: for they will not receive thy testimony concerning me. And I said, Lord, they know that I imprisoned and beat in every synagogue them that believed on thee."* What, we may be led to ask, is Saul's precise meaning in giving this answer? It is as if he had said, "Lord, if there be any place surely where I will have attentive listeners, it will be in Jerusalem, where there are many who knew me well as Saul the persecutor—the murderer of holy Stephen; and when they think of me being at one time as fierce and bitter against Thy name as themselves, and see what Thy grace can do, they will not surely refuse my testimony!"†

"Man proposeth, but God disposeth!" Nay, "but O man! who art thou that repliest against God?" His Divine Master, on that same occasion, answers him in a single sentence, telling him what his future work and calling is to be—"Depart, for I will send thee far hence unto the Gentiles." At this vision his drooping spirit revives. Meanwhile the brethren become ac-

* Acts xxii. 17–19. † Blunt.

quainted with the conspiracy against his life, and they get him persuaded immediately to leave Jerusalem.

Could he leave it, do you think, without a pang? As he passed through its gates, I doubt not he wept, like his Lord, over its hardness and unbelief. We may imagine him pausing on the rising ground outside, and taking one last look of the fated city, under the feeling that he may never see it again; and that when he is sleeping in his grave, "far hence among the Gentiles," the proud towers and palaces and temple which now meet his eye, may be blazing under the torch of the conqueror. Willingly would he have lingered for a while in her streets, to try and convince these hard hearts of their guilt, and bring them to repentance; but the voice of his God has called him elsewhere, and he feels he must obey. The disciples take means to have him privately conveyed to Cesarea. He probably takes a ship from thence to Cilicia, and after an eventful absence, the Apostle finds himself once more in the city and scenes of his infancy. There, it is probable, he was actively engaged in preaching the Gospel. From all we can gather, this was his last visit to Tarsus. We shall leave him seated in his old chamber, looking out on the crags of Mount Taurus, and the shadows of the Roman vessels reflected in the waters of the Cydnus,—talking, perhaps, to his sister about his own great change, and of the Prophet of Nazareth, whom once he scoffed at, now his chiefest boast,—kneeling, it may be, in prayer with her, and asking Jesus to pour his grace into *her* heart, as He had done into *his*. We shall leave Saul in thought in this loved retreat, while we trace what work was preparing for him in other cities.

CHAPTER VI.

The Missionary.

"Up to thy Master's work! for thou art call'd
To do His bidding, till the hand of death
Strike off thine armour. Noble field is thine—
The soul thy province, that mysterious thing
Which hath no limit from the walls of sense.
. . . . . Oh! live the life of prayer,
The life of tireless labour for His sake;
So may the Angel of the Covenant bring
Thee to thy home in bliss, with many a gem
To glow for ever in thy Master's crown."

"Over the vast extent of the Roman empire, Paul everywhere projects his shadow. What are we, preachers or missionaries of a day, before such a man!"—MONOD.

IF my readers will carry their eye along the coast of Palestine, they will see the names of two cities marked, at a considerable distance from each other. The one was Joppa or Jaffa, strikingly situated on a rocky ledge, jutting into the sea. From it, you remember, Jonah fled when God wished him to go to Nineveh. It was also famous as the old port of Jerusalem, to which Solomon floated his rafts of cedar-wood from Lebanon for the building of the temple. The other city was Cesarea, of which we have already spoken. It was situated 35 miles north of Joppa, built by Herod in honour of his royal master, and alled after him. He constructed there, at enormous and labour, a harbour, where ships might ride in safety from the fearful western storms that swept the coast. Also, a large Roman theatre, a remnant of which, at the present day, survives among the other ruins.

While Saul was at his Tarsus home, there dwelt two celebrated individuals in these two towns. The Apostle Peter was living in Joppa, in the house of a tanner.* A Roman officer, of a great family, called Cornelius, was stationed at Cesarea. He was centurion (or captain over a hundred) of a troop of Italian soldiers, which were there in garrison as a body-guard to the Roman governor. Peter one day, as he was engaged in prayer on the roof of his house, "overlooking the waves of the Western Sea—the sea of Greece and Rome—the sea of the isles of the Gentiles"†—fell into a trance, which you will find particularly described in Acts x. 3. He heard a voice commanding him to "slay and eat" some of the animals prohibited to be eaten by the Levitical law.‡ The day preceding this, Cornelius had a vision also in *his* house at Cesarea, telling him to send messengers to Joppa, to inquire there for "one Simon, whose surname was Peter." The messengers just arrived when the latter was returning from his devotions, and wondering what the vision he had witnessed could mean. Their appearance furnished him at once with an explanation. It was nothing less than this, that the Gentiles were now to be admitted to share the privileges of the Jews; and that the distinction between clean and unclean animals,

* The trade of a tanner was generally despised by the Jews, as being connected with dead animals, and many of these in themselves, according to their law, unclean. It was generally carried on in the outskirts of towns near the sea.

† Stanley's *Sermons and Essays*, p. 94.

‡ Lev. xi.

which was till this time the sign or badge of separation, was henceforth to be done away. Peter did not hesitate to obey the heavenly voice. Many years before, his Lord had given him the "keys of the kingdom of heaven." He now understood the meaning of the words. The gates of salvation, which had for ages been locked against the Gentiles, were now to be thrown open to "all people;" and *he* was to have the privilege of first unbarring them. We find him the following day standing in the house or barrack-room of the centurion, where the good Roman soldier had also gathered his kinsmen and near friends. The Gospel of the grace of God is freely proclaimed to Gentile hearers, and, henceforth, "in every nation he that feareth God and worketh righteousness is accepted of him."* The Holy Ghost descended. The officer of Rome, his house, and believing friends, were all baptized. It was a most solemn and joyous moment for the Church of Christ.

The Gospel ship is now fairly launched in Gentile waters. The Gospel seed has now fairly taken root in Gentile soil. There is one spot—a noted city—upon which, at this time, the mind rests with more than ordinary interest. If you again examine your map† of Asia, you will find, far north from Damascus, a little way inland from the Mediterranean, and almost opposite the island of Cyprus, the city of *Antioch*. Antioch was situated on the river Orontes, 20 miles from the sea, and 300 miles from Jerusalem. It formed the great mart of Eastern luxury, and, from its central position, commanded the whole trade of the Mediterranean. It was the outlet for merchants and cara-

* Acts x 35. † See the *green* line in the map.

vans who travelled from the banks of the Tigris and Euphrates, and ranked third (after Rome and Alexandria) among the cities of the Roman empire. Some Jewish converts—natives of Cyprus and Cyrene—had already gone thither and proclaimed the Gospel. Its Gentile inhabitants were beginning to be converted to the faith of Jesus. Many Greeks there "believed and turned to the Lord." Barnabas, whose name has already been favourably before us, crossed from his native island of Cyprus, and preached to them. But the numbers were growing, and he felt the urgency of having an abler minister to argue with Jewish prejudices, Greek learning, and false philosophy. He, as "the son of consolation," was able enough to comfort and direct young inquirers. But he needed some "son of thunder" to rouse the careless, and overturn the wisdom of men by the wisdom of God.* Where can he look? Who can he think of as the fittest man for such a work? I need scarcely name him! The Cyprian apostle embarked in some trading vessel which was bound for the Cydnus, and went, it is conjectured, about the beginning of the year 43, "to Tarsus to seek *Saul*." We may picture their meeting. The heart especially clings to the friends who have been kind to us in times of trial. With what joy must Saul have seen the well-known face that had beamed with kindness and good-will upon him in Jerusalem, when the other disciples were cold and suspicious! "The son of consolation" has, indeed, "consoling" news to give his old friend since they last met—that "God had granted to the Gentiles repentance unto life!" He could tell what he had seen with his own eyes in the city he had

* *The Apostle Paul: a Biography*

left. Saul does not hesitate to obey his wish. He leaves, possibly for the last time, the home of his youth; and the two holy men of God set out together for the great work in store for them at Antioch.

We cannot omit just noting by the way the unselfish conduct of Barnabas. He had himself been doing much good in this city—had gained many converts, and formed many Christian friendships. By his labours, we read, "much people in Antioch had been added to the Lord." If he had been a jealous or selfish man, he would not certainly have thought on bringing another to supplant him or be his rival. But how far removed he was from any such feeling! With simple-hearted joy, we read that, "when he saw the grace of God" displayed in the conversion of so many, "he was glad!" From that moment, he meekly takes the second place in the sacred narrative, saying, in the spirit of the Baptist, regarding a Greater than Saul, "He must increase, but I must decrease." He had but one thought, and that was, the promotion of his Lord's cause and glory; for this he willingly sacrificed self. His was the contented but beautiful feeling of Jonathan of old, when he said to David, "Thou shalt be king, and I shall be *next* to thee."*

We cannot tell whether this was Saul's first visit to a city with which he was afterwards so well acquainted. If it were so, his eye must have gazed with delight on its vastness and magnificence—its towers and temples, Roman villas and gardens, baths and theatres. You will be able to form some idea of Antioch from the picture at the beginning of this chapter. The town itself was nearly five miles long, and lay on the north-

* 1 Sam. xxiii. 17.

ern slope of the rocky Mount Silphius. Walls of enormous height and thickness (fifty feet high, and fifteen wide) extended round about it—spanning, in many places, the deep ravines of the mountain—and the ruins of which remain to the present day miracles of art and labour. A remarkable island was formed in the centre of the city, on which stood the palace of the Seleucidæ, with a bridge connecting it with the northern portion. The crags of Mount Silphius were all of them bold and rugged. One remarkable column of rock overhung the town, which the art of the Greeks had formed into an immense head, with a crown upon it, and which they called "the Head of Charon." If Saul could not see, from the road he travelled, the celebrated temple itself, he must have seen the vast groves of laurels, myrtles, and cypresses, which begirt for ten miles the great shrine at Daphne, erected in honour of Apollo and Diana. In the midst of these thickets, a thousand streams leapt from the neighbouring hills, and refreshed the sultry air. Antioch was well entitled to the name which for a long period it bore "the Queen of the East."

We may imagine the two brothers in the Lord now entering the town. They have perhaps reached the spacious colonnade in the long centre street, which was erected, at enormous cost, by Herod the Great, and where the citizens could assemble for business or pleasure, and be protected either from rain or heat. What a strange and motley crowd would greet their view! —Roman soldiers—servants from the prefect's palace—gay and pleasure-seeking Greeks—the keen dark eye of their brethren according to the flesh; the latter not arrayed in the poor garb they were often found in, in other cities, but bearing the evidences of wealth and prosperity, and worshipping the God of their fathers in handsome synagogues.* But there were other glories which gladdened them more. The cause nearest and dearest to their hearts was fast spreading in Antioch. The *sect* of disciples now began to assume the form of a Church, and, in the year 44, Jews and Gentiles who believed in Jesus as the Son of God and Saviour of the world, had a new title given to them, which they retain to this day, from the Greek word *Christos* ("anointed," or "*the Messiah*"),—"the disciples were called CHRISTIANS first at *Antioch*."

A writer of the sixth century—himself a native of the city—mentions the very spot where the two apostles first engaged in their work of preaching the Gospel. Its situation reminds us of St Paul, at a future period of his ministry, when he stood on Mars Hill, close to the Athenian temples. At Antioch they also took their position near to the Pantheon, in a street called "Singon," close to the busiest thoroughfare.†

Little did Saul think of the wonderful change which the power of God would produce in a few years in that Pagan city. Heathen temples were to give way to Christian churches—hymns to the praise of Jesus were to be heard in every street. In the age of Chrysostom, we find the Christians numbering 100,000, and supporting no less than 3000 poor, besides relieving many more! Antioch became, for many hundred years, the capital of Christendom, and was called by the name of *Theopolis*, a Greek word which means "the City of God." These facts will explain to our readers why we have

* Lewin.

† *Malela*, quoted by Lewin, p. 115.

dwelt more minutely than we should otherwise have done, in giving an account of this interesting place.*

An event in the meantime occurred, which required the two Christian ministers to leave Antioch for a little. Owing to a predicted failure in the harvest, in all the surrounding countries, and especially in Judea, thousands of the poor were about to endure famine. The Christians in Jerusalem, from their poverty, were likely to be among the greatest of the sufferers. Accordingly, they sent some "prophets," and among them one Agabus, to Antioch, to acquaint their fellow-Christians of their coming wants, and request from them what relief they were able to afford. The Gentile believers of the city met. They resolved to do what they could to help their starving friends at a distance; and, having collected some money, they appointed Saul and Barnabas to go with it, and give it to the elders at Jerusalem. God thus overruled this calamity in the world of nature to bring out the spiritual graces of His people, so that Jews and heathen might be brought to say of the Nazarenes they hated, "See how these Christians *love* one another!"

Josephus, in his history, confirms the account given in the sacred narrative regarding the famine. Among other things, he relates that Helena, the Queen of Adiabene (a country not far from Antioch), having become a convert to the Jewish religion, had taken up her abode in the city of Jerusalem, in order to be near the temple. When the famine broke out, she sent her

* *Lewin Conybeare and Howson, Neander, Bible Cyclopædia,* &c.—Antioch is now a small town. It has been six times the scene of fearful earthquakes. That of A.D. 526 is said to have destroyed 250,000 individuals, having happened on occasion of a festival. In 1268 it was laid in ruins by a Sultan of Egypt. In 1822 another earthquake occurred, which destroyed 4000 or 5000.

servants to Alexandria, in Egypt, to procure a large quantity of corn; others she sent to the island of Cyprus for a store of dried figs,—distributing these among the starving Jews. Her son, the reigning King of Adiabene, followed her charitable example, and forwarded large sums of money to Palestine.

When the two holy apostles, Saul and Barnabas, arrived in Jerusalem, there were other events which had made their poor Christian friends very sad and sorrowful. Herod (the grandson of the king who had murdered the little children in Bethlehem at the time of the Saviour's birth) was still reigning Sovereign of Judea, under Claudius Cæsar. Though he was a wicked man, and indulged in many vices, he had always been a strict observer of the Jewish law, and therefore very much hated the new sect of Christians. After eight years' freedom from persecution, the dreaded flames once more burst out. James, one of the disciples of Jesus, he had "slain with the sword." He had put Peter, at the time of the Passover, in prison—set sixteen soldiers to guard him, and bound him with two chains—resolving, in a short time, to bring him forth, and have him killed also. What human power can save him? This apostle must have concluded that the hour of his martyr-death, of which Jesus had forewarned him, had arrived, when he was to "stretch out his hands" like his Lord upon the cross.* But God has work for him to do before he receives his crown. The infant Church could yet ill spare him. No bolts or bars can stop the power of prayer. A prayer-meeting was held in a lowly dwelling in Jerusalem. God heard the voice of his servants. He sent his angel to open the prison doors

* John xxi.-18-22.

and let the apostle free; while the king who put him there was brought to a sudden and fearful end. In the same city where Cornelius the Christian Roman dwelt, there was, as we have already told you, a large theatre, erected by the elder Herod. One day about the beginning of the month of August, this building was crowded with people. The cause of the immense assemblage is to us an interesting one. The Emperor Claudius had gone to join his armies in Great Britain, and remained there for sixteen days. During this time, he obtained several victories, and took, among others, the city of Colchester, which was then, what London is now, the capital of the empire. On returning to Rome, there was universal rejoicing; he was called "Brittanicus," after our island; he had a naval crown put above his palace; and an annual celebration of the event was instituted at Rome, consisting of the usual barbarous sport of fighting wild beasts, with war-dances and chariot-racing. Herod Agrippa, who was both much indebted to Claudius, and desirous of retaining his favour, resolved to keep the festival also in imposing splendour in the theatre at Cesarea. The stone seats, which rose one above another, were a moving mass of human beings. On the second morning all faces were turned towards a private portico, through which in great pomp Herod entered, clad in sparkling robes of silver. He took his seat on a purple throne. When the people saw him, they shouted and cried, "Behold a god!" adding, according to Josephus, "Be thou merciful unto us; for although we have hitherto reverenced thee only as a king, yet shall we henceforth own thee as superior to mortals." The same writer, in his account of it, also relates that at that moment the unhappy being they were thus foolishly worshipping looked up and saw an owl (a bird of "evil omen," that is to say, supposed by the superstitious heathen to bespeak calamity) perched on a rope above his head. He was immediately filled with dread.* The great God of heaven, who will not give his glory to another, made him to be "eaten of worms!" He was carried away to his palace in the agonies of a dreadful death. Josephus adds, that the assembled multitudes fled from the theatre, and, as was the custom with the Jews, rent their clothes and sat in ashes, making a great lamentation—"And the king being laid in a high chamber, and looking down on the people prostrate on the ground, could not himself forbear weeping. And having continued in agony for five days, ... he departed this life." Think of holy Stephen's end, with angels his spectators! Think of *this!* What a comment on the words of the Psalmist!—"I have seen the wicked great in power and spreading himself like a green bay tree: yet he passed away, and lo! he was not; yea, I sought him, but he could not be found. Mark the perfect man, and behold the upright: for the end of that man is peace."†

We cannot tell what time Saul and Barnabas waited in Jerusalem; probably not long. They would give the money they had collected for the impending famine, and make the minds of the Christians there glad and joyful, by telling them of all that the Lord was doing at Antioch. When they prepared to return, they did not go alone, but took with them the nephew of Barnabas.

We have just spoken of a prayer-meeting of dis-

* Josephus, b. xix., chap. viii. † Psalm xxxvii. 35–37

ciples, in a house at Jerusalem, for the deliverance of Peter. It was the house of Mary, sister to Barnabas, and mother of "*John*, whose surname was *Mark*."* It is more than probable that one of those present at this prayer-meeting, who had the joy of welcoming back the imprisoned apostle, was Saul of Tarsus; that there he may have formed his acquaintance with the nephew of his companion, who was to be a future son and fellow-labourer in the faith. We shall have occasion more than once to mention the name of *Mark;* and though at one time, as we shall find, there was an unhappy difference between him and the great apostle, it is interesting to read among the very last sentences which Paul, when he became "the aged," wrote,—"Take Mark," said he to Timothy, "and bring him with thee, *for he is profitable to me in the ministry*."†

After this short visit to Jerusalem, Saul's history becomes more, than it has been yet, a history of preaching among the Gentiles. We shall enter, at this point, on the first of those great missionary tours, with their labours and perils, their joys and sorrows, which only closed when he could say, "I have fought a good fight, I have finished my course." That noble missionary river, whose streams are now fertilising the world, had its little fountain-head in Antioch.

One day, in some house or church in that great city, all the Christians were assembled together. They had met for fasting and prayer. The names of the different prophets and teachers are mentioned at the beginning of the 13th chapter of Acts. There was "Simeon, who was also called *Niger*,"—a word which means

* Acts xii. 12. † 2 Tim. iv. 11.

"black," and from which some have supposed that he was a black African—a negro—the first of the "Ethiopians" who are yet to "stretch out their hands unto God;" there was Manaen, the foster-brother of Herod Antipas; and Lucius, probably the same as *Luke* the Evangelist; "Saul and Barnabas." One or all of these had addressed the assembled disciples, discoursing to them about Jesus and his great salvation. We may imagine the assembled worshippers praising God for all His mercies, or perhaps uniting in supplication, making it the special object of their meeting to receive direction as to their future labours, when suddenly an answer is sent to their prayers. It is one which doubtless must in many ways have made them sorry; for it calls on them to part with the two of their number they had most reason to cleave to and love. But to God's will they joyfully submit. His command was, "Separate me now Barnabas and Saul for the work whereunto I have called them."* That work was to obey the parting commission of their great Lord—"Go and teach all nations, baptizing them in the name of the Father, and of the Son, and of the Holy Ghost."

Another solemn day was fixed to meet the two *missionaries*, before they set sail, to bid them farewell—to hear once more the Gospel message from their lips, and to implore anew God's blessing and guidance. Perhaps some of my readers have been at church when a missionary was set apart, and ordained to go to some far-off portion of the heathen world to preach "the unsearchable riches of Christ." It is a touching and impressive scene, which none can ever forget—a holy man willing to leave home and friends, to "spend and be

* Acts xiii. 2.

spent for Jesus." Here was the *first* of thousands of such scenes which have since taken place—the *first* consecration of three Christian missionaries! "They laid their hands on them, and sent them away."* We may imagine the tears in many eyes which followed them down to the harbour where the boat was in readiness to embark; we may almost hear the farewells that are spoken as the vessel or skiff left the shore. Little did the Syrian onlookers understand these tears, or know all the importance attached to that departure.

We have supposed, what is most likely, that they sailed by ship down the Orontes, with its vine-clad banks, to the harbour of Seleucia. Possibly, however, they saved time by avoiding the many windings in the river, and took the ordinary road which led across the bridge from the city on its north side. In this case, they would enter the sea-town by what was called the "Gate of Antioch"—a noble archway, on the south-east side, supported by pillars and guarded with towers. Seleucia was in those days a large port, with many gallant vessels from all parts of the Mediterranean riding in its harbour. The harbour itself was a famous one. It was built of vast stones fastened together with cramps of iron to which the ships were moored, and which, in the heavy storms and raging seas which broke at times from the west, kept them from being dashed to pieces. The scenery must have been striking to such a mind as that of Saul, standing, as we may suppose him, with his two fellow-missionaries, either on the heights of the fortress, or on the broad pier, with a forest of masts and the din of commerce all around His eye would rest, towards the north, on a

* Acts xiii 3.

bold parapet of Mount Coryphæus, with its rocky sides cut into numerous sepulchres similar to those in Petra cr the Valley of Jehoshaphat. In front he would gaze upon miles on miles of blue sea, whose waters he was afterwards to be familiar with in calm and in terrible storm. In the far distance, the dim hazy tops of the Cyprian mountains rose into view. Barnabas and his relative Mark doubtless loved to look at these, for Cyprus was their old home; and probably this was one among other reasons which had determined them to direct their pilgrim steps first to its shores. They have now set sail; the mountains, which at first they saw at a great distance, come nearer and nearer; their vessel, under a fair gale, is skimming over the waves; and when they are lowering its sails, they find themselves, 100 miles from Seleucia, entering the bay and harbour of Salamis.

Cyprus, known to the Hebrews by the name Chetim or Kittim (from Kittim, the son of Javan), is, next to Sicily, the largest island in the Mediterranean. The many crooked windings and turnings in its rugged coast gave it the name of "the Horned;" but so beautiful and fertile was it, that it was called also by the name of "the *Blest.*" Its situation, and the number of these creeks and havens, made it a favourite place of resort for merchants from Egypt, Phenicia, and Asia Minor. There were large plantations in the interior whose timber was much valued in ship-building. In the cultivated plains, "corn, wine, and oil" were produced in abundance, and its mines and rivers contained diamonds, emeralds, silver, lead, and copper. More valuable and "unsearchable riches" than these had already been brought to Cyprus by the

Christians who were scattered abroad on the death of Stephen; but the efforts of these earlier missionaries were confined to the Jews alone. A great number of Israelites were always resident in the island, and this, we may well believe, was another reason, in addition to what has already been mentioned, for the apostles turning their steps to its shores. Jesus had himself spoken of the peculiar claims of "the lost sheep of the house of Israel;" and Saul and his two companions would doubtless consider that they best fulfilled their Lord's will by seeking first to bring *them* into the Gospel fold. They accordingly began their labours in the Jewish synagogues.

After spending some little time in Salamis, they resolve to cross to the other end of the island to a town called Paphos, now "Baffa,"—a distance of nearly 100 miles. This must have been a place of importance, from being the residence of the Roman governor. The heathen goddess, under whose protection the island of Cyprus was by its Pagan inhabitants supposed to be, was Venus; hence she was called Cypria, and was fabled to have sprung from the foam of the sea. Her principal temple was situated close by Paphos, in the midst of delightful groves and delicious fruit-trees. On the streets of this island town these faithful missionaries stood and preached the glorious Gospel of the grace of God.

Saul says, at a future time, in one of his letters, "Not many noble are called." Here, however, there was *one*,—the first of the few "noble" and great of this world who were, through his agency, to embrace the religion of the despised Jesus. The Roman governor or deputy, Sergius Paulus, is described as "a prudent man, who desired to hear the Word of God." He appears to have been a person of an inquiring spirit, an "open-minded" man, as the word "prudent" means. He could get no comfort in the heathen religion; he found it could not meet the wants of his soul. Mere curiosity prompted, at a future time, other kings and governors to hear Saul; but we believe it was from a deeper feeling that Sergius desired to listen to the Gospel tidings. He was brought to believe and love the Saviour. Let us hear what were the means employed to humble this exalted Roman, and bring him to the foot of the cross. He had with him in his royal dwelling a Jew whose name was Bar-Jesus, or, as he was called also, Elymas,—an Arabian word which means "the wise one" (just as our English word "wizard" is derived from, or rather is a contraction of, "wise art"). But professing himself to be "wise," this man was a "fool." He was one of those false deceivers or knaves, who at that age of the world used to pretend to work miracles, and prophesy, and perform magical arts in connexion with Satan.* They were often found in the houses of the great, and in the palaces of kings.

The East has at all times been famed as the region of wild dreams and fairy tales, of magic and fortune-telling. Many during the age of the Apostle, from whom we might have looked for better things, were silly enough to believe in the magical arts of cunning impostors, and to encourage them by gifts of money. It is sad to think how even some among the Jewish nation lent themselves to this wicked trade. These, certainly, were of the "baser sort," unworthy to be called children of Abraham. They pretended to be possessed of the spi

* See Horne's *Introduction*, vol. ii. p. 366.

rit of their old prophets, and to have the gift of second-sight, foretelling future events. One of this number was Bar-Jesus, who had now found his way to the governor's dwelling at Paphos. Sergius Paulus had been told of the newly-arrived strangers. He had probably heard not a little of the new sect called "Christians," which had grown up in Jerusalem, and whose doctrines were spreading in the capital of Syria. On resolving, therefore, to see and hear its three disciples, Elymas did all he could to prevent their getting into the governor's presence; for as light has no fellowship with darkness, he knew that if his master came to embrace their doctrines, *his* power and influence at court would be at an end. All his arts, however, to exclude the apostle-missionaries were unsuccessful; Saul and his two friends stood in the presence of the high-born Roman. They "preached to him Jesus,"—told him of the only true rest for his troubled soul, and that there was neither happiness nor salvation in any other. Bar-Jesus evidently writhed under the apostles' words. We are not told what he did, or what he said; but we are left in little doubt, from Saul's strong language, that the impostor-Jew had been blaspheming that holy Name which the apostle counted dearer than life. The noble spirit of the latter is roused within him, and by the power of God he prepares to silence the wicked gainsayer by "terrible things in righteousness which he looked not for." In the name of the same Great Being who, on his way to Damascus, had deprived him of sight, "he declared, with divine confidence, that the Lord would punish Elymas with the loss of these organs which he only abused by attempting, through his arts of deception, to stop the progress of Divine truth."* Fixing upon him a stern look, he pronounces the awful sentence, and the miserable man is sent away groping in darkness. Sergius cannot resist the power of this miracle. He believes; and many in the town and throughout the island follow the example of their noble governor. The missionaries doubtless raise their hearts in humble gratitude to God for these first-fruits of the great harvest.†

As this is the first miracle wrought by the apostle, the question may occur to us, What were the extent of Saul's miraculous gifts? Could he work a miracle at any time he pleased, or was it only the result of some special power given him at particular times? Evidently it was the latter alone. "He could strike Elymas blind because he was so directed, but he could not cure Trophimus or Epaphroditus when they were sick, or rid himself of the thorn in the flesh, though it so sorely distressed him. So Paul had the gift of tongues, yet his knowledge in this respect was

* Neander.

† What would the pilgrim-missionary have thought if he had read the following account of his apostolic successor, given by an English traveller in Cyprus 1800 years after?—"I entered the city by the gate of Larnica, and was conducted to the Episcopal palace through a number of narrow lanes, where my horse was nearly buried in mud and filth. The archbishop, dressed in a magnificent purple robe, with a long flowing beard, and a silk cap on his head, received me in the vestibule, and ordered an apartment to be prepared for me in the palace,—a large and straggling building containing upwards of a hundred chambers. These are all required for the accommodation of the bishops, priests, and their attendants; for the archbishop, both in power and affluence, is the second personage on the island. . . . At seven o'clock, supper being announced, he took me by the hand and led me through a gallery into the refectory,—a long and dirty hall, where about thirty priests and bishops sat down to table. The wine and provisions were excellent and abundant, and the bread, which was white as snow, and baked with milk instead of water, was the best I remember to have tasted."—Kinneir's *Journey through Asia Minor*, p. 188.

limited, as we shall see at Lystra, where the Lycaonian dialect was unintelligible to him. So Paul had the spirit of prophecy as to Antichrist; and, when tossed by the storm in Adria, could predict that not a life would be lost, and that they should be cast away on a certain island; but when he parted from the Ephesian elders, on his third circuit, he could not foresee that he should visit them again." *

It is worthy of note, that from this time forward the great apostle always takes the name of PAUL. Saul is never used again, either in the Acts of the Apostles, nor does he use it himself in the course of his own epistles. What was the cause or meaning of this change of name? There must have been some reason for it. We know it was a common thing, with many of God's favoured servants, to have an alteration of name at some important periods of their history. Abram's name was changed to *Abraham;* Simon was changed to *Peter* (the Rock). Some think that Saul took the name of *Paul* in honour of Sergius *Paulus* becoming a Christian—that just as Pagan heroes derived their new titles from the cities or countries they conquered, so Saul adopted a new name from the first conquest he had made by the "sword of the Spirit" in this island. But it is more likely intended to mark his calling as a missionary to the heathen and Gentiles. He dropped his name *Saul*, which was his *Jewish* one; and he takes the title *Paul*, which was his *Roman* one, as it was henceforth not among the Hebrews, but the Pagan Romans, that his greatest triumphs were to be won.† He adopted the change at this particular time, as God had granted him such

* Lewin, vol. i. p. 143.

† Origen. See Calmet's *Commentary.*

marked favour and success in Cyprus,—a place which was always considered very wicked and sinful.

Be this, however, as it may, Paul "thanked God and took courage." He prepared to buckle on his armour for new battles and new victories. He was now about, like Abraham, when he received his change of name, to become the spiritual "father of many nations."

CHAPTER VII.

The Traveller.

"Hark the note!
The natural music of the mountain reed—
For here the patriarchal days are not
A pastoral fable—pipes in the liberal air,
Mix'd with the sweet bells of the wandering herd."

"Once was I stoned, ... in journeyings often, in perils of waters, in perils of robbers, in perils by mine own countrymen, in perils by the heathen, in perils in the city, in perils in the wilderness."—2 Cor. xi. 25, 26.

AFTER this favoured visit to the lovely island of Cyprus, we find Paul and his two companions once more on the Mediterranean, sailing northwards to the coast of Pamphylia, in Asia Minor. We are not told whether God had given them special directions to direct their steps thither, or whether they just took the first vessel they found sailing for another shore,—"the field" being "the world," and perishing heathen souls everywhere equally precious. Perhaps the Great Apostle, now that he had preached in large cities, might be desirous of carrying the glad tidings, with the hopes, too, of greater success, into the less frequented regions of Asia Minor,—upland districts similar to many parts of North Wales, the Highlands of Scotland, or the valleys of the Alps, where the inhabitants were more primitive in their manners, and less corrupted with fashionable vices and sins.

Be this as it may, however, we find the three travellers once more in a Cyprian vessel coming in view of the coast of Pamphylia. On entering, as is probable, the mouth of the Cestrus, their eyes would rest on a flat plain, on either side, running a long way into the interior, till it was hemmed in by a rampart of snowy mountains. Paul's thoughts were occupied with nobler battles and victories than those of earth; but it is not improbable that, as they were slowly steering up the river, some of the crew may have pointed out to him spots which had been rendered famous by contending armies, narrating tales of valour connected with the names of Cimon, Antiochus, and Hannibal. In entering the channel of the Cestrus, he would observe the rugged cliffs which rose perpendicularly from the sea on the east and west. If he had been a few miles further in a westerly direction, he would have seen the leap which the river Catarrhactes (as its name imports) takes over the sea-cliffs into the ocean beneath, and which must have been peculiarly grand after the heavy rains, or the sudden melting of the mountain snows.*

Pamphylia itself occupied about eighty miles along the coast, lying between Lycia on the west, and Cilicia on the east; and as its name, "a land of all tribes," would lead us to infer, it was inhabited by different races—those principally of Greek extraction. At this time, Pisidia and Lycia formed along with it one province, under a Roman governor, having Antioch in Pisidia for its capital.† They have sailed seven miles

* "The river Cataractes, which Strabo places between the cities of Olbia and Attalia, and which, he says, precipitates itself from a lofty rock with a tremendous din."—Beaufort's *Karamania*, p. 127.

† Lewin, vol. i. p. 145.

up the river we have just spoken of, and which bears the modern name of the Aksoo, when they reach the town of Perga. This city was beautifully situated in the valley through which, amid precipitous rocks, the Cestrus winds its way. It occupied chiefly the left bank of the river; it had a wall surrounding it, with the usual edifices of a Greek town—a theatre, stadium, and temples. As at Antioch and Paphos, the great attraction of the place was a temple built on a lofty eminence to Diana, and a yearly festival held in honour of this heathen goddess. Shepherds and their flocks are now found encamping amid broken shafts and columns,—all that is left to mark the spot where Perga stood, and where Paul and his friends lodged.

There was a trial waiting the great apostle here which he little expected. John Mark, who had till now accompanied them, got either timid or weary in his work, and, leaving Paul and Barnabas, he took the first ship that sailed to the land of Judea. We have no means of knowing accurately what induced the younger disciple to take this step, and desert his fellow-travellers, just when they had most need of him. Most probably he feared the "perils of floods (waters) and perils of robbers,"—the dangers and fatigues that were so well known in connexion with a journey across the Pisidian "*Alps.*" He could not make up his mind to "endure hardness as a good soldier of Jesus Christ." It must, at all events, have been cause of deep sorrow and regret to his older companions. May we not conclude this to have been the reason of their brief stay in Perga? The good cause may there have suffered from the unkind and unmanly conduct of Barnabas' young relative. Mark would doubtless have his own sad feelings, when, as he sailed all alone on the midnight sea, he thought of this desertion from his holy and devoted friends. The words of his divine Lord and Master must have been sounding loudly and reproachingly in his ears,—"No man having put his hand to the plough, and looking back, is fit for the kingdom of God." Some have been led in charity to plead, in excuse for him, a commendable desire to be with his aged and widowed mother in Jerusalem; but even this, though it would tend to lessen his blameworthiness, would not be sufficient to justify him; for, after having undertaken his missionary work, he ought to have remembered the words of Him who said, "Whosoever loveth father and mother more than me, is not worthy of me." We have abundant reason to conclude, as we shall by and by find, that he bitterly repented of the step, and did all in his power to atone for present ingratitude and timidity.

The two elder apostles prepare alone to resume their journey. We have already seen them gathered with their fellow-Christians in Antioch (in Syria); we are now to accompany them many miles straight north from Perga, to another Antioch (in Pisidia) in the centre of Asia Minor. There are no gently-flowing rivers, like the Orontes or Cydnus, by which they can approach this remote spot. Desolate paths and rugged cliffs must be climbed and crossed before they can reach the distant capital.

It has been supposed, and perhaps correctly, that the season of the year when the two pilgrims set out from Perga, was about the end of spring or the beginning of summer, when the heat began to be so great in and around Perga, that the inhabitants (as still is the custom in many parts of India) left the intolerable warmth of the lower plains, and went up in companies or caravans to the cool breezes of the mountains.* We are all the more willing to fix this to be the time of their journey, as these lonely passes were infested with thieves, which rendered the route very dangerous to single or unprotected travellers. Many a daring tale of robber chiefs still lingers among these mountain glens; desperate marauders or freebooters, similar to those who kept, a century ago, the Scottish Highlands in a state of lawlessness, frequently pillaged, by sudden incursions, the plains, and then retreated amid their inaccessible rocks and fastnesses. If even Roman armies and Roman valour had to quail before these savage tribes, we need not wonder at Paul speaking afterwards with such feeling (and evidently with reference to his present journey) of "perils of robbers."

It is more than probable that our two travellers selected the period of the year for their journey when they would have that protection on the road which was so much needed. Add to this—it was hardly possible to traverse these regions with comfort or safety at any other season of the year,—there was no travelling during the severe cold and drifting snows of winter, and, in early spring, the defiles were either choked with snow, or else the melting of it on the mountains made what roads and bridges there were, in many places, impassable.

We may imagine, then, the great apostle and his

* See the entire interesting chapter in Howson and Conybeare, where the descriptions of modern travellers are made graphically to illustrate this portion of Paul's life.—Authorities there quoted.

fellow-traveller, staff in hand, on their way from Perga to the mountains of Pisidia. Their eyes are no longer gazing on the walls of a Jewish synagogue or a Roman palace,—the apostle no longer sits wrapped in his warm "cloak" as he floats over the "great sea," but toiling along through difficult and slippery paths, with huge precipices frowning in terror over his head. Now and then some torrent, swollen by the sudden rains, and occupying the whole breadth of the defile, as it rushes down, may remind us also of the "perils of waters" (or "water-floods"), which he couples with the more terrible one of the mountain-freebooters. Those of my readers who are familiar with the floodings of the rivers and mountain-streams in Scotland, when, after the sudden melting of the snows on the higher Grampians, sheep, and trees, and corn-stacks, are often swept along in the furious current, may form some idea of the nature of these "perils" the apostle speaks of.

The fierce heat of the sun is gradually exchanged for the cooling breeze of the uplands; the vine, the orange, the pomegranate, and, above all, the oleander, with its bright crimson flower, at that season must have been carpeting the rocks as they began their ascent.* As they approach the higher regions, these gradually disappear, and the hardier plants and shrubs of the mountain take their place; at last they come to mark only a few flowers shivering in the snow, and are glad to take refuge now and then in some shepherd's cave or grotto, or beneath the shade of pines, to screen them from the cutting winds. Any travellers that might have accompanied them thus far, are

* Spratt and Forbes' *Lycia*, as quoted by Howson.

now left behind, and they pursue their journey alone across a flat table-land of dull and dead scenery. They have bid, for the present, at least, farewell both to the riches of the plain and the stern grandeur of the mountains, and are traversing a vast flat wilderness full of lakes and morasses, where storks and wild swans are raising their necks among the reeds and rushes.* Shepherds' huts and folds are studded here and there, at which fires are kept blazing at night to scare away the wild animals; and the apostle doubtless sees also occasionally encampments formed of the well-known "goats'-hair tents," reminding him of his Tarsus days and childhood happiness.† In the far distance a few scattered specks begin to appear; and, after an hour or two of further journey, they are glad to find their weary limbs reclining in some humble dwelling in the capital of Pisidia.

The Pisidian Antioch, founded by Seleucus Nicanor, stood on an eminence which can still be distinguished as the site of the old city from the numerous ruins which are strewn around. Among these is a magnificent aqueduct of twenty-one arches, and several churches and temples.‡

One Sabbath day, somewhere between the year of our Lord 45 and 50, we may fancy ourselves in the inside of a strange, peculiar building in the city of Antioch. It is built in a circular form; seats, rising one above another, are filled with eager intelligent countenances. In the centre is a raised desk or table of wood, where an individual, with a flowing beard, is

* Fellow's *Asia Minor*, p. 155, quoted by Howson. See the picture at the beginning of the chapter.

† Fellow's *Asia Minor*, p. 155.

‡ *Bible Cyclopædia*, Arundell's *Asia Minor*, &c.

busy reading from some ancient scroll he holds in his hand; beside him is an interpreter, who translates what the other has been reading in Hebrew into the Greek language; close by is an ancient ark or chest, where the roll we have mentioned, along with others, were carefully kept; other bearded rulers sit in stone seats in front, facing the people; and behind a screen or lattice in the gallery, are a number of females—the wives and daughters of those assembled worshippers.* We must not omit to note two other figures in this assemblage—two men, strangers in dress, and yet wearing the covering for the head which was the badge of every Israelite, and, with features like others around them, are seated by themselves, and attract the attention of their fellow-worshippers. I need not tell you what scene this is, nor who these two strangers are—it is the Jewish synagogue in the Pisidian capital. Paul and Barnabas, as their custom was, resorted to the Jews' place of worship to seek an opportunity of preaching the Gospel of their Divine Master.

With what different feelings must they, and the others in that synagogue, have listened to the following prayers which had just been read:—"Blessed be thou, O Lord our God, the God of our fathers, . . . who, in thy love, sendest a Redeemer to those who are descended from them for Thy name's sake! O King, our Lord and helper, our Saviour and our shield! *Blessed art thou, O Lord, who art the shield of Abraham!*" "Look, we beseech Thee, upon our afflictions, . . . and make haste to redeem us with a perfect redemption for Thy name's sake; for Thou art our God, our King, and a strong Redeemer. *Blessed art thou, O Lord, the Re-*

* Philo, ii. 458.

deemer of Israel!" "Make the offspring of David, Thy servant, speedily to grow up and flourish, and let our horn be exalted in Thy salvation; for we hope for Thy salvation every day. *Blessed art thou, O Lord, who makest the horn of our salvation to flourish!*" What a solemn "Amen" must the two Christian missionaries have pronounced over these answered prayers!

The "President" has just finished reading, as was the custom, the allotted portion of the Law and the Prophets; he has carefully rolled back the parchment or vellum scroll, and given it to the officer to be replaced in the chest. He then sends a messenger to the two strangers to ask them if they have any instructions to give the audience.

We may wonder at the notice thus taken of these unknown travellers; but it seems to have been understood in Jewish synagogues, that whenever any strangers took a seat, "*sat down* as Paul and Barnabas now did, it was an intimation that they were in the habit of addressing their countrymen, and were desirous of doing so."*

Paul was waiting ready to obey the invitation. We are told that, upon being asked, "he rose and beckoned with his hand,"—his usual mode of imposing silence when he was about to speak.

His sermon possesses a peculiar interest in being the first and the only one that we have on record as preached during this missionary journey. Though in itself only an outline of what he delivered, we may feel assured it contains a complete summary of his address, and much of it in the very words he employed. He secures at its commencement their attention by reminding them how

* Lightfoot

God had selected *them* to be His peculiar people—recounting His manifold mercies to their nation; briefly touching on various leading incidents in their miraculous history, till he comes to the promise of Messiah given to His servant David, of whom, according to the flesh, Jesus was to be born. He then began to open up the great subject of his teaching, viz., that that Messiah promised to their royal ancestor *had* already come, and that by faith in Him they were "justified from all things from which they could not be justified by the law of Moses." Neander observes, that the whole discourse is a specimen of the peculiar wisdom and skill of Paul in the management of men's dispositions. We may well be pardoned for quoting this memorable sermon in full. Imagine, then, the great apostle standing up in the synagogue of this distant city, and thus "preaching to them '*Jesus*:'"—

"Men of Israel, and ye that fear God, give audience. The God of this people of Israel chose our fathers, and exalted the people when they dwelt as strangers in the land of Egypt, and with an high arm brought he them out of it. And about the time of forty years suffered he their manners in the wilderness. And when he had destroyed seven nations in the land of Chanaan, he divided their land to them by lot. And after that he gave unto them judges about the space of four hundred and fifty years, until Samuel the prophet. And afterwards they desired a king; and God gave unto them Saul the son of Cis, a man of the tribe of Benjamin, by the space of forty years. And when he had removed him, he raised up unto them David to be their king; to whom also he gave testimony, and said, I have found David the son of Jesse, a man after mine

own heart, which shall fulfil all my will. Of this man's seed hath God, according to his promise, raised unto Israel a Saviour, Jesus: when John had first preached before his coming the baptism of repentance to all the people of Israel. And as John fulfilled his course, he said, Whom think ye that I am? I am not he: but, behold, there cometh one after me, whose shoes of his feet I am not worthy to loose. Men and brethren, children of the stock of Abraham, and whosoever among you feareth God, to you is the word of this salvation sent. For they that dwell at Jerusalem, and their rulers, because they knew him not, nor yet the voices of the prophets which are read every sabbath-day, they have fulfilled them in condemning him. And though they found no cause of death in him, yet desired they Pilate that he should be slain. And when they had fulfilled all that was written of him, they took him down from the tree, and laid him in a sepulchre. But God raised him from the dead: and he was seen many days of them which came up with him from Galilee to Jerusalem, who are his witnesses unto the people. And we declare unto you glad tidings, how that the promise which was made unto the fathers, God hath fulfilled the same unto us their children, in that he hath raised up Jesus again; as it is also written in the second psalm, Thou art my Son, this day have I begotten thee. And as concerning that he raised him up from the dead, now no more to return to corruption, he said on this wise, I will give you the sure mercies of David. Wherefore he saith also in another psalm, Thou shalt not suffer thine Holy One to see corruption. For David, after he had served his own generation by the will of God, fell on sleep, and was laid unto his fathers, and saw corruption: but he, whom God raised again, saw no corruption. Be it known unto you therefore, men and brethren, that through this man is preached unto you the forgiveness of sins: and by him all that believe are justified from all things, from which ye could not be justified by the law of Moses. Beware therefore, lest that come upon you which is spoken of in the prophets; Behold, ye despisers, and wonder, and perish: for I work a work in your days, a work which ye shall in no wise believe, though a man declare it unto you." *

When Paul had finished, the Jews and Gentile proselytes† came crowding around him. The minds of the latter had been deeply impressed—they had been conscience-stricken, and the good seed sown was ere long to manifest its growth in a Christian church. They were not content with what they had just heard from his lips, they ask the apostle to return again on the next sabbath, and repeat these wondrous glad-tidings of great joy. He gladly agrees to do so. Meanwhile, ere he leaves the synagogue, he entreats them, with fatherly affection, "to abide in the grace of God."

We may imagine how the two Christian teachers would be employed before the return of another sabbath; how busily they would be engaged in going from house to house, explaining more fully the great salvation. The strange and startling sermon which this Jew of Tarsus had preached would doubtless be the topic of general conversation during the week. Greek merchants would talk of it at their place

* Acts xiii. 16-41.

† Proselytes were those heathens or Gentiles who had been converted to Judaism, and worshipped the only living and true God.

of business—peasants, at the market—Jews, as they met in groups on the streets. When the next sabbath came round, the fame of the apostle had spread far and wide, and at the hour of service a dense crowd of Greeks, Romans, Hebrews, and Pisidians, was collected both in and around the synagogue. "Almost the whole city came together to hear the word of God."* The greater number of these worshippers were Gentiles. Their presence excited the envy of the Jews, who would not, as on the former sabbath, listen patiently to what Paul had to say. Filled with spiritual pride, they were offended at the thought of salvation coming in any other way but through their law, and given to any other but their nation. They drowned his voice, therefore, with their clamour, and "interrupted him, contradicting and blaspheming." Paul tried in vain to quiet them. He offered them anew "the grace of God," but when he found all his pleadings were to no purpose, he speaks as the apostle to the *Gentiles,* "magnifying his office." "It was necessary that the word of God should first have been spoken to you; but seeing ye put it from you, and judge yourselves unworthy of everlasting life, lo! we turn to the Gentiles."† There were, however, many sincere converts made to the faith of Jesus as the result of these sabbath-days' services; indeed, we are told the word of God spread through the region round about. His word never returns to Him void. It is added at the close of the narrative in the Acts, that "the disciples were filled with joy and with the Holy Ghost."‡

But the apostle was not allowed to remain and watch the bread he had thus cast upon the waters. Some

* Acts xiii. 44. † Acts xiii. 46. ‡ Acts xiii. 52

women of influence in the city prevailed on the chief citizens to take part with the Jews against Paul. He saw that it would be needful for him again, as at Damascus formerly, to obey his Lord's command, "When they persecute you in one city, flee to another." They left, therefore, the gates of the Pisidian capital, and "shaking the dust from their feet," as a testimony against its unbelieving citizens, made their way to Iconium.

This town is situated at the foot of Mount Taurus, sixty miles from Antioch, on the great highway connecting Ephesus with the Syrian Antioch. Under the modern name of Konieh, or Cogni, a corruption of its ancient one, it still exists a Turkish city, but has few remains of its antiquity, saving some slabs, columns, and pedestals, with Greek and Roman inscriptions. Iconium rose many ages after Paul visited it to much greater splendour and importance, under a bold race of eastern princes or sultans. Here they had their palace, and adorned the town with many spacious buildings. To this day, although there are few ancient remains, its walls are extensive, numbering many towers and eighty gates. A traveller already mentioned was peculiarly struck with the imposing appearance of the mosques and colleges. "Several of the gates of these old colleges," he says, "are of singular beauty. They are formed entirely of marble, adorned with a profusion of fretwork, and a fine entablature in the Moresco fashion, far excelling anything of the kind I have seen."* However altered in many other respects, the natural features of the city and neighbourhood must have undergone little change since the days of Paul.

* Kinneir, p. 219.

The same gardens and pleasant meadows which the modern traveller observed stretching along the base of the hills—the same mountains, covered with snow on all sides but one, must have been seen by the apostle. An extensive plain stretches towards the east, the largest in Asia Minor. The Saracens who conquered the country are said to have been forcibly reminded by it of their own eastern deserts; and modern tourists speak of their camels stooping to crop the same tough herbage these animals are so familiar with in the boundless and arid plains of Eastern Asia.* It is not improbable that the great apostle may have had suggested to *his* mind its resemblance to the plain of Damascus — standing as both cities did like green spots in a waste wilderness; the heights of Taurus, with its scantier streams, reminding him of Hermon and Lebanon, and the dry and dusty plain of Lycaonia recalling "the wilderness of Damascus."

Our two travellers seem to have remained at Iconium for some time, preaching in the synagogue and in private dwellings. The same treatment, however, awaited them here as at Antioch. The envious Jews stirred up the people—who threatened to stone them; but, on being informed of the plot against their lives, they resolved yet again to renew their journey, and preach the Gospel in "other cities."

The two places to which they next directed their steps, seem to differ from any they had yet visited. We have followed them hitherto chiefly into the streets of great capitals, full of wealth and learning. Now their route lies through the desert and little-travelled region of Lycaonia, to the cities of Derbe and Lystra. Here

* Ainsworth, Col Leake, as quoted by Howson.

the inhabitants seem to have been a pastoral race, rude, uncultivated, and plunged in gross paganism. There seems, indeed, to have been neither Jew nor synagogue in either city. The very name of the God of Israel was unknown to them. As they approached the gates of Lystra, they saw a large temple, with a statue within it, or before it, of Jupiter, the king of the pagan gods. This shewed at once what the religion of this city of the desert was. Jupiter was patron or presiding deity; the ignorant citizens imagined that he watched over it, and protected it. Day after day these pagans brought animals to the temple for their priests to slay to him in sacrifice.

We have abundant evidence from pagan writers that Lycaonia was a country wholly given to heathen idolatry. The very name (Lycaonia) had a strange fabulous meaning, which it may be interesting to note, as it bears on the occurrences we shall have presently to mention in connexion with the two apostles. The word Lycaonia is said to be derived from the Greek word λυκος, a *wolf*, and the story, as related by the Latin poet Ovid, is in outline as follows:—

There was a king of Arcadia, by name Lycaon, who was directed by an oracle to found a city in that region. Jupiter, the king of the gods, descended one night in bodily shape to the palace of Lycaon; and the subjects of the king, recognising the deity, wished to pay him adoration. Lycaon was angry; he resolved to shew to his people that they were under a delusion in supposing this inmate of his house was really Jupiter, and he took the following method of proving their mistake. Some legates had been sent to treat with him from a neighbouring kingdom. He issued the cruel order to kill one of these, and to serve up his flesh at dinner to the reputed king of the gods. The horrible order was obeyed; Jupiter, in dreadful wrath, overturned the table—caused flames to burst forth in the palace, and laid it in ashes. Meanwhile, Lycaon fled in terror—his speech forsook him—his human form was gradually changed into that of a *wolf*, and he turned growling with fury on the unprotected flocks browsing on the fields around.*

Such was the very foolish story and fable currently believed by the blinded pagan citizens, whose gates Paul and Barnabas were now approaching. No sooner did the two apostles arrive in town than they proceeded to sound the Gospel trumpet. It does not seem that in doing so they went into any building or house. Probably in the open streets or squares, in the market place, or under some shady trees, they began to preach the great salvation. We may imagine the strange groups that were gathered around them,—men of rude garb and rougher manners, whose city was rarely visited by learned strangers; whose ears, though doubtless they understood it, seldom listened to the polished tones of the noble tongue in which Paul afterwards spoke to the philosophers of Athens, and in which he addressed his hearers now. As the preacher, with the stately figure of Barnabas at his side,† waxed in fervour and power, the thought may have occurred to the Lystrian crowd, with the temple of their patron god in view, What! can it be, that Jupiter can have come from his throne on Olympus, attended with Mercury, the god of eloquence? The idea, as we have seen, was neither new nor unwelcome to superstitious

* Ovid, *Met.* lib. 1. † Described so by Chrysostom and others.

minds, and an incident presently occurred, which either led to their delusion or confirmed it.

As Paul was proceeding with his discourse, his eye was attracted by a lame man who lay on the ground unable to walk, but whose face was turned with ardent gaze on the lips of the speaker. The same, we read, "heard Paul speak." He was, doubtless, "hearing him speak" on the great theme of salvation through a crucified but now exalted Redeemer. We have every reason to conclude that he had been brought to believe in that holy name, by which the power of the servant of Christ was about to perform on him a "notable miracle." There are few towns, or even villages, which have not some such helpless object as now met the eye of Paul at Lystra. They are generally well known from their infirmity; and dependent, as they generally are, on public charity, they take their station at any notable place of resort, to be in the public eye. Anything, therefore, performed on this poor Lystra cripple in the shape of a cure, would be sure to attract attention. Paul saw that "he had faith to be healed." "Stand upright on thy feet," exclaims the great apostle, in a strength mightier than his own. In a moment the limping sufferer springs from the ground, and walks whole and restored before the gazing crowd.

Soon the tidings of the wonderful miracle spread. The town is in an uproar. The people rush away to the temple we have spoken of; they get the priest to adorn some oxen with flowers and garlands, and walking with these in procession, they advance towards the residence of the apostles. What can be the meaning of all this? These deluded heathens verily believe that the story of Lycaon has again come true,—the king of gods and men is once more in their streets, with his constant companion! They need not worship Jupiter in his temple, for they have him in the person of Barnabas, and Mercurius has come to them in the person of Paul. The people, in the fever of their excitement, had made these remarks to one another in the old Lycaonian dialect, so that the apostles were not at first aware what they had been purposing, until, to their amazement, they beheld the procession of garland-crowned oxen close by their lodging. How it grieves and saddens the heart of Paul to see such ignorance and superstition! He and his companion rush to the door of their dwelling—they rend their clothes—they rebuke the folly of the citizens, assuring them that they are "men of like passions with themselves," and that it is by the power of Jesus alone they can perform such mighty works as had just been witnessed in the case of the lame man.

Ye men of Lystra, "why do ye these things? We also are men of like passions with you, and preach unto you, that ye should turn from these vanities unto the living God, which made heaven, and earth, and the sea, and all things that are therein: who in times past suffered all nations to walk in their own ways. Nevertheless he left not himself without witness, in that he did good, and gave us rain from heaven, and fruitful seasons, filling our hearts with food and gladness."* The conduct of the Lystrians affectingly shews us "how much more willingly the world is led by the power of Satan than by the Spirit of God." The apostles had wrought many miracles to prove the divinity of their Lord and Master; few, comparatively, believed on Him

* Acts xiv. 15–17.

But here one single miracle is enough to bring these blinded pagans to worship and serve the creature rather than the Creator! They refuse to believe in the divinity of *Jesus;* but they dishonour His holy name by desiring to pay divine honours to two poor sinful mortals He had redeemed with His blood.* I may just add, if Paul and Barnabas had been impostors, designing men, who wished to get for themselves honour or wealth or dignity, how easily might they have worked on the credulity and ignorance of the people of Lystra! Gold and silver were generally stored in abundance in pagan temples—how easily might these two reputed "gods" have got access within the gate of the temple of Jupiter, and demanded the offerings treasured there! All their thoughts, however, were bent on undeceiving the ignorant minds around them; their only desire was, that they themselves be nothing, and that their Great Lord might be "all in all."

But where do we find the apostle next? We should surely at all events expect the Lystrians to shew him every kindness and respect, to lodge him in a comfortable home, and listen with solemn earnestness to his preaching. Alas, what a changeable thing the human heart is! What an instance have we before us of the vanity and emptiness of human applause! He whom they would have worshipped one hour, is lying the next apparently a lifeless man, covered with wounds and bruises, outside their city wall! Some wicked Jews had followed the apostles from Iconium. They had made the citizens of Lystra believe that they wrought these miracles by *magic,* or by the power of the Evil One. The fate of the martyr Stephen very nearly

* Blunt, p. 178.

PAUL NOT DEAD.

becomes Paul's own. They stone him in the midst of the street. He is dragged, cut and bleeding, outside the ramparts of the town, and left to lie there. The few disciples that loved him are gathered round the dying man with tears. Doubtless many feared he was breathing his last. Barnabas would have all the sad thoughts of preparing a grave for his honoured friend in this far off pagan city, and of a return back alone to Jerusalem with the terrible tidings—"Paul is dead!" But the Lord, in whose hand is the breath of every living thing, had more work yet for his dear servant. "Though cast down, he is not destroyed." The Church could not spare him, and these tears are soon to be turned into joy. We know not the names of those in that mourning crowd who were bathing his throbbing temples, and staunching his wounds; but we have good reason to think that there was a little boy there, who never forgot that scene and the lessons it conveyed. It was one whom Paul was afterwards proud to call "his own son in the faith." TIMOTHY beheld in that meek but suffering countenance before him, what the grace of God could do. We find the great apostle, when far advanced in life, reminding Timothy, in the second epistle he writes to him, of the persecutions which "he had fully known" at *Antioch*, *Iconium*, and *Lystra*.* The old saying was here again made true, that "the blood of the martyrs was the seed of the Church." Timothy's young name was that night added to "the glorious company of the apostles." Paul, doubtless, when he thought of the ingratitude and cruelty of the Lystrians, would go forth from them "weeping," bearing elsewhere the precious seed they

* 2 Timothy iii. 10.

had rejected; but at his second visit, two years afterwards, he came "with rejoicing" to bear away this precious sheaf with him.

The apostle, so far recovered from his wounds, proceeds with his companion from Lystra to Derbe. The route between these towns, and indeed their position, is only a matter of conjecture. It has been supposed that the distance between them was twenty miles. They were separated from one another by a huge mountain called *Karadagh* or the *Black Mount*, spoken of by travellers as remarkable both for its sombre colour and great height, rising like a giant in the midst of the boundless plain which, "level as the sea,"* stretches from Iconium. It has its summit capped with snow, and a thousand and one churches are said to be built upon its sides. A recent explorer mentions having looked down from the top, and seen its slopes covered with these edifices, or ruins of them.† Like the Pisidian mountains, the neighbouring range of the Taurus was infested with robbers. The historian Strabo mentions Derbe as the stronghold of a famous freebooter of the name of *Antipater*, who made this a central point for his daring feats, and kept the neighbouring country in terror.‡ He was at last killed by Amyntas, King of Galatia.§ To the city of Derbe,

* Kinneir. † See Hamilton's *Asia Minor*, Kinneir, &c.

‡ Strabo, xii. 1. 6, as referred to by Lewin.

§ Modern travellers in the same spot have to record similar perils of robbers with those Paul experienced. "I was desirous of visiting it" (a place at the foot of the Black Mount), says Kinneir, in 1818, "but could not prevail upon any person to accompany me, or even to hire me horses, as they said that the country, in addition to being covered with snow, was now the resort of a band of Delhi Bashees, who gained a subsistence by plundering travellers, and laying the adjacent countries under contribution."—Kinneir's *Travels in Karamania*, p. 212.

which we may note, in passing, was the native town of Gaius, the future friend and companion of Paul, the apostles now bent their steps. It was but a few hours' journey from Lystra, and here they seem to have enjoyed a short season of quiet after the stirring scenes through which they had passed. If Paul had been a selfish man or a coward, or rather, if love to the Lord Jesus had not burned in his bosom, he might have resolved from this place to go straight through the mountain passes to the south-east, and, like Mark, have avoided further danger and peril by retiring to his old home at Tarsus.* But he was the servant of Him who "pleased not himself;" and already "he counted not his life dear unto him that he might finish his course with joy, and the ministry he had received of the Lord Jesus."

It has, indeed, been conjectured that the original purpose of the travellers may have been to cross into Cilicia, through the well-known pass called the "Cilician Gates," but that they were prevented by the swelling of the great lake which lay between them and the mountains. We think it, however, more probable that the apostle, having already proclaimed the Gospel in his native Cilicia, was desirous rather of returning by Iconium and Antioch, to water the seed which had been sown amid much discouragement and persecution, and to strengthen and confirm the disciples there.

Whatever their motive was, we know that they returned by the same way they came, passing through

* "About twenty hours to the northward of Tarsus there is a remarkable defile through a great chain of mountains, which are everywhere else inaccessible. This pass admits about eight horses abreast, and has been cut through the rock to the depth of forty feet. The marks of the tools are still visible in its sides."—Beaufort's *Karamania*, p. 264.

Lystra, Iconium, and Antioch,—there making elders in the Church, choosing among the disciples those they thought best fitted for the ministry,—telling them all, from their own experience, not to expect release from trial, but rather "that through much tribulation they must enter into the kingdom of heaven." Once more they descended through the precipitous rocky paths to Perga; and after pausing there for a brief time, instead of sailing, as formerly, down the Cestrus, they journeyed by land south-west to Attaleia,—a city beautifully situated in the curve of a sheltered bay. There they embarked for the Syrian Antioch, to tell with joy that the name "Christian," first known within its walls, was now gloried in within the palace of a Roman, and in sight of the temples of Diana and Jupiter!

CHAPTER VIII.

The Delegate.

"On! champions blest, in Jesus' name,
Short be your strife—your triumph full,
Till every heart have caught your flame,
And, lighten'd of the world's misrule,
Ye soar, those elder saints to meet,
Gather'd long since at Jesus' feet;
No world of passions to destroy,
Your prayers and struggles o'er, your task
All praise and joy."

"It surely is of no slight importance that the history of the first age of Christianity should present us with one undoubted instance of a character which unites all the freedom and vigour of a great reformer with all the humbleness, and holiness, and self-denial of a great apostle"—STANLEY'S *Essays on the Apostolic Age*, p. 173.

OUR two travellers, then, are once more, after a probable absence of a year and a half, approaching the shores of Syria, and looking forward to a happy meeting with their loved disciples and friends at Antioch. The above picture represents them in their vessel, under a bright Eastern moonlight, about to cast anchor at the port of Seleucia. We may imagine with what fond haste they would complete the rest of the land journey; and, when the "Christian city" was at last reached, how many things they would have to tell!—their mercies, their escapes, and, above all, their missionary success. How they would long, also, to hear how the Gospel had been flourishing since they left! The writer of the "Acts" does not tell us the particulars of the meeting. When a great earthly hero returns from great exploits, he has earthly honours decreed to him. and receives the applause of senates and kings. Paul and his brother hero return from the mightiest of victories, but their reception at the Christian capital is thus briefly and simply recorded:—"And when they had come, and had gathered together the Church, they rehearsed all that God had done with them, and how he had opened the door of faith to the Gentiles."*

But Paul only comes back to fight a battle of a different kind. It is sad to think how, even at this early period of the Church, divisions were beginning to arise, not between Christian and heathen, but between Christian and Christian. Tares were beginning to be sown among the wheat. "An enemy hath done this!" That great enemy has well known, in every age, that to disunite believers is the surest way to cripple and weaken the Church. Moreover, how often does he seize upon the very time when a Church is prospering, thus to destroy its peace and mar its usefulness! It was so now with that at Antioch. When its outward foes were silenced, he takes the opportunity of exciting an unhappy discord among the members themselves. I must explain to you shortly, in this chapter, what these divisions arose from, and what the Apostle Paul did to heal them.

I daresay you are aware that, at this moment, when our missionaries go to India, one of the great difficulties they have to contend with is that of *caste*. Some Hindus consider themselves of a higher rank than others, and will hold no social intercourse with those they imagine to be beneath them. They will not eat with them, or admit them into their families. Also, in slave states, it is well known that those who

* Howson, vol. i. p. 218; Acts xiv. 27.

are either slaves, or have any African blood in them, are (sad to think) frequently not allowed to mingle in company with the rest of the people, or to visit them; not even to occupy the same cabin in a steamer, or the same seat in a public conveyance.* They are looked upon as a lower and inferior race, and cruelly treated as such. It was with feelings very similar to this that the Jew of old regarded the Gentile. The former was proud of his birth and descent from Abraham, and, when he went into foreign countries, he refused to have any dealings in private life with the Gentiles around him. They might meet in the same market and transact business together, but their families had no intercourse. They might live side by side in the same street, but there was "a wall of partition between them" in more ways than one. They had, indeed, higher authority than their own for this rigid exclusion. The law given by Moses, which commanded them to abstain from different kinds of meat, *forbade* them to eat with the Gentiles. By doing so, they might become unclean, as the latter were often in the habit of taking various sorts of food which the Jew was not allowed by the law to touch.

The question then was, *Are* JEWS *who have become* CHRISTIANS, *and* GENTILES *who have become* CHRISTIANS, *to forget their differences, and to meet together? or must they continue, as before, separate?* Are those who are now baptized into the same Christian name, still to live apart, and eat apart, and keep up, as in former times, the old national distinctions? Paul found the whole Church in a very unhappy and divided state about this question. Let us hear how he tries to settle it—

* So we were informed by a friend lately in the Slave States in America.

the prudent and discreet method he adopts to bring his brethren to a right mind.

You will remember what I have already told you about Peter's vision of the great white sheet, containing clean and unclean animals, which he was commanded to slay and *eat*,* and the great truth which God had by this means taught him, viz., that "He was no respecter of persons," but intended now that the separating wall between Jew and Gentile was to be for ever taken down. When the news of Peter's vision, and his conduct afterwards in eating with uncircumcised Gentiles, reached Jerusalem, the Church there was much displeased. Peter was blamed and called severely to account; but he brought along with him the six brethren who had gone with him from Joppa to Cesarea; these declared how they had, with their own eyes, seen the gift of the Holy Ghost poured out on the Gentiles. Those who had at first expressed themselves unfavourably to "the apostle of the uncircumcision," were obliged to own the Divine hand in the matter, and, indeed, they even "gave thanks that God had also granted to the Gentiles repentance unto life." But, notwithstanding all this outward show of satisfaction, many were still displeased; they could not bear the thought of losing their national distinction; they remembered that Jesus himself, on one occasion, had said, that He was "sent to the lost sheep of the house of Israel." They were slow to believe that, as there was but "one Shepherd," so there was to be but "one sheepfold." Could they not be Christians, and yet still have a separate Jewish and Gentile Church? Perhaps these feelings increased in strength

* Acts x.

when the accounts reached them of how Paul and Barnabas had been freely mixing with Gentile converts in Crete, Antioch, Lystra, and Derbe; and that "He who had wrought effectually in Peter to the apostleship of the circumcision, the same had been mighty in Paul toward the Gentiles." At that time some Christians, who belonged to the sect of the Pharisees, had gone down from Jerusalem to Antioch, and did all they could to induce the Jewish Christians there to refuse holding fellowship with Gentile converts. They taught them the dangerous doctrine, that unless they observed the Jewish law, they could not be saved; that Christian baptism would be of no avail, unless accompanied with the old Jewish rite of circumcision. "Except ye be circumcised after the manner of Moses, *ye cannot be saved!*" Paul was, like Moses, a meek man of God, gentle and loving; but whenever he saw the truth of his God assailed, like Moses, too, he could be bold as a lion; and at present, when he observed the damage these false teachers were doing, he tells us "he could not give place by subjection, no not for an hour." He discovered at once the great danger that would arise to the souls of the disciples, if this doctrine were tolerated; since whatever was thus put upon an equality with the one great sacrifice of our Lord, whether it were ceremonial or moral observances, would dim the glory of the Redeemer's work, and render the cross of Christ of none effect.* This most unfortunate dissension continuing thus so sorely to vex and disturb the minds of the Gentile converts, Paul and Barnabas were requested to go up to Jerusalem, to lay the matter before the apostles and bre-

* Blunt, p. 188.

thren there, and get their advice. It is probable that Paul gladly availed himself of the opportunity, that he might give in to the mother Church the first great missionary report, and tell how the Lord had prospered his work among the heathen. Moreover, he had a higher inducement than his own wishes in taking the journey—God himself had told him to go. He mentions expressly, in his epistle to the Galatians, that he went "by revelation."*

His two companions were well selected. Barnabas was himself a Jew and a Levite. Titus, his other fellow-traveller, and of whom we shall hear more afterwards, was a young and uncircumcised Greek, and therefore a good sample of a heathen convert. They journeyed along the coast-road through Phenicia; thence to Samaria. It would seem they were not travelling among strangers to the gospel, for we are told that, as they passed through, "declaring the conversion of the Gentiles, they caused great joy to all the brethren."†

We have the old scholar of Gamaliel, then, once more, after many eventful years, entering the scene of his youth, and of his first persecuting fury. He would likely pass by the well-remembered Damascus gate, and skirt the ridges of the valley of Jehoshaphat. Perhaps, since his last visit, some of those who had "sat with him at Gamaliel's feet," had been brought to sit at the feet of Jesus. But if they had, he had come upon the present occasion, it is to be feared, to dispute with many of them, and oppose them. For while they sat at the feet of Christ, they wished to sit at the feet of Moses too. Though they had taken the name of Jesus, they were not willing to part with the

* Galatians ii. 2 † Acts xv. 3

name of Pharisee, and, like himself, to suffer the loss of "*all.*"

On reaching Jerusalem, the Great Apostle determined, before meeting the brethren in public, to see Peter, James, and John in private. After holding a meeting with these "pillars of the Church," the General Assembly, or, as it is called in Church history, the *First General Council,* was convened. There seems to have been at first much "disputing" on the question. The Pharisees "who believed" strongly held to the views already stated. We have only, however, four speeches mentioned—those of Peter, Paul, Barnabas, and James. They all took the same view. Peter, who held the "keys of the kingdom of heaven" in the sense I have explained, rose first to address. He was heard with marked attention. He declared again what God had revealed to him by means of the vision at Joppa—that there was now no longer "any difference"—that "the same Lord over all was rich to all that call upon Him." He reminded his hearers that the Holy Spirit had been poured out upon the Gentile converts, and that the yoke of the Jewish law was "a burden which neither they nor their fathers were able to bear." Peter's words made a deep impression on his audience. After a few moments' silence, Paul and Barnabas followed. We may readily imagine the interest which pervaded the assembly as the two "foreign missionaries" rose to tell all that God had done in their behalf. The last speaker was James "the Just" —so called, the historian Eusebius mentions, on account of his eminent virtue. Hegesippus (a converted Jew, who lived in the second century) tells us that he led a life of great sanctity;* and other traditions further picture him as an old and venerable man, with a bald head and long unshorn beard, with his feet bare, and wearing a linen ephod, yet so greatly esteemed that the people vied with each other to touch even the hem of his garment.† He was equally decided with the others in his opinion that nothing should be done to prevent the free admission of the Gentiles into the Christian Church, or to stop a work which God had so evidently favoured, by continuing to impose the old ceremonial observances. The glorious truth was then finally proclaimed, that there was to be "neither Jew nor Greek, circumcision nor uncircumcision, barbarian, Scythian, bond or free, but Christ was all and in all."

The settlement of this question was in every way important. For although Christians have never sought since that time to unite the service of Christ with obedience to the old ceremonial law, there has ever been a tendency in the human heart to combine some good works of our own with the one great work of Jesus. Some would look to their virtues and moral duties, and mix up *these* with the one only salvation; others would look to church observances and church forms, to sacraments and penances, and mix *these* up along with the "one only way." To do so is sadly dishonouring to Him who will not give His glory to another. The *First Council in Jerusalem* gave forth a decree to the whole world, and to the Church in every age, as to what forms a true Christian in the sight of God—

* *Biblical Cyclopædia.*

† See Stanley's *Sermons on the Apostolic Age*, p. 295.

"*Neither circumcision availeth anything, nor uncircumcision, but faith which worketh by love.*" We may just further note, with reference to this Church Assembly of the brethren, that Paul was publicly acknowledged by them as "*the Apostle of the Gentiles.*"

One of the three "pillars of the Church" here mentioned was silent in the Council! It was "the Apostle of Love," John, who leaned on Jesus' bosom; "who, beyond any other of the sons of men, had received the impression of the Divine character; . . . . one simple, unadorned spectacle of moral and spiritual excellence, enshrined as if in its own heavenly light, irradiating everything that fell within its sphere . . . . by the crystal purity of a heart and mind penetrated through and through with the indwelling spirit of Christ."* It is the only time we ever read of Paul and he meeting one another. They were very different in natural disposition; but they were one in intense affection for their glorified Master. Though John made no speech, so far as we know, in the Jerusalem Assembly, he gave at the end of the discussion the right hand of fellowship to his "brother Paul," and cordially joined in the decision which was given.† A letter was drawn up in the name of the Assembly, in order to be conveyed by the hands of Paul to the Gentile brethren at Antioch. It is short, but of much interest, as being the first document of the kind we have given forth by a Church court.

It was the custom, in these ages of the world, when a letter of any importance was sent, to appoint some noted individuals to be the bearers. This was done not only to prevent any accident befalling such com-

* Stanley's *Sermons*, p. 256. † See Howson, vol. i. p. 235.

munications, and to secure their safety, but that these messengers might be able to enter into any explanations which might be required. Judas and Silas (Silvanus) were appointed to accompany Paul, Barnabas, and Mark for this purpose.

We may imagine the great interest excited in the Church of Antioch, when the tidings spread, "The brethren with envoys have arrived! and they have a pastoral letter with them from the assembled apostles at Jerusalem!" We may picture a crowded church in the great Syrian city, where the following communication was read amid breathless silence :—"The apostles, and elders, and brethren, send greeting unto the brethren which are of the Gentiles in Antioch, and Syria, and Cilicia: Forasmuch as we have heard that certain which went out from us have troubled you with words, subverting your souls, saying, Ye must be circumcised, and keep the law; to whom we gave no such commandment: it seemed good unto us, being assembled with one accord, to send chosen men unto you with our beloved Barnabas and Paul; men that have hazarded their lives for the name of our Lord Jesus Christ. We have sent therefore Judas and Silas, who shall also tell you the same things by mouth. For it seemed good to the Holy Ghost, and to us, to lay upon you no greater burden than these necessary things; that ye abstain from meats offered to idols, and from blood, and from things strangled, and from fornication: from which if ye keep yourselves, ye shall do well. Fare ye well."* Judas and Silas still further explained the scope and contents of the letter by word of mouth. What was the result? It was a very

* Acts xv. 23-30.

happy one; the storm was immediately changed into a calm, and the agitated minds of the Antioch disciples soothed.

Judas, after spending some further time in this city, returned to Jerusalem. Silas, as we shall afterwards find, remained, and became Paul's companion on his second missionary journey, as Barnabas had been in his first.

There was an occurrence which took place at Antioch, before setting out on this second missionary tour, which greatly grieved and troubled Paul. The first of those who had so decidedly spoken in the assembly at Jerusalem, about the necessity of doing away with all distinction between Jew and Gentile, was the Apostle Peter; yet he was himself (on a visit he paid to Antioch) the first to act contrary to his public declaration. On going there, he mingled freely with the Gentile converts, dining with them at their meals, and sharing with them their "*Agape*" or love-feasts. But, soon after, when some of the Judaising party had come down from Jerusalem (who he knew would be displeased at seeing him sitting at the same table with his Gentile friends), the apostle began to waver; he changed his manner altogether towards the converted heathen; he no longer ate with them, nor would sit at the same Lord's table with them; he raised, once more, the old wall of separation! He performed, in this, a double and sinful part. It was the same lamentable weakness which led him, three times before, to deny his Lord and Master. Paul was roused to a holy indignation against his erring brother, and "withstood him to the face because he was to be blamed." It was an unworthy fear of man which made the former desert the path of duty, and his conduct was likely to produce much mischief, as "even Barnabas was carried away with his dissimulation."* We cannot wonder, therefore, that Paul was obliged to do what must have pained him much—to "rebuke Peter before all."† We believe that sharp as the rebuke was, it was given and received in love. Peter's character was bold and rash, and this was not the first time in which he had been a traitor to truth, and a coward; but we have reason to think also that he was kind and forgiving—ready to "weep bitterly" when he saw his faults. This would seem to have been the case now; at all events, he died twenty years after, loving Paul, and speaking of him to all the Churches as a "beloved brother."‡ We should have been sorry to have wanted this short clause in the end of one of his letters—"*Our beloved brother Paul!*" We might have been apt, otherwise, to fear that Paul's rebuke had created a sore quarrel between them, which they had carried to the grave; but no such thing: grace brought about what nature might not have done.

"It is pleasing," says an able writer, "to trace the traditionary confirmations of their entire unity—the unity which joins St Peter to St Paul, rather than to his own early friend, St John—the legends which represent them as joint rulers of Antioch, Corinth, and Rome—both confined in the Mamertine dungeon—both receiving the crown of martyrdom on the same day—and, in all the early works of Christian art, both ever exhibited side by side; the one with his inverted cross—the other 'with the executioner's sword.'"§

* Gal. ii. 13. † Gal. ii. 11. ‡ 2 Pet. iii. 15, 16.

§ Stanley's *Sermons and Essays on the Apostolical Age* p. 101. See also Howson, p. 243.

These, doubtless, are no more than vague legends and traditions, and must be received with caution; but they are sufficient to show what the impression of the early ages of the Church was as to the sacred harmony existing between these two truly great men—that they died faithful to their blessed Master's last bequest—"This is my commandment, that ye love one another."

CHAPTER IX.

The Second Journey.

"Friend after friend departs—
Who hath not lost a friend?
There is no union here of hearts
That finds not here an end.
Were this frail world our final rest,
Living or dying none were blest."

"He exhibits to us, notwithstanding an infirm body and a feeble speech, what a man can do, even one single man, when his will is in harmony with the will of God."

PAUL continued for some time with Barnabas at Antioch, preaching to their converts, and "building them up in their most holy faith." He would not, however, allow himself to forget his special work as a *missionary*. He thought, with fond affection, of the many believers he had left behind in Asia Minor, exposed to dangers and trials; and of the multitudes elsewhere, still strangers to a Saviour's name. He resolved, accordingly, along with his former companions, to visit the churches which they had already planted. "Let us go again," he said to Barnabas, "and visit our brethren in every city where we have preached the word of the

Lord, and see how they do."* They would doubtless take along with them the important circular letter, or "decree," lately issued by the Council at Jerusalem, in case the same question which had so disturbed the believers in Antioch might be marring the peace of converts elsewhere. This visitation of these churches gives us the first specimen of the tender and affectionate love which Paul bore to all he had been honoured to call to the faith of Jesus. It is more like the love of a father to his children, than that of a stranger to strangers.

There is a painful commencement, however, to this second missionary tour. We have spoken, at the close of last chapter, of an unhappy cause of difference between Paul and Peter. A still sadder estrangement took place now between him and Barnabas, showing us that the best of *earthly* friends, and the holiest of mere *human* hearts, can never be depended on. Barnabas was desirous that his nephew, Mark, should go along with them. Paul objected to this. We can easily understand the feelings in the latter apostle's mind which constrained him to act contrary to the wishes of his brother missionary. Mark, you will remember, had already been tried as a companion. He had grown weary of the work, and, on reaching Perga, had returned home. The Great Apostle might be afraid, and justly so, lest the cause of his Master might suffer by the employment again of so heartless an agent. Barnabas, on the other hand, was naturally fond of his kinsman. He had doubtless received from him assurances of penitence and sorrow for his past conduct, and a determination to act better for the future. We can

* Acts xv. 36.

therefore make allowance also for the feelings of the good uncle, in whose character we have seen so much to admire. We are not called upon to decide who was right and who was wrong, in this painful quarrel. They must both have felt the sad truth they told the Lystrians, "We are men of like passions with you!" As Mark did not disappoint the hopes of his uncle, we may have reason to regret that Paul adhered so strongly to his determination. On the other hand, as a great writer remarks, "We see, on this occasion, the severe earnestness of Paul's character, which gave up, and wished others to give up, all personal considerations and feelings when the cause of God was concerned." * Another commentator gives the following as perhaps the truthful verdict on the case:—"The attempt of many to justify both completely, or, at least, Paul, I cannot approve. If both had been perfect men, no quarrel would have arisen, for there must always be two to a quarrel. Yea, there should have been no contention, if even only ONE of them had been perfect." †

God, however, overruled the infirmities of these two apostles for the promotion of His cause. "He can make the wrath of man to praise Him." Meanwhile, we find that the contention grew "so sharp" between them, that they were forced to separate! It had evidently been their intention to have gone over the very same ground which they had traversed in their first journey—together to revisit and confirm the churches they had already planted. They agree, on separating, to begin at the two extreme points. Paul took the northward direction, to the interior of Asia Minor, tak-

* Neander, p. 169. † Olshausen—note *in loco*.

ing with him Silas (one of the brethren sent from Jerusalem); while Barnabas, with Mark, took the island part of the tour, sailing towards Cyprus, which, you will remember, was Barnabas' native country. Of the latter, we hear no more after this. We know not whether he and Paul ever met again. It is supposed by some, that reference is made to him by Paul in 2 Cor. viii. 18, as "the brother whose praise is in all the churches;" but this is uncertain. Tradition gives us an affecting account of his death. It is said that, when he came with his nephew to Salamis, in Cyprus, he entered into the Jewish synagogue, and made many converts to the faith of Jesus—that some Jews had followed from Syria, under the guidance of Bar-jesus, and, rousing the people against him, had cruelly stoned him to death; but his nephew rescued the body, and his tomb was shown for centuries after at Salamis. Paul and Mark *did* meet again. We have the same assurance with regard to them, as in the case of Peter, that they came to speak of one another as esteemed fellow-soldiers, fighting under the same great banner. Tradition also (although—we deem it necessary always to add the caution—no safe guide in general) further mentions what we would fondly believe was the case—that Barnabas' dying injunction to his nephew was to go without delay and rejoin Paul. We love to think of the good old disciple, who showed our Apostle so much true kindness at the first, and especially on his flight from Damascus, going down to his grave with the name of one on his lips he had long loved so well!

Leaving the island-missionaries, Barnabas and Mark, as they sailed down the Orontes, let us follow Paul and Silas as they crossed the bridge over the same river, and made for the passes of Mount Amanus.* There were various narrow and precipitous gorges leading across this lofty range. The principal of these was a singular defile, called the "Syrian Gates," and which is known by the modern name of the "Beilan Pass."† On reaching the other side, they would doubtless visit several of the smaller towns of Cilicia, although the names are not given us, and scatter among them the precious seed. There was one which we have every reason for supposing would not be omitted, and which Paul would enter with very peculiar feelings. It was his own native Tarsus—the city and home of his childhood. Though still heathen—the temples and statues of false gods lining its streets—he must have had a peculiar joy in knowing that many had, by means of his preaching, "been turned from dumb idols to serve the living God." How it must have cheered his heart, when "far hence among the Gentiles," to think that, in his own birth-place, there were some who loved the Saviour, and who prayed on his behalf, that the word he preached might "have free course and be glorified!"

We must follow him and his companion as they continued their journey still further north, across Mount Taurus. It was probably in the early part of the year 51, when they were wending their way along the banks of the Cydnus on this mountain journey.‡ It is with probability supposed that they crossed through the "Cilician Gates,"—a gorge much more remarkable than the Syrian, and one, too, through which more than one large army in ancient and modern times has with

* The reader will now follow the *crimson* line in the map.

† Reasons for supposing this to be the probable route of the apostle, see Howson and Conybeare, vol. i. p. 276.

‡ Ibid. p. 278.

difficulty and danger passed. Cliffs several nundred feet high frown on either side above the head of the traveller, the width in some places being only a few yards. Small patches of vegetation are seen here and there among their summits, while rushing torrents come tumbling down, often covering or undermining the road. The old military highway may itself to this day be traced from the many fragments and inscriptions which have been found by curious travellers. They have now reached an elevation of 4000 feet above the sea, and begin gradually to descend among the wooded uplands of Lycaonia. We may imagine here also the joy of Paul in revisiting the old scenes of his first missionary journey. How his heart must have beat as the well remembered form of the "Black Mount," with its snowy summit, rose in the plain before him! He was approaching at present in the opposite direction, and therefore he comes to Derbe first. Interested he must have been to see and hear all about his beloved converts there. He would doubtless not be without anxiety. He knew well the deceitfulness of the human heart, and could not fail to dread lest many of those who had promised well had "fallen from grace." There is no account given us of his reception at Derbe; we may easily imagine, however, what it would be—the kind-hearted man of God, coming once more into the midst of those for whom, night and day, he had "prayed exceedingly," and they with hearts overflowing with gratitude towards the honoured minister who had been the means of rescuing them from a blind superstition. Lystra was the town next in order to which they came. You will not have forgotten that it was here the citizens wished first to worship the two apostles as gods; and then behaved so shamefully—stoning Paul, and leaving him as dead. Lystra was heathen still! The large Pagan temple rose as it had done the year before at the city gate, and the priest (perhaps as Paul was passing) was offering animals in sacrifice to Jupiter. There was *one* face which, among others, he had not forgotten since his last visit. I daresay you remember the youth who stood among the crowd when the great apostle lay bleeding from his wounds. That young convert, doubtless, never forgot that night;—the patience, and resignation, and forgiveness of the cruelly-treated servant of Jesus. We believe that none of all the Christian converts in Lystra welcomed with greater joy the return of the great missionary than this promising young man, whose name was in future ages to be so linked with that of his spiritual father. As I have already said, he had been brought up under the tender religious training of his grandmother Lois, and his mother Eunice. Eunice was a Jewess, a Christian convert, and her husband was a Greek. We can picture to ourselves that holy Christian home of the infant apostle. His pious mother, and aged grandmother, had, from his earliest years, instructed him in the knowledge of the ancient Scriptures. Like Simeon, Anna, and others, they had been waiting in humble faith for the "consolation of Israel"—not unprepared for the glad tidings which Paul had proclaimed to them, that the types and promises of the Jewish dispensation had been fulfilled in Jesus of Nazareth, of whom "all the prophets bear witness." Paul's letters to Timothy at a later time tell how affectionately he loved him. There doubtless must have been something very winning and engaging about this young stranger, that could induce the apostle at once to fix upon him for so signal an honour as to be the companion of his journeys. Notwithstanding their great difference in age, notwithstanding Paul's great learning and accomplishments, he seems to have esteemed Timothy as the most valued of all his friends. "Son Timothy," "My beloved son," "My own son in the faith," "My work-fellow," "My brother," are expressions which bespeak no common affection. Well has it been said, "What mother ever wrote to her son a letter more full of solicitude than the Second Epistle to Timothy?" * Hear how he writes of him when he is looking back on the manifold friendships of a whole life: "I have *no man* likeminded, who will naturally care for your state. . . Ye know the proof of him, that, *as a son with the father*, he hath served with me in the gospel." † He had been converted during Paul's former visit. The seed then sown had ripened in his heart to good fruit; and now, when the apostle returned a second time, he found him all equipped and ready for that "good fight of faith," about which he afterwards discourses. "Him would Paul have to go forth with him." ‡ He was circumcised at Iconium, and there solemnly ordained and set apart for his great work. It was a day never to be forgotten by the young Lystrian. Paul afterwards speaks of it in one of his letters. "Thou hast professed a good profession before many witnesses." §

From Iconium, they proceeded to the cities farther north, leaving in each of these, where Christian converts were, a copy of the decree of the Jerusalem Council. Very considerable difficulty, however, has

* Monod. † Phil. ii. 20, 22. ‡ Acts xvi. 3. § 1 Tim. vi. 12.

been felt by writers on the life of Paul as to the *direction* of this journey. The high road he and Silas had now been traversing the length of Antioch, led on to Ephesus, a distance of 230 miles; and some have supposed they went by it the length of Colosse, a town situated half way. Other writers, of equal authority, assign to him a route more directly north, not supposing that he visited Colosse at all. If you examine the map, you will see what his course would be if he and his fellow-travellers followed the great highway of Asia Minor; they would come to the valley which is watered by the river Lycus, and on the south bank of which stands the city of Colosse—a few scattered ruins now only remaining to mark the spot. Had they pursued the same great road twelve miles further along the valley, they would have reached two other famous cities fronting each other on either side of the river. On the right, Hierapolis rose on a commanding situation; it crowned the summits of a bold cliff, and had within its walls the temple of Pluto and its famous cavern. Upon the opposite bank, on the slope of Mount Cadmus, and a mile from the river, stood Laodicea, whose vast ruins, at the present day, attest its former extent and greatness. We have every reason to believe, however, that neither of these cities were the apostle and his companions allowed *at present* to enter; "they were forbidden of the Holy Ghost to preach the word in Asia."*

We can, with greater certainty, follow them as they retrace their steps north-east to *Galatia.* This province we *know* they now visited;† and from the epistle Paul wrote to the churches there, as well as

* Acts xvi. 6. † Acts xvi. 6.

from the peculiar history of its people, it deserves more from us than a passing notice. Much interesting light, moreover, has been thrown upon the subject by recent writers.

The Galatians (or *Gaul*atians) were not the original inhabitants of that country; they were a colony of *Gauls*. Who were these *Gauls?* Gaul, as you know, was the ancient name of *France*. Greek historians, in speaking of the inhabitants of France, call them "*Galatians*." The Gauls, however, seem not to have been confined to this portion of Europe, but to have spread themselves also over Spain, Great Britain, and Ireland. They were a bold, warlike, and manly people; their name and invasions indeed became so terrible, that the countries they sought to people did what they could to destroy and extirpate them. Those that remained, had to take refuge in fastnesses and wild uninhabited districts, where they could do comparatively little harm. In France, they were driven into Brittany; in England, into Wales, which was called from them Wallia, or *Gallia*, (and indeed Wales is called by Frenchmen still, "the country of the Gauls.") In rugged Scotland, they got a suitable refuge among the wild Highland glens and passes—hence the name of the Highlanders and their country, as the *Gaels*, the land of the *Gael*, or *Gaul;* and their language, *Gaelic*, or *Gaulic*. The place, however, in the west of Europe which they retained strongest hold of was Ireland; they peopled the whole of it, with the exception of a portion of the north-east.

But how came they, it may be asked, to find their way to the province which the Apostle Paul was now treading in the centre of Asia Minor? After th-death of Alexander the Great, a swarming host of 300,000 Gauls, like the Huns and Vandals of the middle ages, made an irruption over the plains of eastern Europe, forcing a passage along the banks of the Danube. We need not pause to describe their march; suffice it to say, the greater number of them met on the shores of Asia Minor. Their wild war-songs were heard on the plains of ancient Troy, and around the tomb of Achilles. From thence they marched hither and thither on a mission of pillage and plunder, leaving behind nothing but the ashes and smoke of conquered countries. A portion of them (with which we are now principally concerned) had withdrawn from the main body, and were still in Europe; they were lured, however, at last across the Hellespont by Nicomedes, king of Bithynia, who was at that time engaged in war with his brother. By their means he obtained a complete and decisive victory, and, as a reward for their assistance and valour, granted them the north-east portion of Phrygia, which ever afterwards bore the name of GALATIA, or *Gallo Græcia.* Not contented with this royal recompense, they seem to have inspired great fear among the inhabitants of Mount Taurus by their warlike incursions, and to have exacted tribute from all around. Their numbers at their first settlement, according to a Roman historian, did not exceed 20,000, and the half of these were unarmed. This may give an idea of their power, and of the influence their ferocious name and character exercised over the timid tribes among whom they settled. We can imagine, from what is related of them, the terror these barbarians would inspire, especially in the hour of battle, with their wild native war-whoops, clanging their long swords or claymores on their targets, and rushing madly against their foes.

For many centuries this remarkable race retained their language and native manners. Even when Paul now visited them, though they could speak the Greek of the country, they never had forgotten their own tongue,—just as in Wales, or in the Scottish Highlands, that same tongue, with little variation, continues to be spoken. St Paul's epistle to them, however, was written in Greek; and any inscriptions of the period, found on their sculptures, are in the same language. Their independence, as a people, was, at the age of the apostle, like all the rest of the world, laid low under the iron hand of imperial Rome. They had been suffered, till the reign of Augustus, to retain it nominally, and had at that time a king of their own, called Amyntas; but a Roman pro-prætor was now at the head of the province. What their precise religion was when Paul first found them, we cannot say. More than probably their ancestors would carry along with them their Druidical superstitions; but we know also, that Jupiter and Cybele, the deities of Greece and Rome, were worshipped at two of their principal cities. It is among this strange people, then—strange even in their complexion and appearance, with their tall figures and long flowing yellow hair*—that the Apostle of the Gentiles is now about to sojourn.

We are not informed to what localities Paul went in Galatia, or how long he remained there; this, however, is certain, that he preached in many places, and that a

* See the picture, at the beginning of the chapter, of a "Galatian hero."

vast blessing attended his labours. Nay, more, that warm-hearted people seem to have received the "stranger apostle" with great readiness and cordiality, and he appears, ever after, to entertain towards them feelings of deepest affection and love.

If we have spoken of France as the original country of the Gauls, and Ireland as the land in western Europe where they chiefly abounded, we have, in the well-known sprightliness and warm-heartedness of these two countries at this day, a living picture of the character the Apostle Paul had to deal with in Galatia 1800 years ago. In other respects, too, the likeness seems to hold good—while warm and loving in their natures, they were fickle, unsteady, excitable, "carried about with every wind of doctrine." May we not say, in no unkindly spirit, that the charge which he brings against them might, in a modified shape, be made to apply not inaccurately to others in later years, and nearer our own shores?—"O foolish Galatians, who hath bewitched you that ye should not obey the truth?" While at one time "they received the apostle as if he had been an angel," "they were soon removed from him that called them to another gospel."*

On the occasion of this his first visit, Paul was overtaken with sickness. None but those who have experienced it, can know how painful it is to be laid, in the heart of a foreign land, on a couch of illness; nor, on the other hand, how grateful, in such circumstances, is the kindness of strangers. The apostle felt deeply the warm and affectionate solicitude which the Galatians manifested towards him at this trying hour. They saw his body bowed with intense suffering; but when

* See Mr Lewin's interesting chapter on Galatia.

they beheld his noble mind rising superior to all, and enabling him joyfully to bear all for the everlasting good of others, they were struck with a heroism that would have done honour to their own bravest and best. We may well believe that Timothy would not be behind in bestowing dutiful attention on one he so loved, while it would doubtless tend to draw out more than ever the heart of the apostle towards him whom "he had begotten in the Gospel."

Connected with Paul's illness in Galatia, and with many references in his epistle, this seems the proper time to refer to the nature of that bodily infirmity or ailment under which he so often laboured, and which he calls "*the thorn in the flesh.*" * What could this have been? The answering of this question may help us in forming our impressions of his personal appearance, and account for many allusions he makes in his writings which could not otherwise be explained.

From this bodily malady, whatever it was, he evidently was suffering during this his first visit to Galatia; for, in his "Epistle to the Galatians," which was written after his second visit, he says—"Ye know how through infirmity of the flesh I preached the Gospel unto you *at the first*" (*i. e.*, the former visit). "And my temptation which was *in my flesh* ye despised not, nor rejected; but received me as an angel of God. . . . I bear you record, that, if it had been possible, *ye would have plucked out your own eyes, and have given them to me.*" † These striking words appear to afford a key to the nature of the "thorn in the flesh," to which they, in all probability, allude.

We have the strongest reason, then, to infer that it

* 2 Cor. xii. 7-10. † Gal. iv. 13-15.

was a *disease in his eyes*, which greatly injured his sight, and at times his appearance. It has been thought that, ever since being struck blind at his conversion, on the way to Damascus, his eyes and eyesight had been much affected—just as if his Lord had wished him to carry about this continual remembrance, at once of his guilt, and of the grace which saved him. Writers have specially noted besides (what was mentioned in a former chapter), that the climate of Damascus is most injurious to the vision; many in the neighbourhood of that city to this day suffering severely from its pernicious effects. What can more naturally explain the verse I have, a few sentences before, quoted from his Galatian epistle, than this? He wishes to tell his converts there, how greatly he felt their attention and affection; as if he had said—"So great was your kindness to me, a poor half-blind stranger, with my eyes painful to look upon, that you would have willingly plucked out *your own*, if it had been in your power, and exchanged them for *mine*, if this could have cured me of my sad malady."

There are other similar references made in the same epistle: as when he says, at the close of it, "From henceforth let no man trouble me: for I bear in my body the *marks* of the Lord Jesus." The word translated "*marks*," literally means "*brands*," and refers to the old custom of branding the forehead or arm with a hot iron, more particularly in the case of runaway slaves. A name or device was thus impressed on the skin as a punishment, as well as to prevent them in future deserting their masters. "In this sense," says Paul, "I, who was a fugitive slave rushing away from my Master, was 'arrested' by Him on the way to

Damascus, when he cried after me, 'Saul, Saul, why persecutest thou me?' and when He caught me, or 'apprehended me,'* He put His own brand or mark upon me; these eyes, which He struck blind with the blaze of His glory, I am to bear continually about with me as the 'marks of the Lord Jesus.'"

There is one other verse in the epistle, to which I shall refer, bearing upon the same; it is in the concluding words of it. He says, "Ye see how large a letter I have written unto you with my own hand."† From the weakness of his eyesight, Paul was always in the habit of employing another to write for him. To show his affection, however, for this warm-hearted people, he says, "See, I have made an exception in *your* case. Suffering though I am from these eyes of mine, I have sent you a letter in my own handwriting." It has been rightly observed, that the expression, "See how large a letter," does not refer to the *length* of the epistle, but to the *clumsy writing*. He apologises to them for this. "See," he says, "in what awkward characters I have written unto you; but you cannot expect otherwise from my eyesight. You will pardon their inelegance, and understand what I mean by putting myself to this piece of unusual labour; it is to give you a proof of my cordial love for you, and my interest in your welfare."

We have strong reason to infer, then, on these and other considerations, that Paul's "thorn in the flesh" was no other than a disease in his eyes; so bad, too, as to have made him occasionally, when it increased, nearly blind, as we read, in an after-portion of his life, that he was "*conducted*" by others to Athens.‡ It

* Phil. iii. 12. † Gal. vi. 11. ‡ Acts xvii. 15.

must indeed have been a severe trial to the great missionary apostle; not only from the ridicule which the bodily defect might draw down at times upon him from his enemies, but think of his constant exposure to the open air, and the sudden changes from the burning heat of the summer plains to the cutting breezes and cold of the mountains. How acute often must have been his sufferings in an organ so sensitive to pain as we know the eye is! Three times, he tells us, did he pray that his malady might be removed. The prayer was granted; not, however, in the manner he wished or expected, but in the way which God saw best. The thorn still remained; but his Lord gave him, in answer to his prayer, "more grace." "My grace is sufficient for thee; for My strength is made perfect in weakness."* The great and holy man was satisfied; he saw that all was for his good. He was led triumphantly to say, "I take pleasure in infirmities;" "Most gladly will I rather glory in my infirmities, that the power of Christ may rest upon me."† "This giant apostle—this spiritual conqueror of the half of Asia and the whole of Europe, had a bodily weakness which attracted the attention of all, which emboldened his enemies, which troubled himself, and which seemed to render him for ever disqualified for his work. Well! God thus made him weak for the express purpose of glorifying Himself in him."‡

We cannot, immediately after this, very accurately trace the course which the missionary band took. I

* 2 Cor. xii. 9.

† See on this also the full and satisfactory statement of Mr Lewin, vol. i. p. 213.

‡ Monod's *St Paul*, p. 151.

have already noted that they were forbidden to go to Asia or Bithynia. "The Spirit suffered them not." Why they were not suffered, it is not for us to inquire. It has been thought, from the dedication of Peter's first epistle, that these regions, including Bithynia, were specially allotted to *him.* "Peter, an apostle of Jesus Christ, to the strangers scattered throughout Pontus, Galatia, Cappadocia, *Asia,* and *Bithynia.*"* We need not, however, attempt to explain, where the Word of God is silent. Bending their course directly westward, they probably went to a sea-port town on the Ægean, called Adramyttium; from thence along the coast to Assos, where a beautiful road, of nineteen miles, brought them through the oak woods that skirted Mount Ida to *Troas.* This was, and still is, a spot of deep and sacred interest. It was the scene of the oldest and greatest war of antiquity—the Trojan. Greek and Latin poets have vied with one another to celebrate its scenery. Mount Ida rose behind it with its beautiful woods and sparkling streams—the island of Tenedos lay on the bosom of the sea in front of its harbour—while, far off in the blue distance, the nearest land of Europe was in sight—the lofty Grecian Mount Athos. . Perhaps the time when Paul approached it answered to the description of a modern traveller, who thus speaks of the close of his first day's visit to Troas:—"The beauty of the evening in this country surpasses all description. The sky glowed with the rich tints of the setting sun, which now, skirting the western horizon, raised, as it were, up to our view the distant summits of the European mountains. We saw Mount Athos distinctly, of a conical form, and

* Chap. i. 1.

so lofty, that on the top, as the ancients relate, the sun-rising was beheld four hours sooner than by the inhabitants of the coast; and, at the solstice, its shade reached into the Agora or market-place of Myrina, a town in Lemnos, which island was distant 87 miles eastward."*

The town of Troas itself must have been a very considerable one. It stood on a height, sloping gently down to the sea. A deep ravine separated it from Mount Ida, and a large plain stretched on either side by the sea-shore.† Large masses of hewn stone, walls that include a circuit of nine miles, and the ruins of piers and arches, remain to this day to bespeak its former greatness. The situation was so striking in itself, and so renowned in story, that Constantine, before he fixed on Constantinople as the site of his new capital, is said to have wavered between it and Troas;‡ indeed, at this day, it retains the name of Eski-Stamboul, or Old Constantinople.

We have supposed the apostle and his friends approached this classic city by the winding road that skirted the sea-beach, unless, from the expression, "they *came down*" to Troas, we are to infer that they crossed one of the shoulders of Mount Olympus, and looked from the summit on the celebrated "Trojan plains." If so, Paul, with his taste and scholarship, could not surely feel unmoved and uninterested on a spot which, while the world lasts, will be remembered in connexion with Homer—its oldest and, in many respects, greatest poet. On those very sandy plains and knolls along which they passed, the prancing war-

* Chandler's *Travels in Asia Minor*, p. 23. † Ibid. p. 26.
‡ Gibbon's *Decline and Fall*, quoted by Howson.

steeds and chariots of the Trojans and Greeks had rattled along. "But who would recognise, in those shallow reedy streams, the Simois and Scamander of the poet's fancy? The storm of war had swept over the spot, and now it was the path of the messengers of peace. Europe had poured forth her thousands to desolate and destroy; and Asia, in return, sent her three wayworn pilgrims—Paul, Silas, and Timothy—to proclaim to Europe the glad tidings of the Gospel! They passed on, and entered Troas."*

That night was one never to be forgotten. When the great apostle lay himself down on his pillow, and composed himself to sleep, a vision appeared at his bed-side. A figure, like "a man of Macedonia," stood over him, and beckoned to him, saying, "*Come over and help us!*" It was the voice of his God telling him there were perishing millions in Europe, who were waiting to receive the bread of life. He could not resist the solemn pleadings of that nightly apparition. The next day we may imagine the four strangers (for Luke, "the beloved physician," who writes so faithfully his history, had now joined them)—we may picture them by the harbour of Troas, entering some trading vessel about to convey them to Greece. The ship weighs anchor—the sails are spread; and, on the bosom of the surging Ægean, riches more precious than the gold of Ophir are carried to the civilised countries of Europe. Each of *us* were deeply interested in that vessel as it flies before the south wind to Samothracia! Ah! little did poor heathen Britain think at that moment there was then advancing nearer her shores so rich a prize for her children's children!

* Lewin, vol. i. p. 223.

CHAPTER X.

The Prison.

"When Persecution's torrent-blaze
Wraps the unshrinking martyr's head;
When fade all earthly flowers and bays,
When summer friends are gone and fled;
Is he alone in that dark hour
Who owns the Lord of love and power?

Or waves there not around his brow
A wand no human arm may yield,
Fraught with a spell no angels know,
His steps to guide, his soul to shield?"

"None of these things move me, neither count I my life dear unto myself, so that I might finish my course with joy, and the ministry I have received of the Lord Jesus."—ACTS xx. 24.

THE Apostle, when he entered Troas the day before, had probably very much the feelings of his great ancestor Abraham, of whom we read that "he went out, not knowing whither he went." It has been indeed supposed that Paul had some serious thoughts at this time of going to the city of Rome. He wished to carry the gospel of his Divine Master within hearing of the world's capital, and the palace of the Cæsars. God was at a future time to fulfil his wish; but he graciously "hindered" him now. It shows how far better the Lord knows what is the right path for us than we know ourselves. If Paul had trusted to his own wisdom and guidance, and gone direct at this period to Italy, he would have shared in the violent expulsion which took place of all the Jews from Rome by the edict of Claudius. The time would have been wasted which he profitably employed elsewhere. He could feelingly say of a kind Providence afterwards, regarding his intentions of visiting the city of the Tiber, "Oft times I purposed to come unto you, but was let (or hindered) hitherto." The striking vision mentioned at the close of the last chapter "hindered" him at present, and determined his journey to the regions of Macedonia.*

We have also just referred to a new name added to their little band—that of *Luke.* As he is not only the companion of the Great Apostle, but his biographer, we may well pause, on this the first mention of him in the narrative, to say a few words regarding his history. If you look at the chapter in the Acts describing their leaving Troas, you will see that the plural pronoun "*we*" is used for the first time. "After he had seen the vision, immediately *we*" (indicating that Luke was one of the number) "endeavoured to go into Macedonia."†

Luke, or Lucius, was most probably, from his name, not a Jew, but a Gentile by birth. The opinion, too, has been hazarded, that he had been once a slave at Rome—that he had there practised the art of medicine in his master's family—and that, after a certain period, in reward for his services, freedom had been conferred on him. He seems to have returned thence to his native city of Antioch;‡ and while there, carrying on his profession as a physician,§ he was brought

* Lewin, vol. i. p. 224. † Acts xvi. 10.
‡ Eusebius and Jerome. § Col iv. 14.

under the power of the truth as it is in Jesus. Some have thought that he acted as a ship surgeon, or what is equally probable, he was what in modern days we call (in connexion particularly with China) a "*medical missionary*"—a physician inspired with love to the "Great Physician of Souls," and who, while he exercised his healing art on the *bodies* of men, at the same time tried to lead them to "the balm in Gilead, and the Physician there." It is interesting thus to think of this earnest man, sailing about from island to island in the vast Archipelago with healing medicines alike for soul and body. It is interesting to think of him, also, as the attendant and friend of our apostle on this and a future voyage. I have recently spoken of Paul's dangerous illness in Galatia; it is not at all improbable that he may have sent a message to the beloved physician to meet him at Troas, and give him the benefit of his medical skill and Christian counsel. One of the last short entries in the Great Apostle's life tells us at once of the faithful and devoted friendship of this Christian physician, and Paul's estimate of his services. He is mentioning, with a sorrowing heart, how all had forsaken him; but he adds, "only *Luke* is with me."*

The little band are now fairly on their way. A prosperous wind brings them in two days to the north of Greece. They seem to have anchored for the first night at the island of Samothrace, where the mountains rise to a great height above the sea, forming a landmark to the Grecian sailors for a long distance, and regarded by these Pagan mariners of old with a sacred reverence. Neptune, the god of the sea, in the heathen mythology, was supposed to have his throne

* 2 Tim. iv. 11.

on the cliffs of Samothrace; from thence it was thought he had looked down on the scene of the Trojan war, animating its heroes; and the caves which he made his ordinary dwelling were imagined to be deep down in the ocean, between Imbros and Tenedos. Such were the false but beautiful dreams of the heathen world, which a feeble pilgrim, who had now moored his bark near these fabled caverns, was to be instrumental more than any other in dispelling for ever! From thence they sailed north-west to the harbour of Philippi; it was called Neapolis, or "New City" (now *Cavallo*), situated in a sheltered bay or haven. Here travellers landed when they wished to pursue the Via Egnatia, the great military road which led to Italy. Between Philippi and this port-town, a distance of ten miles, was a craggy ridge, rising steep from the sea, by which it was necessary for the apostles to cross. We may imagine them pausing when they reached the summit, and seating themselves on one of the masses of rock, which modern travellers speak of, looking down on the prospect on either side. Behind them their eyes would rest upon a vast wilderness of blue waters, with Mount Athos rising in the far distance; on the inland side they would behold a spacious plain, watered by many little streams, the richly wooded valley of Seres running towards the west. Situated in the midst of these streams, on account of which it was originally called Crenides, or Fountains, is the town of Philippi. The city, I need not say, from its name, was built by Philip of Macedon, father of Alexander the Great. In its immediate neighbourhood there was a famous hill, called "Bacchus-mount," rich in golden treasure, from whose mines the king was said to have gained annually one thousand talents. The town itself was enclosed with a wall, which stretched down on either side from the fortress. Two American missionaries, who some time ago travelled in that region, give us some interesting details about the present appearance of Philippi. They observed the ruins of the castle on the top of the hill, and traces of a *forum*, the seat of justice—perhaps the very same within which we shall presently find Paul and his companion standing, and submitting to the rods of the lictors. The ruins of a palace, built of the finest white marble, is the grandest of the old monuments still existing, although it is fast disappearing under the hands of the Turks, who are despoiling it to form their gravestones.* Those who have read Roman history know well how famous Philippi and its neighbourhood was, from being the scene of a great battle. Here Brutus and Cassius, Octavius and Antony, pitched their camps. The two former were defeated; and, at their own request, slain by the hands of their comrades, rather than fall into those of the enemy. In honour of the victory, Augustus declared Philippi to be in future the capital of the province, and seat of the government. Paul is about to make it renowned as the scene of a greater moral victory, with weapons which are not "carnal, but mighty, through God, to the pulling down of strongholds." Philippi itself was a sort of little Rome, it was peopled by Romans, its citizens spoke the Roman tongue, and prided themselves in Roman manners and customs. There were few Jews, indeed *so* few, that there was not even a synagogue. Their only place of worship was one of the *Proseuchæ*,—slight and uncostly

* Dwight and Schauffler, as quoted by Dr Kitto.

buildings for prayer and religious service. Some of these were open at the top, and exposed to the weather. They were most generally situated in a grove, or under a tree, either by the sea-side, or, more commonly still, by the banks of a river, as many of the Jewish ceremonial observances required water for performing ablutions.* The one at Philippi was outside the city, by the banks of the river Gaggitas, or *Zygactes*,—a word which means "pole-break," and which is said to have been so called by the Greeks from another absurd legend they had, that one of their false gods, *Pluto*, in crossing it broke the pole of his chariot on the banks! † A few women, "proselytes of the gate," as they were called, believers in the God of Israel, Sabbath after Sabbath had been accustomed to meet here for prayer, both those who were by birth Jewesses, as well as other residents in the town. Among these there was one of the name of Lydia, a stranger from a province in Asia, for it is expressly said she belonged to "the city of Thyatira." This city had been long celebrated, and, indeed, is to this very day celebrated, ‡ for its purple dye; and she was one of many who made her livelihood by selling it. It was among this handful of lowly women that the glorious gospel of the blessed God was first preached in Europe! In no splendid temple, or gorgeous cathedral, but at a simple *prayer-meeting* in an oratory by a river side! The heart of Lydia was

* Horne's *Introduction*, Olshausen, Epiphanius, &c.

† Appian iv. 105, as quoted by Lewin.

‡ So far back as the time of Homer we read of the Lydian purple—

"And as by Lydian or by Carian maid,
The purple dye is on the ivory laid."—*Iliad.*

Dr Kitto gives the following extract from Sir Emerson Tennant's *Letters from the Ægean*—"Large quantities" (of scarlet or purple cloths) "are sent weekly to Smyrna for the purposes of commerce."

opened as Paul and Silas unfolded the great salvation. She was convinced that Jesus of Nazareth was indeed the true Messiah, and Son of God, and in His name she and her household were immediately baptized. It is striking here to observe how God finds out his people, and brings them under the power of the truth. Lydia was an inhabitant of one of those very cities in Asia where Paul had been "forbidden" to preach. Probably she lived almost constantly at Thyatira; but her passing visit at Philippi was ordained and overruled by a higher Hand to bestow a nobler "citizenship" upon her! She was just following her wonted trade as "a seller of purple," when the Lord sent his servants to declare to her the way of life. It is another of the many striking examples given us in His Word, of how He delights to meet His people in *the ordinary business and employments of life.* He called Matthew when he was seated at his toll-bar—Peter and Andrew at their nets, and here he meets Lydia when in a strange city she has taken up her abode to prosecute her trade. It teaches us the great lesson—that we do not require to leave the duties of life in order to be religious. With that Christian love and hospitality, so common in these primitive ages, this earliest convert at Philippi took the apostles to her own house, and made them take up their abode during their stay at Philippi. This was the first of many proofs of personal kindness Paul received at the hands of the Philippians. Four times we find during his life did they liberally contribute to supply his wants; and we shall afterwards see how his Roman dungeon was cheered with the gifts of their bounty.

God seemed to smile upon these early labours of

his servants at Philippi. The church grew, men and women were added to it, and for "many days" their teaching was allowed to go on undisturbed. A terrible furnace, however, was at hand—although grace was to be given these faithful men to pass boldly through.

I must proceed to tell you the cause of this "fiery trial" which was about to "try them." There were some wicked heathen masters, whose female slave or servant had "a spirit of divination," or "spirit of Python"—that is, the Prince of darkness had sent some of his evil spirits or agents to take possession of her mind; for at this time, when Jesus, the true light, had come into the world, the powers of darkness seem to have exercised an unusual influence over both the bodies and souls of men. This female, by wild gestures and words, and ravings, called "oracles," practised on the weakness of the ignorant by pretending to foretell the events of the future. The Greeks and Romans supposed such unhappy persons to be possessed by the god Apollo, and that through his agency they had this "spirit of divination." Apollo was often called by the title of the "*Pythian* Apollo,"—Python being a serpent which he was said to have destroyed with arrows, so soon as he was born. These masters thus made a gain of this poor girl, getting money from those whose future history or fortune she pretended to read. Paul and Silas seem, after the conversion of Lydia, to have been in the habit of going for some time to the oratory at the river's side. The number of hearers was daily increasing, and the devout women had probably brought with them their relatives and friends, to listen to the words of eternal life. The "possessed" slave had followed the apostles several times when they were on their way thither, crying after them, "These men are the slaves of the Most High God." She may possibly have been herself a Jewess; she may have had some idea about the coming of the Christ; and the preaching of Paul may have produced some singular effect on her mind,* for she added, "They show unto us the way of salvation." Day after day she seems to have returned to the same spot, repeating her wild ravings. Paul feared lest such a testimony might bring discredit on their cause, and wishing to show the superiority of the Christian religion to the powers of imposture, he turned round on one of these occasions, and in the name of his Divine Master rebuked the evil spirit. It immediately came out of her, and the sufferer was restored to her right mind.

You may imagine the rage and anger of her masters when they saw the demon expelled, and all hope of further gain gone. They resolved to have a full revenge, and they knew the multitude would heartily second them. Accordingly, they seized on the apostles, and dragged them before the magistrates in the forum, or market-place. They accused them of having thrown the whole city into confusion, and of unlawfully trying to introduce a new religion among Roman citizens. I have already mentioned that some offending Jews had shortly before been driven from Rome; the Philippians doubtless thought they might well follow the example. The violence of the mob was great, and the magistrates gave orders to the lictors to strip the two apostles and scourge them. What a sad and sorrowful sight, these holy men dragged along to receive this fearful punishment! Their garments are

* Lewin.

torn off their backs;* the lictors untie their "fasces," or bundle of rods, made of elmwood, and these descend upon them in heavy blows. Paul may have all the time been calling out, with righteous indignation, "Scourge me not! It is at your peril if you do, without even the form of a trial. I am a Roman!"† But if he did, they refused to hear. His voice was drowned in the clamour. There is no doubt this was regarded by the apostles not only as a severe, but as a degrading punishment. It was much more cruel than the Jewish manner of scourging, which Paul once endured. The latter was inflicted with leathern thongs. Moreover, by the Jewish law, they were restricted to *forty* stripes. The apostle, in referring to the ills he had endured at the hands of his countrymen, says, "Five times I received forty stripes *save one.*" Thirty-nine seems to have been the usual number; but in the case of the Roman rod-scourging, he speaks of suffering stripes "*above measure.*" There was in it no limitation.‡ We have already noted the occasion of the reference in his letter to the Corinthians to the "perils of waterfloods," and "perils of robbers." Here we have another, which he speaks of in the same passage, "*Thrice was I beaten with rods.*" §

But the Prætors in the present case were not contented with the scouring; they gave the jailer strict orders to keep them "safely." It was a significant

* "The lictors being sent to inflict punishment, beat them with rods, *being naked*."—*Livy*, ii. 5. "He commanded the men to be seized, and to be stripped naked in the midst of the forum, and to be bound, and rods to be brought."—*Cicero*, quoted by Barnes.

† Cicero, *Verr.* v. 57.

‡ Dr Kitto's *Bible Illustrations.*

§ 2 Cor. xi. 25.

hint to deal as harshly with them as he might. Faint and bleeding, they are hurried away to a dark prison; their limbs, still quivering under the scourge, are thrust into the stocks, and so fastened that they will be unable to move them.* No wonder Paul should, in an after period, when he was writing to the Thessalonians, speak of the way in which he was "*shamefully treated at Philippi.*"† It must be observed, too, that it was the *inner* prison into which the apostles were thrown,—doubtless one of those dark cells that had such a terrible name in the Roman world, where the heavily-bound captives were left to endure the tortures of a living death! "We must picture to ourselves something very different from the austere comfort of an English jail. . . . . The inner prisons of which we read in the ancient world, were like that 'dungeon in the court of the prison' into which Jeremiah was let down with cords, and where 'he sank in the mire.' They were pestilential cells, damp and cold, from which the light was excluded, and where the chains rusted on the limbs of the prisoners."‡ We can think of the apostles, when, under the guidance of a rough jailer, they passed from cell to cell, and heard the clanking which told of miserable beings who were already their inmates. They have reached the appointed dungeon, and have bidden farewell to the cheering light of day; but they are not downcast. Though they have nothing to expect but a dreadful morrow, there is an inner sun-

* "ξυλον, *nervus*. A wooden block furnished with holes, into which the feet were put, and, according to the severity of the torture, stretched far from one another. Origen, in his extreme old age, was obliged to bear this torture, and for several days to lie in such an instrument, with limbs far spread out from one another."—Olshausen *On Acts*, p. 557.

† 1 Thess. ii. 2.

‡ Howson and Conybeare, vol. i. p. 326.

shine which is lighting up their souls, which the poor jailer, as yet, knows nothing of. The magistrates who so cruelly condemned them, are now perhaps sleeping tranquilly on their pillows, but suffering seems to have banished sleep from the eyes of the prisoners. We may picture to ourselves the deep darkness that has gathered around them; perhaps the tempest howling piteously through their vaulted cell, and now and then, when there was a pause in the storm, the heavy-measured tramp of the sentinel reminding them of their terrible situation. Or shall we imagine the storm has spent itself? It is the stillness of the midnight hour! The other prisoners are startled from their chains by a strange and unwonted sound; it is the two Jews, brought, on the previous evening, who are making their dungeon resound, not with piteous groans and lamentations under the torture of their torn backs and fettered limbs, but with songs of joy and praise. "Paul and Silas prayed and sang praises to God!" What these praises were, we are not told. They probably were the songs of the sweet Psalmist of Israel, many of which were so suitable to their case. Their voices would join together in earnest entreaty, that the same God, who had rescued Joseph of old when "his feet were bound with fetters of iron," would "hear the groaning of the prisoner, and free them that were appointed to death." How strange the feelings of those must have been who were listening to them! —wretched outcasts, robbers, murderers, thieves, rebels, traitors, profligates.* How strange for them to hear, in such a place, sweet strains of gratitude and love! —no complaining under their torture, but, perhaps,

* Howson and Conybeare, vol. i. p 328.

PAUL AND SILAS IN PRISON.

like Stephen, or Stephen's Lord, praying for their very enemies, and committing their cause to the God they served.

At that very moment, when prayer and praise were ascending together at midnight, an earthquake shook the prison walls to their foundations. The bands of all the prisoners are loosed—the doors are shattered on their hinges, and fly open! It is God Himself, who has "heard them while they are yet speaking"—come to give them release. Do they immediately avail themselves of the opened doors to make their escape? We might have thought so; but no! Paul and his companion had work to do in that prison; they had troubled souls to comfort and save; and, forgetful of themselves, they remain quietly in their cell. There is *one* much agitated spirit, who, roused by the earthquake's crash, comes rushing into them with a flaming torch in his hand: it is the morose and hard-hearted jailer, who feels that his honour and his life are at stake. He knows the terrible vengeance that will wait him on the morrow if one prisoner be missing. In a state of hopeless despair, he draws his sword, and is about to plunge it into his heart, in order to escape certain infamy and disgrace. It was one of the false maxims of ancient Paganism, that there was something meritorious in self-destruction. We have, a little ago, noted it in the case of two Roman generals, Brutus and Cassius. Cato was guilty of self-murder in Utica; and it was doubtless the same mistaken idea which prompted, at this moment, the jailer of Philippi to attempt suicide, and rush unprepared into the presence of his God. But Paul cries out, "Do thyself no harm, for we are all here!" The keeper must have been struck with the conduct of these noble-minded prisoners. He had just been listening, doubtless, to their prayers and praises; he may have heard of the good news of salvation that had been for several days preached by them in the city; he may have heard the ravings of the "possessed" Pythoness, proclaiming them to be messengers from Heaven; the terrific earthquake shook the walls of his seared and hardened conscience as well as of the prison; he wondered at the conduct of these two suffering Jews; he had treated them with nothing but harshness—they had returned nothing but kindness; the door was open for their escape, but they remained still, only to speak words of comfort to him. His heathen heart wondered, and trembled. Holding a blazing torch (*Greek*, "lights"), he rushed into their cell with the anxious question, "What must I do to be saved?" It was, doubtless, a far higher salvation the poor man was in search of, than mere safety from the vengeance of Roman prætors. His sins, more terrible than a scourge of scorpions, rose up before him. The answer was joyfully given—"*Believe on the Lord Jesus Christ, and thou shalt be saved, and thy house.*"

What a strange scene immediately followed: the trembling jailer and his family were standing, in wonder and terror, in the apostles' inner cell—the glaring torch-light flickering on the damp walls! Along with them, we may believe, other prisoners, loosed from their fetters, crowded around, and listened to a strange sermon from the lips of the scourged Christians, at that strange hour, and in that strange place. We may imagine what it would be. *Jesus!*—His work—His life—His agony—His death—would be fully unfolded. The storm was changed into a calm. Like Elijah in the wilderness, after the earthquake and the hurricane came the "still small voice." The jailer grasped that golden assurance which Paul himself had seized at a similar hour,—"This is a faithful saying, and worthy of all acceptation, that Jesus Christ came into the world to save sinners."

The first place Paul preached at in Europe was a river-side; the second, in a dungeon at midnight! Truly God is not confined to temples made with hands. He could make a pillow of rude stones to Jacob, and a Roman dungeon to "the chief of sinners," the gate of heaven! Nor is He confined to any particular *manner* of bringing His people under the power of the truth. *Generally* He employs means. In the case of Lydia, the means was a *prayer-meeting.* Prayer ascended—prayer was heard—her heart was opened. But He can work, too, independently of instrumentality. He sometimes shows how his grace can triumph over every obstacle, —a rough heathen jailer, whose only prayers before were probably his dreadful oaths, is brought in a moment to the foot of the Saviour's cross!

We believe that more in that Roman prison than the jailer had their hearts touched that night,—other criminals *there*, were probably made the monuments of the same wondrous grace. The simple history of Luke completes the interesting account. He, who was so lately a stern jailer, now becomes a Christian friend; he feels that he owes his two prisoners a debt which never could be repaid; he does his best to show them how much he felt it; he takes them first of all to the fountain or well in the prison-court,* and there washes their wounds. In the water of the same cistern, he

* See the picture, beginning of the chapter.

and his household are at the same time also baptized. He then conducts them to his own dwelling, and sets food before them. They rejoice together in one blessed Saviour, who, in a nobler sense, "proclaims liberty to the captives, and the opening of the prison to them that are bound." Can we not picture that strange family scene? While yet the town of Philippi was hushed in sleep, all ignorant of what had taken place that night in its gloomy prison,—the jailer seated in his own house, with his relatives gathered around him,—his eye every now and then filled with tears of mingled sorrow and joy, as he casts them upon the two holy strangers who had been the means of ushering him into the glorious liberty of the children of God!

What takes place in the morning? The tidings of the earthquake reach the ears of the Roman magistrates. In their fear and terror, they send orders by their lictors, "Let these men go." We know the superstitious ideas attached by Romans of old to an earthquake; they invariably imagined it to indicate the anger of their gods, and it would not be difficult, in the present instance, to refer it to this cause. The magistrates began to tremble when they reflected on their own conduct. Such an outrage on law! Indeed, if their doings had been reported to the Proconsul of Macedonia, they might even have been called to answer at Rome in the presence of Cæsar, and be deprived of the powers of magistracy for life.* They were very anxious, therefore, to hush the matter up; but Paul was a lion-hearted man as well as a true Christian, and he nobly and bravely sent word back that they would *not* go in that underhand way until their judges came

* Biscoe *On the Acts*; Livy, iv. 9; Cicero's *Orations against Verres*, &c

and made an apology; for they had violated the very laws they were there set to uphold. "They had beaten them publicly and uncondemned, being Romans." "Nay," says the apostle, "let them come themselves, and fetch us out!" * The prætors saw at once that they had exceeded their powers, and might be severely punished for their illegal treatment of "Roman citizens." So they had to go themselves to the jail, and *beseech* the apostles to depart. What a humiliating position for these proud Roman magistrates! See them now coming as suppliants to the prison doors, as Paul had required, and courteously leading out those whom, the day before, they had unmercifully scourged!

We must not suppose, from the apostles' resolute conduct on this occasion, that there was anything like revenge, or want of meekness and submission to injury. If they had left the prison merely at the solicitation of the rulers, without asking an apology, it would more than probably have been said, that they had bribed the jailer, whose fears they had worked upon, and thus made their escape. This would inevitably have damaged their own reputation and the success of the gospel in the city and neighbourhood. On the other hand, their bold and manly conduct, followed as it was by the magistrates coming personally to request them to leave their cells, must have told with powerful effect on the minds of the Romans, and prepared the way for the future preaching of the truth in Philippi. Had Paul, on his return in future years, been only known there as a poor Jew, who had left the public jail covered with scourging and contempt, he

* Acts xvi. 37.

would have attracted little attention; but Paul, the bold and manly Roman citizen, who had the fortitude to protest against an unjust and iniquitous act of tyranny, had the way paved for that happy success among rich and poor which attended his labours, afterwards, in the same town. If he had demanded no such apology, he would have gone away with the name of a "pestilent fellow" and a "coward." As it was, he departed an innocent and a brave man—a holy, patient, and devoted Christian. As an excellent writer observes on this subject—"St Paul, in this instance, affords us a remarkable example of the union of the two Christian duties, firmness and forbearance. He compels the magistrates to humble themselves, and to reverse their unjust sentence, by going to the prison in person and fetching him out; but he does not, as he might have done, institute a rigorous prosecution against them, and subject them to heavy penalties for an obvious violation of the well-known Roman law." *

Unmoved by the past cruelties which had been inflicted on them, Paul and Silas repair to the house of their first convert, Lydia. There they meet other Christian brethren, who have assembled to receive the apostles' farewell blessing. Timothy and Luke are left behind to nourish the infant church planted in the city of Philippi. Although Lydia and the jailer, with their houses, are the only converts specially mentioned, we have reason to believe that many others, during the weeks of that memorable visit, were added to the church. "Paul and his companion, full of gratitude and courage, set out on another stage of their great missionary journey."

* Blunt's *Lectures on St Paul.*

CHAPTER XI.

Thessalonica and Berea.

"As some tall cliff that lifts its awful form
Swells from the vale, and midway leaves the storm,
Though round its breast the rolling clouds are spread,
Eternal sunshine settles on its head."

"He might have filled hundreds of *martyrologies* with his sufferings; . . . all which he generously underwent with a soul as calm and serene as the morning sun. No spite or rage, no fury or storms, could ruffle and discompose his spirit; nay, those sufferings, which would have broken the back of an ordinary patience, did but make him rise up with the greater eagerness and resolution for the doing of his duty."—CAVE's *Life of St Paul*, 1676.

We are soon to meet the Great Apostle in the streets and halls of the most polished and learned city of the Old World; but before we follow him thither, let us briefly track his steps from the city of Philippi, where we last left him, weary and faint with scourging, but his spirit full of joy at all the great things which God had done for him.

Travelling still along the Via Egnatia by Amphipolis and Apollonia, he reached, in three days, the city of Thessalonica. Thessalonica was the largest town at that time in Macedonia, and is one of considerable note at the present day, under the slightly-changed name of Salonica. It reckons, indeed, third in importance in the Ottoman empire in Europe. If you look at your map, you will observe that it is situated at the north of Greece, close by the shore near the head of the Thermaic Gulf. It occupies, as you will also see from the picture, the slope of a hill at the corner of the bay. It was built by Cassander, one of the generals of Alexander the Great, who was struck with the beauty of the site,* and compelled, at the same time, the inhabitants round about to leave their own cities and villages, and take up their abode in the new seaport which he called, after his wife, *Thessalonica.* At the time of St Paul's visit, it was the capital of the province—a Roman proconsul, with his lictors and officers, held his court there. It was what we may call the Liverpool of northern Greece—a great place for commerce—ships sailing from its harbour to all places of the known world. It became very soon a great Christian capital, and continued so for many hundred years; so that the truth of Paul's words was not confined to his own age—"From you the Word of God hath sounded forth; not only in Macedonia and Achaia, but in every place."† Dr Clark visited the city in the year 1801, and describes many ruins of ancient buildings with Roman inscriptions. Among others, he mentions a Turkish mosque, containing an old and singular marble pulpit, from which, tradition says, Paul preached in a vault under ground.

On arriving at Thessalonica, we may follow in thought the weary apostles as, after their long journey of 90 or 100 miles, and still suffering under their recent tortures at Philippi, they approached the gates of its terraced walls. We cannot tell whether it may then have possessed the same striking appearance it presents to modern travellers, with its white-painted buildings, its walls glittering in the sun, and, in a calm day, casting their pearly shadows in the beautiful bay,

* Strabo. † 1 Thess. i. 8.

which, whatever changes the city may have undergone, remains the same now as when Paul and his friend gazed on its sparkling waves.

On arriving in the city, they took up their abode with Jason, a Jewish convert; by some supposed to have been a relative of the apostle;* by others, one of "the brethren" to whom the believers in Philippi had given him "letters of commendation." For three successive Sabbaths (Jewish Sabbaths—our Saturday) Paul spoke in the synagogue. It seems to have been the place of worship to which the Jews all around resorted; for, in speaking of it, he does not say, "where there was *a* synagogue," but "THE synagogue." The Israelites, at the towns of Amphipolis and Apollonia, seem to have been too few or too poor to have a synagogue, or even a *proseucha* of their own, and to have attended, therefore, the one at Thessalonica.† We may picture to ourselves the Great Apostle, bearing in his body some new and recent "marks of the Lord Jesus," standing up in this Jewish church, on the first Sabbath after his arrival, to speak to his "brethren according to the flesh."

Thessalonica, I may add, is as celebrated at the present day, for its large Hebrew population, as it was then; for, out of 70,000 inhabitants, more than one half are Jews.‡ Of these, many are engaged in the manufacture of *cloth* for tents,—a circumstance which is curious in connexion with the employment of the apostle during his present residence, and to which we shall immediately refer.

If you read the letters he wrote at an after period to the Thessalonians, you must be struck with a sub-

* Rom. xvi. 21. † Kuinöel. ‡ Dr Kitto.

ject which he dwells much upon in these, viz., "the kingdom and second coming of the Lord Jesus." You are aware that the Jews had long looked forward to the Messiah as a great temporal deliverer. Their country was now under the Roman yoke; but they clung to the fond hope that once more, under the promised "Prince of Peace," it would regain the independence and glory it possessed under the reign of David and Solomon. One great object of the apostle, both now in his address in the synagogue and in his future epistles to the Thessalonians, was to correct these mistaken ideas about the *nature* of Christ's kingdom. He proved to them from their own prophecies that He was to come, not as a triumphant, but as a lowly suffering Messiah; and that though a King, His kingdom was "not to be of this world:" it was to be a spiritual, not a temporal one. "He reasoned with them out of the Scriptures; opening and alleging that Christ must needs have suffered and risen again from the dead; and that this Jesus, whom he preached unto them, was Christ."*

As I have just hinted, he again found here the trade he learned in his boyhood at Tarsus of use to him. He did not wish to be "burdensome" to any, and though the converts at Philippi sent him on two occasions gifts and presents, he preferred doing what he could for his own support. It is interesting to think of him, evening after evening, when the labour of teaching and preaching was over, seated with his bundle of goats' hair at his side, busy at the manufacture of the hair-cloth

It is, indeed, a striking picture to see the holy man

* Acts xvii. 2, 3.

of God, the polished scholar, the great missionary, not considering himself demeaned in taking up this lowly occupation; and, though still severely smarting under the stripes he received at Philippi, bending with cheerfulness over his laborious task. It has been supposed, however, that at this time the apostle must have been in great bodily want. Historians of that period mention a famine which prevailed throughout Greece, and which raised provisions to six times their usual price—a peck of wheat costing in their currency four shillings and sixpence.* But the many kind hearts Paul had left behind him in Philippi, would not allow him at present to fall into straits; and on two occasions afterwards, we shall find they sent some Christian messengers with a similar supply of money. "Now, ye Philippians, know also, that in the beginning of the gospel, when I departed from Macedonia, no church communicated with me, as concerning giving and receiving, but ye only. For even in Thessalonica ye sent once and again unto my necessity."†

His success among his own Jewish countrymen does not appear to have been great at Thessalonica. His converts seem to have been principally heathens "who turned from dumb idols to serve the living God." "How new and how comforting to *them* must have been the doctrine of the resurrection from the dead! What a contrast must this revelation of life and immortality have been to the hopeless lamentations of their own pagan funerals, and to the dismal teaching which we can still read in the sepulchral inscriptions of heathen Thessalonica, such as told the bystander that after death there is no revival, after the grave

* Eusebius. † Phil. iv. 15, 16.

no meeting of those who have loved each other on earth!"*

It is more than probable that Paul, in commending the new doctrine to these idolatrous pagans, made use of *miracle* in proof of his Divine commission. In writing afterwards to them, he says, "Our gospel came to you in *power*, and in the Holy Ghost." That word "*power*" would seem to imply (as elsewhere) the use of extraordinary and miraculous agency. We know that he did not deceive them by any bright pictures of earthly or carnal glory. He did not say that if they left their dumb idols they would become great and powerful and glorious in the world. It was quite the reverse; for he writes thus afterwards, "Verily when we were with you, *we told you before that we should suffer tribulation*, even as it came to pass, and ye know."†

The envy of the Jews was stirred up against these "preachers of strange doctrine." The scum and refuse of the city—"lewd fellows of the baser sort,"—that is, a number of those dangerous idlers who were always found in a place like Thessalonica, hanging about the pier and the forum ready to join in any tumult,—were easily prevailed on to take part in this assault on the innocent apostles. The house of Jason was stormed, but not finding their victims there (they having been previously warned of the attack), Jason and other Christians were seized by the mob, and dragged before the magistrates. They were accused of sedition and rebellion, of harbouring in their house those who were preaching treason against Cæsar—speaking of another kingdom and another King, "one *Jesus*." They thus

* Howson and Conybeare, vol. i. p. 355.
† 1 Thess. iii. 3, 4. See Lewin, vol. i. p. 256.

easily perverted Paul's words about the kingdom of Christ into a meaning to suit their own purposes. The magistrates bound them over to keep the peace, taking money from them as bail or security in the meantime, that the quiet of the town should not again be broken. Paul immediately saw with a sorrowful heart that it would be needful to withdraw elsewhere. The rage alike of the multitude and the Jews was roused, and if they remained, and continued to preach the gospel, their faithful friends, to whom they were indebted for a home, would be sure to become the victims of popular fury. He would, perhaps, leave behind him with his inquiring pagan disciples, as the only substitute for the *preaching* of the gospel, a copy of the Old Testament Scriptures, and probably the Gospel of St Matthew, the only one of the four inspired histories which at that time was written. It is to this gospel he is supposed to allude, when he says in his future letter, "But of the times and the seasons, brethren, ye have no need that I write unto you. For yourselves know perfectly, that the day of the Lord so cometh as a thief in the night."*

We are not told to what extent Jason and his friends afterwards suffered. Though the magistrates had accepted bail from them in the meantime, it is not probable they would be freed from a future trial, and the result, most likely, on a charge of aiding those guilty of treason, would be severe fining, or else the forfeiture of their goods. Be this as it may, we know that the danger of the apostles was so great that the very night of the assault they were obliged, under covert of darkness, to leave the city.

* 1 Thess. v. 1, 2. Compare with this Matt. xxiv. 36-41

Timothy, probably, may now have rejoined Paul. If so, he would accompany him and Silas at their departure. Passing out by the arch at the western gate, they proceeded fifty miles' distance to the lovely city of Berea, situated, among its gardens, streams, and groves of palm and plane trees, on the eastern slope of the chain of mountains of which Olympus is the chief.

This town was founded by one Pheres, and called Pherea; but from a singular difficulty the Macedonians had in pronouncing the *Ph*, it was corrupted by them into *Berea*. The modern inhabitants, however, who work in the red marble quarries in its neighbourhood, seem able to pronounce what their forefathers could not, for it has resumed the name of *Pheria.**

Berea, at the time the apostle fled to it, was a secluded place. It was a considerable distance from the great Roman road (the Via Egnatia), and probably was selected by him and his companions on that account. Moreover, being in another district of Macedonia, he was safe from the power of the proconsul of Thessalonica.

After the treatment he had received at the former city from his Jewish brethren, we could not have wondered, on reaching this new abode, if he had resolved in all time to come to preach only to the Gentiles. But no; he was far too true a patriot, to allow ingratitude or opposition to damp or cool his love for his countrymen; "apostle of the Gentiles" as he was, it was still with him "to the Jew *first*." It is pleasing to be able to add, that the encouragement he met with among his countrymen at Berea was very different from that which he received at Thessalonica. He found the

† See Wetstein *in loco*, &c., quoted by Lewin, vol. i. p. 265.

Jews there "more noble" than those of the former city, because they did not, like the others, shut their ears against the truth, but "searched the Scriptures" every day, comparing the prophecies about the Messiah with their alleged fulfilment in Jesus of Nazareth.

Let us picture to ourselves the scene in the Berean synagogue. The Rabbis and ministers, attired in their flowing robes, hold in their hands the well-thumbed scrolls of parchment containing the writings of Moses and the Prophets. The apostle directs them in these to reference after reference, proving that Jesus was indeed the Christ. May we not imagine him saying, "Turn to your roll containing our old prophet *Micah's* predictions—you will find there mentioned the *birth-place* of the Messiah." The presiding minister reads aloud—"But thou, Beth-lehem Ephratah, though thou be little among the thousands of Judah, yet out of thee shall He come forth unto me that is to be Ruler in Israel; whose goings forth have been from of old, from everlasting."* "Jesus," Paul may be supposed to say, "was born there."

"Turn again to your Pentateuch-scroll, and you will find his predicted *tribe*,—'The sceptre shall not depart from Judah, nor a lawgiver from between his feet, until Shiloh come; and unto Him shall the gathering of the people be.'† Our Jesus," Paul might add, "was born of the tribe of *Judah*. Turn again," might he not say, "to our great prophet, and see what Isaiah's roll says about his royal *line*,—'And there shall come forth a rod out of the stem of Jesse, and a Branch shall grow out of his roots : . . . . . . And in that day there shall be a root of Jesse, which shall

* Micah v. 2. † Gen. xlix. 10.

stand for an ensign of the people; to it shall the Gentiles seek: and his rest shall be glorious.'* Jesus was born of the *Virgin Mary*, the lineal descendant of *David!* Turn again to the prophet of Babylon—unroll the parchment of *Daniel's* prophecies—see what was the *time* your Messiah was foretold to come,—'Seventy weeks are determined upon thy people, and upon thy holy city, to finish the transgression, and to make an end of sins, and to make reconciliation for iniquity, and to bring in everlasting righteousness, and to seal up the vision and prophecy, and to anoint the most Holy. Know therefore and understand, that from the going forth of the commandment to restore and to build Jerusalem, unto the Messiah the Prince, shall be seven weeks, and threescore and two weeks: the street shall be built again, and the wall, even in troublous times. And after threescore and two weeks shall Messiah be cut off, but not for himself: and the people of the prince that shall come shall destroy the city and the sanctuary; and the end thereof shall be with a flood, and unto the end of the war desolations are determined. And he shall confirm the covenant with many for one week: and in the midst of the week he shall cause the sacrifice and the oblation to cease, and for the overspreading of abominations he shall make it desolate, even until the consummation, and that determined shall be poured upon the desolate.'† Above all, turn again to Isaiah's prophetic roll, and read the very *history of this Jesus* whom I have embraced as the true Messiah,—'For he shall grow up before him as a tender plant, and as a root out of a dry ground: he hath no form nor comeliness; and when we shall see

* Isaiah xi. 1, 10. † Daniel ix. 24-27.

him, there is no beauty that we should desire him. He is despised and rejected of men; a man of sorrows, and acquainted with grief; and we hid as it were our faces from him: he was despised, and we esteemed him not.' "*

Many were converted; and among these, Greeks and heathens as well as Jews, and several females of higher rank.

But the apostle was learning every day to "cease from man whose breath is in his nostrils." He was becoming more familiar with the "much tribulation" through which every saint, and more especially every faithful minister, must enter into glory. The "less noble" Jews at a distance, stirred up with envy on hearing of his success, compelled him to leave a city which gave promise of much fruit. He saw that it would be hopeless, from the furious hatred of his own countrymen, to remain for the present longer in Macedonia. They were tracking, like bloodhounds, his footsteps from place to place; he would be sure, humanly speaking, to fall a victim to their malice; he resolved, therefore, to quit it altogether, and make for the nearest point at sea where he could take a vessel to some other field of labour. It was judged advisable to leave Timothy and Silas behind, to nurse the good seed which had been scattered. But how could the persecuted apostle—perhaps, too, at this time suffering from his eyesight—start by night and travel through an unknown country all alone? He was wearied and pained both in mind and body—his stripes, his blindness, his mental sorrow at the sadder spiritual blindness of his brethren,—all forbade a solitary journey. His friends

* Isaiah liii. 2, 3.

at Berea, in these circumstances, undertook to convoy him to the sea-shore. They conducted him, doubtless by the nearest road, close by the woods and olive-groves of the great Olympus. Olympus was the spot celebrated in all ancient song as the seat of the gods. Jupiter, whose name is now familiar to us from his temple at Lystra, was thought to have his throne there, and other divinities haunted its groves and temples. Thousands upon thousands of Pagans revered that spot as the most sacred on earth. Christians may look back with interest at this moment of which I am now speaking, not to the snow-capped mountain as the haunt of false deities, but to one who was now passing in a little skiff under its shadow. It was a Jew of Tarsus who, by the power of the great God of heaven and earth, was to shatter in pieces many a shrine and temple of Olympian Jupiter—"to turn," in a sense the Thessalonian Jews never dreamt of, "the world upside down," and to demonstrate that there was "none other name given under heaven among men by which the sinner could be saved, but the name of Jesus." Paul's companions from Berea had now returned to their own city, taking from him a special message to Silas and Timothy to lose no time in following him to the south.

CHAPTER XII.

Paul at Athens.

"Behold, the Apostle of the Cross sublime—
The warn'd of Heaven, the eloquent, the bold!
Who spake to Athens in her hour of prime,
Braving the thunders of Olympus old,
And spreading forth the Gospel's snowy fold
Where heathen altars pour'd a crimson tide,
And stern tribunals their decrees unroll'd,—
How does his zeal our ingrate coldness chide!"

"Who can calculate the mighty influence of his life upon maxims, upon manners, upon literature, upon history,—in short, upon the whole development of humanity!"

We have, in former chapters, followed the "footsteps" of St. Paul into regions where both nature and man were seen in their savage state. You remember the rugged mountain-passes of Pisidia, and the still more rugged hearts of the Pagan Lystrians? We lately accompanied him, in the quiet of a Sabbath morning, to a river-side, where his listeners were a handful of devout females. We found him, immediately afterwards, in a place more unpromising still, when an inner dungeon and a jailer's iron soul were made as "the house of God and the gate of heaven." We are to follow him now to a grander arena,—amid the philosophers and wise men of the city which then ruled the world of mind and thought, as Rome ruled the outer world by force of arms.

We can easily imagine what his journey thither would be. How many spots of classic interest would open before his eyes! After passing the long island of Eubœa, on the eastern coast of Attica, we may think of him standing on the prow of his vessel and gazing on the splendid temple of Minerva, on the height of the promontory of Sunium. The vessel has now entered the magnificent bay whose waters wash the southern shores of Attica. Soon a glittering object catches his eye on a distant rock: it is the colossal statue of Minerva, on the Acropolis, with a helmet on her head and a spear in her hand, made out of the brazen shields and spears taken at the battle of Marathon.* Temples and columns gradually unfold themselves. The Great Apostle has got his first glimpse of the civilised capital of the ancient world—the seat and centre of art, eloquence, philosophy, and science—Athens, "the eye of Greece!" And now they are nearing the shore:—to the left, he sees the well-known island of Ægina; to the right, that which has given its own name to one of the greatest naval battles ever fought—the island of Salamis. Behind it rises the hill of Hymettus, famed for its honey; and right in front, as you see in the foreground of our large picture, is the *Piræus*, the port of Athens, with its two high moles on either side. "The Piræus," it is said, in a graphic description of it as it appeared to Paul on his landing, "doubtless retained many of the outward features of its earlier appearance,—the landing-places and covered porticos; the warehouses where the corn from the Black Sea used to be laid up; the stores of fish brought in daily

* Conybeare and Howson, vol. i. p. 371. The picture we give is the "Athena," from the Hope collection.

from the Saronic Gulf and the Ægean; the gardens in the watery ground at the edge of the plain; the theatres into which the sailors used to flock to hear the comedies of Menander."* The city and port are distant from one another about five miles. Houses had at one time been built the whole way between, consisting of one narrow street, guarded by walls of sixty feet in height, and with towers in various parts of them. These, however, had at this time greatly fallen into decay,† for we must remember, that by this time the political greatness of Athens had ceased. The Roman eagles had hither, as elsewhere, winged their flight, and the seat of government had been changed to Corinth.‡

And now we may imagine the Great Apostle entering by the gate of the Piræus. He finds himself in a city of temples—a city literally "wholly given to idolatry." Statues of Neptune, Jupiter, Ceres, Minerva, Apollo, Mercury, and the Muses, meet his eye one after the other; porticos, too, with battle-pieces painted on their walls, and bronze figures of illustrious Athenians. On the left is the Pynx, with its tribunal cut from the solid rock, guarded by a statue of Jupiter and the nymphs of the Demus, and which remains to this day uninjured by the ravages of time. Passing further onwards, the statues of Conon, Epaminondas, and, most illustrious of all, Demosthenes, meet the eye of the Christian pilgrim. The soul of the young Tarsian, in bygone days when seated at Gamaliel's feet, had doubtless often kindled under the burning words of the Grecian orator,—now he was gazing on the statue reared

Howson and Conybeare, vol. i. p. 375.

† Ibid. See the entire account given by them of ancient Athens.

‡ Dr Kitto.

on the very spot which had listened to his living tones.

It would weary the reader to dwell on this colossal statue-gallery through which St Paul now walked. Warriors were there—the commanding forms of Philip and Alexander of Macedon, Themistocles and Miltiades; lawgivers were there—such as Solon, standing in front of a portico richly adorned with the recollections of Troy and Marathon. Well was it said of Athens by Petronius, that it was then easier to find in it an idol-god than a man. How striking this idol-crowded capital of the world must have been to one who had been so much in Jerusalem as Paul, where not so much as one image was to be found! *

The Apostle is all at once in a little world of busy thought. In passing along the great central street, the citizens are listening, or gathering in groups "to hear or tell something new." † When he reaches the end of this thoroughfare, with colonnades on either side, we may suppose him turning to his right hand into the *Agora* or market-place,—a square surrounded with the same temple buildings and shady porticos; bazaars filled with every article of luxury; circular booths, some for the sale of slaves, others for provisions. Flowers and fruits were ranged out on one side to tempt the eye, and books and parchments on another, for those who preferred food for the mind.‡ Students

* See Mr Lewin, vol. i. p. 272, with authorities referred to.

† "Demosthenes represents the Athenians as inquiring in the place of public resort, '*If there were any news?*' Meursius has shown also that there were more than three hundred public places in Athens of public resort, where the principal youth and reputable citizens were accustomed to meet for the purpose of conversati n and inquiry."—Barnes *On the Acts*, p 298.

‡ Lewin.

from all quarters of the world might be found there, taking their hours of recreation, their masters standing close by, discussing weighty points of religion and philosophy. Right in front were the rocky crags of the Acropolis, with the temples and statue of which we have already spoken, and its beautiful Parthenon built of white Pantelican marble, whose remains are to this hour so much admired. We may imagine what it must have been then, when its magnificent friezes were all complete, and the statue of the goddess Minerva, from the hand of the great sculptor Phidias, was inside, glittering with gold and ivory. We shall find Paul immediately saying in his address, "The Lord of heaven dwelleth not in temples made with hands;"* as if he had said, "If any temple on earth were befitting for *Him* to dwell in, it would surely be such a masterpiece as this."

We must not forget to note two of the buildings in the Agora. They were the Schools of Epicurus and Zeno, the founders of the two sects the Epicureans and Stoics, to whose followers the Apostle was about to unfold the way of salvation.

I am sure our young readers will be wearying to hear what Paul thought of this great city, with its temples and schools, and sculptures, and other magnificent works of art. He had a mind that was well able to enjoy these treasures of a great people; but the God he served was so despised and neglected in the midst of all this light of nature and philosophy, that we find the only effect produced upon him was, "His spirit was stirred within him, because it was a city wholly given to idolatry!" He himself touchingly says, regarding

* Acts xvii 24.

this visit, "I was left in Athens alone." Timothy and Silas were still at Berea. We may well imagine the feelings of a lone Christian stranger, without one single heart to share his sorrow, pacing the streets of that mighty capital, and feeling, amid all the glory and world-wide fame of its people, that his God was not in all their thoughts. Somewhat of Jonah's experience in going through the streets of Nineveh, nine hundred years before, must have been that of Paul of Tarsus now. If anything could have added to his sorrow and grief, it was that so much seemed to be done *about* religion, while the unholy, profane, and vicious lives of the Athenians showed that true piety had no place in their hearts. Although they knew something *about* a deity, "they glorified him not *as* God, neither were thankful, but they became vain in their imaginations, and their foolish hearts were darkened."

Anxious, however, as he was for the return of his two fellow-labourers, Paul could not remain idle and silent in the midst of the stirring scenes and throngs around him. Though alone, he resolves to unfurl the Gospel banner.

The Apostle first of all, as we have invariably found him doing elsewhere, sought out his own "brethren according to the flesh." He commences in the Jewish synagogue. It was not, however, with *them* he came hither to fight the battles of his Heavenly Master, but with the teachers of those false systems of philosophy and pagan superstition, which had then in Athens their principal seat, and which formed in many other places the main hindrance to the spread of the Gospel. We may follow him, therefore, once more into the hum of the *Agora* or market-place, going from one group to another of those who were standing or strolling under the shady plane-trees or porticos, till he joined in the conversation, and introduced the great subject of his thoughts and labours—"Jesus and the Resurrection!"

How was his preaching listened to? How did these proud wise-men receive the great Christian ambassador? They loved oratory. Demosthenes and others, by their marvellous eloquence,

"Wielded at will that fierce democracy."

How, then, will the Christian orator and philosopher fare when he unfolds things in heaven and earth, that were "never dreamt of in their philosophy?" Socrates and Plato had long laboured in vain to discover, by the light of nature, the great realities of the future. Paul is about to unlock the wondrous secret; to reveal to them One, who is at once the "power of God and the wisdom of God," the "Abolisher of death," the "Resurrection and the life!" How will they receive such doctrine and testimony as this? How will proud reason be content to seat itself at the foot of the cross of Jesus? Doubtless he would not find it difficult to draw them into converse, as there was nothing these sharp and keen intellects enjoyed more than a discussion upon difficult points, and all the better if these were connected with some new religious system. Moreover, we must remember that Paul was not altogether unprepared to meet them, as Epicureans and Stoics were found in abundance in his own native town of Tarsus, where doubtless he had acquired a familiarity with their doctrines. The leading doctrines of the Epicureans were, that the world was made, not by an Almighty Framer, but by an accidental or "fortuitous" concourse of atoms; that pleasure was the highest human pursuit:

also, that the soul was matter, and did not survive the dissolution of the body. This sect were truly "without God and without hope." The Stoics had a better creed: they believed in a Supreme Being, the creator and sustainer of all things, and in the immortality of the soul; but they had dim and imperfect notions about the character of a future state. They rejected the idea of coming punishment, and opposed those fundamental doctrines of Christianity which demanded true repentance, and set forth the nature and method of forgiveness of sin and justification by faith.*

It is evident that Paul was not long in gathering around him an attentive knot of hearers. They were struck with the acuteness of the Jewish stranger. He was mean in his bodily appearance, his face wan, and his garb ragged; his speech lacked the rich, mellow, musical tone they were wont to hear. But he was no weakling in other things. Jew as he was, he was a scholar. He could speak their pure Attic tongue—he could quote their poets. If his eyesight was at times dim, he had an inner taste for the sublime and beautiful; for he conversed with them, as he did with the Lystrians years before, of "Him who had made the heavens and the earth, and the sea; who had never left Himself without a witness, in that He was continually doing them good, giving them rain from heaven, and fruitful seasons, filling their hearts with food and with gladness." Though his doctrines were strange, he defended them well. He was an acute reasoner. Indeed, they had got so interested in his conversation, that they proposed he should go with them, for quiet and retirement, if not for space, to the top of the *Areopagus*, or Mars'

* See Neander, p. 188.

Hill. This was another famous spot in the Athenian capital. It was the place of sacred judgment; and as it was especially intended as a place of arbitration on *religious* matters, it was all the more suitable for hearing the new doctrines of this Christian missionary. We may imagine to ourselves the spot where Paul now stood and preached. It was where Pericles and many other great men had raised their voices before him. The stone seats of the judges hewn out in the rock were in front, probably occupied now with Dionysius and other Areopagites, who were the noblest of Athenian citizens. In the same rock was the reputed sanctuary of the Furies, which gave additional awe and solemnity to the place; while the temple of Mars rose immediately in view, crowning the rock to which it gave its name. It was a most impressive moment in the history of the Christian faith. The religion of the despised Jesus of Nazareth, preached at first by a few humble fishermen of Galilee, now finding its way to the very fountain-head of the world's boasted wisdom. Paul is placed on the tribunal, and the question is courteously put to him by this courteous people, "May we know what this new doctrine whereof thou speakest is?—for thou bringest strange things to our ears. We would know, therefore, what these things mean." Christianity had now a bold and fearless advocate. We may imagine him standing up, his face and countenance worn and sad with the traces of recent suffering and bonds, and sadder still with the spectacle of godless splendour all around. He does not at first openly attack their heathen divinities; had he done so, they would at once have refused tc listen. He tells that it is his desire to direct them to the God, whom all their religious edifices showed they were "in ignorance" trying to "worship." He applauds the strength of the religious feeling among them—that they were "exceedingly devout" (the word which is not so correctly rendered in our translation by "too superstitious"). He makes some of the temples and their inscriptions, which he had seen passing along the street, the text of the following stirring address :—

"Ye men of Athens, I perceive that in all things ye are too superstitious. For as I passed by, and beheld your devotions, I found an altar with this inscription, To THE UNKNOWN GOD. Whom therefore ye ignorantly worship, him declare I unto you. God, that made the world, and all things therein, seeing that he is Lord of heaven and earth, dwelleth not in temples made with hands; neither is worshipped with men's hands, as though he needed any thing, seeing he giveth to all life, and breath, and all things; and hath made of one blood all nations of men for to dwell on all the face of the earth, and hath determined the times before appointed, and the bounds of their habitation; that they should seek the Lord, if haply they might feel after him, and find him, though he be not far from every one of us: for in him we live, and move, and have our being; as certain also of your own poets have said, For we are also his offspring.* Forasmuch then

* Paul's quotation occurs in no less than two Greek poets. They are both, of course, celebrating the praise of Jupiter (or Jove), the king of their gods I subjoin a translation of both, given by Mr Lewin, vol. i. p. 284 :—

"He animates the mart and crowded way,
The restless ocean and the shelter'd bay.
Doth care perplex? is lowering danger nigh?
We are his offspring, and to Jove we fly."—*Aratus.*

"Hail! unto thee may mortals lift their voice,
For we thine offspring are. All things that creep
Are but the echo of the Voice divine."—*Hymn of Cleanthes*

as we are the offspring of God, we ought not to think that the Godhead is like unto gold, or silver, or stone, graven by art and man's device. And the times of this ignorance God winked at; but now commandeth all men everywhere to repent: because he hath appointed a day, in the which he will judge the world in righteousness by that man whom he hath ordained; whereof he hath given assurance unto all men, in that he hath raised him from the dead."*

This is doubtless only an outline of Paul's oration; but what a scene! what an auditory! His pulpit, the tribunal where Socrates had once spoken, at the age of seventy, on the same charge of introducing strange gods—his canopy, the intense blue of an Attic sky—the craggy mountains all around—the blue waters he had lately crossed—the crowded monuments of art before and on every side! He looks above them all, and proclaims that his "God, who made the world, and all things therein," owns, as the most hallowed of temples, the hearts of those who devoutly "seek" Him; and that the noblest forms their marble and gold and silver can assume, are poor mockeries of the majesty of His glory.

It has been thought by some†—and the opinion seems not unsupported—that the "*unknown* God" of which he speaks, may have referred to none other than *Jehovah*, the living and true God of the Jews. Moreover, that the fact of no statue being erected on that altar, is sufficiently accounted for by the expressions which Greek writers themselves use when speaking of

* Acts xvii. 22-31.

† See Cave, p. 79, with references to Justin Martyr, Plutarch, Tacitus, &c.

the God of Israel (referring to his spirituality of nature),—*e. g.*, "not to be expressed;" "Him that may not be named by you;" the "All-hidden." If this were the case, what an appropriate and significant text was Paul thus furnished with! He found the empty altar—he places upon it the revelation of a *hidden* God; and, better still, the all-glorious Sacrifice. Jesus he first sets forth as the Saviour, and then as the Judge! The existence of such an altar, however, may be traced to an altogether different cause. It may be referred to the custom which, in the Athenian capital, was not unfrequent, of erecting shrines to "unknown deities." "At Athens," says Pausanias, "there are altars of gods which are called 'the UNKNOWN ones.'" We have from one of their own writers a singular account of how one of these was reared 600 years B.C. Laertius informs us regarding Epimenides, that, "taking white and black sheep, he led them to the Areopagus, and there allowed them to go where they would, commanding those who followed them to sacrifice to the god to whom these things pertained (*without giving the name*), and thus to allay the pestilence from which it has arisen." He adds, that "at this day, through the villages of the Athenians, altars are found without any name." *

But to return to St Paul. Regarding his whole address, it has been well said by a writer from whom, in this chapter, we have already largely drawn—"Simple throughout as is the language of the preacher, yet, in the compass of these few words, he tells them the noblest truths. That there was *one God;* that He

* Diog. Laer. b. i. § 10, quoted by Barnes *On the Acts*.

dwelt not in temples; that the world was not only made but *sustained* by Him; that all mankind were of *one blood;* that they had *fallen away from righteousness;* that God had *sent His Son Jesus* to redeem them; that He *had raised Him from the dead* as an earnest of future life; that *all men must be judged* at the last day."*

Beautiful and comprehensive, however, as the address of the apostle was, one cannot help being struck with its great simplicity. Although in the presence of the world's sages, he just preaches to them as we heard him preaching to the rude Lystrians or the fierce ailer! There is no display, no eloquence, no deep and profound reasoning. In writing afterwards to his Grecian converts, he explains the reason of this unadorned simplicity. "And I, brethren, when I came to you, came not with excellency of speech, or of wisdom, declaring unto you the testimony of God: for I determined not to know anything among you, save Jesus Christ, and him crucified. . . . And my speech and my preaching was not with enticing words of man's wisdom, but in demonstration of the Spirit and of power; that your faith should not stand in the wisdom of men, but in the power of God."† The great Raphael, I doubt not, has both truthfully and strikingly treated this eventful scene, in his famous cartoon of "*Paul preaching at Athens.*" When you next see this well-known picture, if you begin with the figures at the extreme left, and go gradually round to those on the right, you will observe he represents, step by step, from hardened unbelief to full and perfect faith. The figures on the left are frowning with indignation

* Lewin, vol. i. p. 285.

† 1 Cor. ii. 1-5.—See Blunt's *Lectures.*

on the new preacher; those next in order are beginning to reason with one another; the next are arrested, the next convinced, till it ends with the hands stretched out in "believing joy."

The Apostle was stopped in the midst of his discourse. Some (evidently the Epicureans) laughed and ridiculed, saying, "What can this babbler mean?" Others (the Stoics) said "they would hear him at some other time." They affirmed him to be a "setter forth of strange gods." The Greeks had gods and goddesses personating every passion and affection of the soul, such as Pleasure, Hope, Shame, Fear, Peace, Fame, &c. And when Paul spoke of "*Jesus* and the *Resurrection*" (*Anastasis*), they imagined these two words indicated some novel and strange deities they never heard of before.* Lovers as they were of "mythology," the punishment of death was decreed in their laws against any person who, without authority of the state, would presume to introduce a new divinity. The court of the Areopagus, before which Paul had just been standing, was that which was empowered to pronounce what were lawful objects of worship, and to punish those who ventured to be "setters forth of strange gods." By it Socrates had the cup of hemlock put into his hands, which he drank without a murmur.† They seem, in the present instance, not to have exercised any of the severities of the law against the Apostle. The court adjourned, the

* Chrysostom, Pausanias, i. 17.

† If Socrates, "the apostle of natural reason," had been one of Paul's present hearers, who knows but his noble soul would have opened, like the sunflower, to the light of life! Had they been spoken of the true God, his own words at his trial were worthy of the Apostle Paul himself, "Ye men of Athens! I am obliged to you and thank you, but I must obey God rather than you."

crowd dispersed, and, so far as we know, Paul never again preached in this city. We read only of two converts which he made—"Dionysius the Areopagite, and a woman named Damaris." But who can tell what precious seed may have been sown that day among those who hung on the lips of the apostle of Jesus? Who can tell what thoughts they may have carried away with them to their homes, as they remembered the closing sentences of the solemn appeal, that "God had appointed a day in which he would judge the world in righteousness by that Man whom he had ordained"? The expression used regarding his few Athenian converts is worthy of note: "Howbeit, certain men *clave* unto him." It must have cost them a strong effort to be wrenched away from an idolatry to which they were so attached; but, having made the bold resolution to forsake all and follow Jesus, their faith was strong, and they were enabled "to *cleave* to the Lord with full purpose of heart." It is of the nature of faith to grow out of difficulties. We have reason to conclude that the saints in Nero's palace, of whom we shall afterwards hear, were the most devoted converts in Rome; they had much, in their exalted station, to endure for the sake of Jesus; and, unless their faith had been strong and vigorous, they would not so readily have suffered the loss of "*all*" for it. So also with the converts at Athens. We may well believe that an Areopagite, a member of that proud court of philosophers, would not, on slight grounds, have taken the publican's place at the cross of a crucified Redeemer. Regarding Dionysius, we have no further information. If we can credit the traditions of historians respecting him, he had been a witness, when in Heliopolis in

Egypt, of the supernatural darkness which attended the Saviour's crucifixion, and, on beholding it, exclaimed, "Either the God of nature suffers, or the frame of the world will be dissolved." If aught of this tradition be true, his mind had received a previous training for the happy result which made an Athenian philosopher become a lowly disciple of Jesus. He was said afterwards to have been appointed over the Church at Athens, and to have crowned his labours with an heroic martyrdom, being burnt alive in the same city, in the year 93.*

When, however, we witness the effect of the Apostle's labours and eloquence in a city of wise men, we see how true is the Bible saying, that "the world by wisdom knew not God," and that "not many mighty, not many noble, not many wise after the flesh, are called." Paul's abode at Athens was only for a short season. Originally he does not seem to have had any intention to be there at all. He landed at Philippi, with the purpose of carrying the Gospel to the cities and villages of Macedonia; but, having been obliged to flee by night from Berea, he had taken refuge at Athens till he was rejoined there by Silas and Timothy. At last Timothy arrives. It is, however, with no cheering tidings. The rage of the Jews at Thessalonica is still unabated, and Paul's fervent desire to return could not be attempted without endangering his life. What was to be done? The good Apostle could not bear the thought of his dear Thessalonian converts being left "as sheep without a shepherd;" and therefore, young though Timothy was, and ill as he could spare his company, Paul resolved to remain "at Athens

* See Blunt's *Lectures*, p. 260, Cave, Calmet.

thus alone,' sending him back to comfort them, and bring him tidings of their welfare. Listen to his own words in the letter he sends to them :—" We would have come unto you (even I Paul) once and again. . . . Wherefore, when we could no longer forbear, we thought it good to be left at Athens alone, and sent Timotheus, our brother, and minister of God, and our fellow-labourer in the gospel of Christ, to establish you, and to comfort you conecrning your faith." *

After remaining some time in Achaia, preaching the Gospel, the Apostles passed over to the adjoining city of Corinth.

* 1 Thess. ii. 18: iii. 1, 2.

CHAPTER XIII.

Paul at Corinth.

"They have mocked
At Heaven's high messenger, and he departs
From the mad circle. Athens! is it so?
* * * * * *
Thou who didst smile to find the admiring world
Crouch as a pupil to thee, wert thou blind?
Blinder than he, who, in his humble cot,
With harden'd hand, his daily labour done,
Turneth the page of Jesus and doth read?
Yet shall that poor wayfaring man lie down
With such a hope as thou couldst never teach
Thy king-like sages!"

"His letters (say they) are weighty and powerful."—2 Cor. x. 10.

"St Hierom cries him up as a great master of composition; that as oft as he heard him, he seemed to hear, not *words*, but *thunder*."—Cave, 1676.

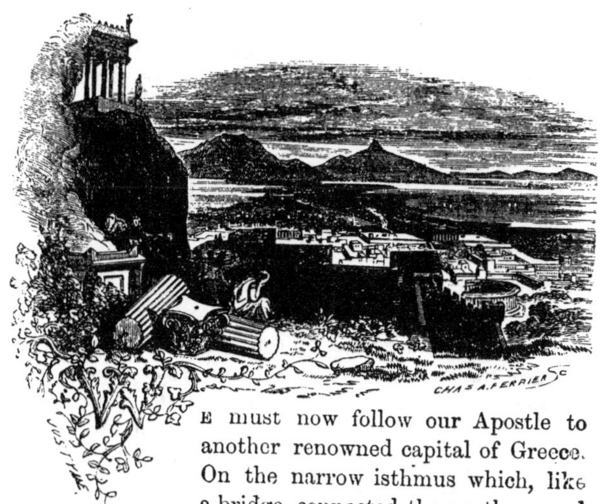

WE must now follow our Apostle to another renowned capital of Greece. On the narrow isthmus which, like a bridge, connected the northern and southern divisions of this ancient kingdom, was situated the city of Corinth, well called, by an old writer, "the city of the two seas." Again and again had Corinth been strongly fortified by high walls to resist invaders from either side. Nature, too, supplied her with noble fortifications. There is one lofty rock especially, on the south, called Acro-corinthus, with the temple of Venus on its summit, which still towers to a height of two thousand feet above the level of the sea, overlooking the city. From its ridge a magnificent view is obtained on every side. At a distance of forty-five miles the Athenian Acropolis might be distinctly seen,* and appearing in that clear atmosphere

* Conybeare and Howson.

not to be nearly so far off as it really was. There was a spacious harbour on either side of the isthmus, in which ships of commerce from every shore might be seen riding at anchor, Cenchrea in the east, and Lechæum in the west. Lechæum was nearest the city, and was very much to Corinth what the Piræus was to Athens, a range of long walls connecting them together. Corinth itself was more especially noted for its metals, dyes, and porcelain;* while the far-famed Isthmian Games attracted thousands upon thousands every year from all parts of Greece, and gave a celebrity to the spot, independent of every other claim.

The ancient city had been entirely destroyed before Paul's time. The citadel on Acro-corinthus had been burnt to ashes, and the numerous statues that studded the rock being melted on that occasion by the heat, formed in their fused state the well-known and highly-prized "Corinthian brass." The town lay thus in ruins for one hundred years; but Julius Cæsar, seeing its maritime importance, built it afresh, and peopled it with a Roman colony of freedmen, among whom doubtless were many Jews.† When Paul, therefore, now visited it, it had been restored to its former splendour; not only were its buildings gorgeous, and its wealth great, but its population was vast and varied, consisting of Jews, Greeks, and Romans.

We cannot imagine a greater contrast than existed, at the period of which we write, between the cities of Athens and Corinth. The one was the renowned centre of learning, venerable with age, art, and worldly wisdom; the other was a magnificent mercantile capital, far exceeding the former in wealth and population,

* Conybeare and Howson. † Strabo, viii. 6.

but without any pretensions to learning or philosophy. In its splendid harbours would be seen riding the ships of all nations, and particularly Roman vessels,—the town being included in the empire of the Cæsars.

We may picture the Great Apostle approaching this city after his residence at Athens. As he travels along the isthmus, he must have witnessed, in passing, the celebrated Stadium and Theatre where those famous games were celebrated, to which he has such frequent reference in the course of his writings. If his mind had not been so familiarised with the splendid sculpture of Athens, he could not fail to be struck with the long line of busts and statues erected along the road in honour of the victors in these world-renowned meetings, —the temple of Neptune, with its sacred grove, overlooking them all.* Avenues, or clumps of pine, shaded or beautified the highway,—those very trees which yielded the "corruptible" wreaths which, in an after letter to Corinth, he so touchingly contrasts with the better "crowns of glory," in the Christian race, which "never fade away."† Close to the gate was a monument to the memory of Diogenes the cynic. The traveller entered the city, and the market-place opened to his view. In the centre was a bronze Minerva, and around were temples and statues, and a fountain gushing from "the mouth of a dolphin supporting the figure of Neptune."‡ Corinth, at that time, was one of the most expensive places to reside at in the east of Europe,—so much so, that it was a common proverb, "Not every man can go to Corinth." Alas! alas! if Paul's spirit was stirred within him in Athens, because it was wholly given to idolatry, much more must

* See the picture. † 1 Cor. ix. 25. ‡ Lewin, vol. i. p. 292.

he have mourned and grieved over a city wholly given to vice in its most debasing form. If we have likened Thessalonica to our modern Liverpool, the comparison made by a writer, of Corinth to modern Paris (in its worst aspect) is perhaps an equally truthful one. It was the world's fashionable capital—full of show and glitter—but all this gilding covering corruption in its worst form.

What perhaps at first attracted the Apostle the more to it, was the number of Jews who, on account of a severe edict of Claudius Cæsar, had been recently expelled from Rome, and had there taken up their abode. The Hebrew population in Rome had for long—as, we know, is still the case there—occupied a "Jewish Quarter," where they were allowed to have their own "oratories," similar to what we found in the neighbourhood of Philippi. The cause of their present expulsion we give in the remarkable words of the historian Suetonius:—"The Jews, who were constantly exciting tumults (*Chrestus* being the mover), he banished from Rome." The word "Chrestus" is more than probably intended for *Christus*, or Christ. The Roman historian, who was not intimately acquainted with the Jewish religion, might easily fall into the mistake of speaking of a tumult occasioned *under* Christ, when it was only *about* Christ.* There were other causes, however, which operated in rousing the jealousy of the emperor. Judea itself had been in a state of revolt from the Roman power at this very time. Tacitus informs us, among other acts of violence, of a royal servant, named Stephen, being assaulted by a gang of Jewish thieves, the baggage

* Lactantius.

plundered, and the Roman soldiers killed who were appointed to guard it.* When so great an enmity existed betwen the nations, the authorities deemed it unsafe to permit so many of the Hebrew people to remain with the walls of the capital;—hence the edict for their expulsion, which had brought so many of them at present to Corinth. Among these banished Jews were two natives of Pontus, Aquila and Priscilla. As we learn afterwards that they returned to the city of the Tiber, we may gather that the latter formed their regular place of residence. They were by trade tent-makers, and probably had made money by their profession. In consequence of their expulsion, like others, they had been making their way to their native place, Pontus, in Asia, by way of the Corinthian isthmus, when all at once, for reasons we are not told, they paused at the Grecian capital, and hired a house and workshop. Perhaps the riches and extent of Corinth gave promise of a flourishing trade.

It is more than likely that it was their trade also which induced Paul to take up his abode with them, that he might the more easily obtain his own livelihood. As there were Jews from Pontus who heard Peter preach his first sermon,† it is very possible Aquila and Priscilla may have first heard of the Messiah from the lips of that apostle. Be this as it may, it does not seem that they were converted to the truth when Paul first went to reside with them; but it was while carrying on their joint labours at their tent-looms, that they were led cordially to embrace the salvation of the Gospel. It does indeed give us a beauti-

* Whitby's *Annotations*.

† Acts ii. 9.

ful specimen of Gospel humility, as well as a pattern for duty in every sphere of life, to see this great man, who had so lately been keeping company with Athenian philosophers, now plying his needle on the rough hair-cloth along with two refugee Jews; and, at the same time, during these hours of hard and laborious toil, unfolding the riches of the great salvation! If, as some suppose, Aquila and Priscilla had a workshop at Corinth, with a number of workmen employed, we may well believe that Paul would form among them his "church in the house,"—preaching, as he advised another, "in season and out of season,"—"becoming all things to all men, if by any means he might gain some." At all events, with Aquila and Priscilla he now commenced a sacred friendship, which lasted till the Apostle's death. This is not the last time we shall find their names and Christian deeds mentioned together

There was another new kind of ministerial labour St Paul undertook in the midst of his handicraft. His mind often wandered back in fond solicitude to his beloved Thessalonian converts. He is prevented seeing them or visiting them; but he resolves to *write them a Letter;* and this brings us to a most interesting period of the Apostle's history,—the composing of the first of those inspired Epistles, which have so cheered and comforted the Church in every age. "You yourself," says an able living writer, who inherits much of the great Apostle's spirit, "have never had any connexion with St Paul but by his writings, and yet you seem to know him personally. So much of life and heat palpitate in his words, that it only seems necessary to touch the hand in order to feel the pulsations of that heart which has ceased to beat for eighteen hundred years." * What a blessed consolation every Christian feels it, at a time of bereavement or sorrow, to receive a letter of sympathy and solace from a loved friend! How interesting for us to read *the first of such letters ever written!* It is from the great Apostle of the Gentiles to the Church at Thessalonica. It would do well for my young readers to take up their Bibles and peruse this Epistle for themselves. I shall merely tell you the circumstances in which it was composed:—Timothy and Silas, you will remember, had been left in Macedonia; Paul—alone in Athens—had been wearying much for their return; and his anxiety for their coming was increased, as he dreaded lest his converts in Thessalonica might be beginning to fall away, and be forgetful of their "first love." He tells us he was now among the Corinthians "in weakness, and in fear, and in much trembling." He may have felt the almost hopeless wickedness of this dissolute city, and despaired of making any progress in his great work. At last Timothy and his companion did return. The Apostle was indeed glad to see them. In addition to his other trials, he must have been suffering much from the famine at that time prevalent in Greece; and we know he refused to his dying day to receive any pecuniary assistance from the Corinthian Church, lest they might accuse him of unworthy motives. These two faithful brethren brought him relief from Macedonian Christians. We find him thus referring afterwards to his circumstances, in a letter to the Corinthians:—"And when I was present with you, and *wanted,* I was chargeable to no man: for

* A. Monod's *Discourses,* p. 31.

that which was lacking to me the brethren which came from Macedonia supplied; and in all things I have kept myself from being burdensome unto you, and so will I keep myself."* Timothy and Silas also brought the Apostle cheering tidings about the spiritual condition of those he had so recently left. Paul, with a joyful heart, employed what time could be spared from his other labours in writing "*The First Epistle to the Thessalonians.*" In it he expresses his joy and affectionate regard for them; and sends some salutary warnings, urging them still to remain faithful in the midst of all the persecutions which, for the sake of Christ, they were called to endure.

He had commenced his labours in Corinth by preaching to the Jews; but here, far more than in any other place, was their envy and hatred manifested against him, and against that holy Name he loved to proclaim. So much so, that at last, with a heavy heart, he was obliged to leave their synagogue altogether, shaking off the dust from his garment—the expressive testimony used in these times against the hardened and reprobate. "And when they opposed themselves, and blasphemed, he shook his raiment, and said unto them, Your blood be upon your own heads; I am clean: from henceforth I will go unto the Gentiles."†

He and his two friends, who had now joined him, and were strengthening his hands, set themselves to procure another place of meeting where they might address the Gentiles, and such Jews as still chose to attend their ministrations. There was a house or room, next door to the synagogue, which belonged to a proselyte called Justus. This became hereafter the

* 2 Cor. xi. 9. † Acts xviii. 6.

place of the Apostle's preaching. He seemed still to continue his residence with Aquila and Priscilla; but their house had probably no space to contain the increasing worshippers. Among those who became converts, under his instructions, were Stephanas and his family, who is called by him "the first-fruits of Achaia unto Christ." A more important and influential convert still, was Crispus, the ruler of the synagogue, whose high character and office must have added great weight and influence to his adoption of the religion of Jesus. These, and other things, caused the rage of the Corinthian Jews to increase. It bowed down Paul's spirit with grief, to see that his worst foes were those of his own brethren and household. It was at this trying time he wrote his "*Second Epistle to the Thessalonians*," in which he refers to (what he seldom cares dwelling upon) his *own* vexations and sorrows on their account, and requests an interest in the prayers of this distant church.

There was ONE, at least, who was at this moment no unconcerned witness of His servant's struggles and conflicts: God himself had seen how sorely and heavily his spirit had been weighed down. He appeared to him in the middle of the night in a vision, and spake "comforting words"—telling him not to be afraid, nor to hold his peace, for that He would uphold and strengthen him in the midst of every difficulty; and all the more so, "as He had much people in that city."*

It may be well here to peruse the Second Epistle to the Thessalonians. The messenger he had sent with the First Epistle, had just returned with the singular

* Acts xviii. 10.

tidings that the Thessalonians had taken up the strong impression that the end of the world was at hand. You will find that one of the main objects of this second letter was to correct these erroneous views which many of the converts had been entertaining about the second coming of Christ; some of whom were even giving up their daily trades, under the impression that the Lord was about to appear. The Apostle assures them how false this expectation was; for that great advent could not take place until sundry events had occurred, of which he had often before spoken.

We need only further add, with reference to the Apostle, that he seems to have continued his residence in Corinth for the space of eighteen months; during that time visiting various places in Achaia, and particularly Cenchrea, the busy seaport on the opposite shore of the isthmus. It was an important and interesting period in his history, and an important spot in the civilised world. It was either *from* Corinth, or *to* Corinth, that his choicest epistles were written. The numbers of his converts there seem to have been very considerable. He speaks, in his Epistle to the Romans, of the *churches* in Corinth; and there would appear to have been a special church in Cenchrea, for Phœbe is described as deaconess of it.*

It was near the end of this year and a-half to which we have referred, that Gallio was made governor (or proconsul) of the province, by Claudius Cæsar. He was the adopted son of Junius Gallio. Who had been in the office before him, we are not told; but whoever he was, he must have been lenient towards the Chris-

* Rom. xvi. 1.

tians, else Paul could not have continued undisturbed in his teaching and preaching for so long a period as eighteen months. I need not say that the comfort and well-being of the inhabitants of a Roman province greatly depended on their governor. The Corinthians and Achaians had obtained in Gallio one who was remarkably distinguished for his kindness, integrity, and honour. Roman writers tell us, just what we should have expected from what we know of him in sacred story, that he was a man of gentle and amiable disposition, besides being of superior abilities. Seneca, his own brother, who had the responsible office of tutor to the young Emperor Nero, speaks of him as "without a fault, whom every one loved too little, even he who loved him to the utmost. In him there was such a natural power of goodness, that there was no semblance of art or dissimulation." * The Jews, whose envy we have already found was stirred up against Paul, were anxious to test what the feelings of the new proconsul were to themselves and their religion; or knowing perhaps his easy and obliging temper, they thought they might presume upon it for the overthrow of an adversary they hated. They resolved, therefore, to accuse the Apostle at Gallio's judgment-seat. They were enabled with greater plausibility to do so, as their religion was protected to them by Roman statute, and they could charge him with doing violence to the laws of the state. "This fellow persuadeth men to worship God contrary to the law." † It was wisely ordered that so kind and benignant a ruler had been sent to Corinth. Had Gallio been stern and rigorous—had he been fired, as many others were, with hatred to the Christian cause, the Apostle

* Lewin and Barnes. † Acts xviii. 13

might have been expelled, or imprisoned, and the flourishing little church left to droop in sadness. But Gallio's verdict contributed greatly to the strengthening of the Gospel cause; for after Sosthenes (probably the successor of Crispus in the Jewish synagogue) had led the accusation, the governor, without even allowing Paul to speak a word of defence, dismisses the case. He tells the Jews that he was not sent there to act as judge in their petty quarrels, and to be the settler of religious disputes. Had it been a question affecting the peace of the province, his conduct would have been different; but he would certainly not meddle with matters of mere party violence and feeling. "And when Paul was now about to open his mouth, Gallio said unto the Jews, If it were a matter of wrong or wicked lewdness, O ye Jews, reason would that I should bear with you: but if it be a question of words and names, and of your law, look ye to it; for I will be no judge of such matters." * The Greeks were standing around the tribunal, anxiously waiting the decision; they heard it with gladness and satisfaction; they even laid hands on Sosthenes and beat him. It is evident, moreover, that Gallio's feelings were by no means of a friendly kind towards these accusing Jews; for we are told that he "took no notice of any of these things." † Paul, therefore, on account of this important decision, was allowed to remain in safety in the Isthmian city. The assurance he received in the night vision was

* Acts xviii. 14, 15.

† This seems to be the true meaning of what is rendered in our version, "And Gallio cared for none of these things." "This has been usually charged on Gallio as a matter of reproach, as if he were wholly indifferent to religion. But the charge is unjustly made."—Barnes *On Acts*; note in Olshausen, &c.

already fulfilled, that no man would be allowed to hurt him, and that he might fearlessly proclaim the cause of his Divine Master. A judgment-day only will reveal the fruit of these many months' devoted labour. We know, however, that he had in that city many souls for his hire. Wicked Corinth, with all its dreadful sins, became a striking comment on Paul's own words elsewhere, "Where sin abounded, grace did much more abound."

It may just be worthy of notice here, that Sosthenes, who appears at this trial a leader of the Jews, and the bitter opponent of St Paul, himself became a convert to the faith of Jesus. He has his name joined with that of the Great Apostle in the 1st verse of the First Epistle to the Corinthians. Nay, as Paul was himself unable to write his own letters, and always employed a scribe, it is more than likely Sosthenes penned that Christian epistle from Ephesus to his old fellow-citizens of Corinth!

At the end, however, of "a year and six months," our Apostle was desirous of paying a visit to Jerusalem, and there keeping one of the great annual feasts, most probably the Feast of Pentecost. He avails himself of the opportunity of his two friends, Aquila and Priscilla, going to Ephesus. They embark together in the same vessel, taking, doubtless, many affectionate farewells, with the solemn feeling that they might never again meet in the flesh. Their road first conducted them to the Eastern port of Cenchrea, where an occurrence took place we must not pass by without notice. It was customary for the Jews, whenever they had experienced any great mercy or deliver ance at the hand of God,* to take the "vow of the Nazarite," which you will find particularly described in the 6th Chapter of the Book of Numbers. It consisted in abstaining for thirty days from the use of wine, the hair and beard being left to grow, and at the end of this period the head was shaven. There were also several appointed sacrifices; but as they could only be offered in Jerusalem, it was customary for those who made the vow at a distance, to defer presenting them till their next visit to the Holy City. Paul, though he looked in no degree to the law of Moses for salvation, still loved to retain any Jewish custom which the higher claims of Christianity would admit of. It has been supposed, indeed, that one great object he had at present in making this vow was, to convince the Jews that he was no enemy to their law, but that he still looked with the veneration of a child of Israel to the rites of the old dispensation; and feeling at this time the great goodness of God in his merciful preservation from the hands of his accusers, he had made, thirty days before arriving at Cenchrea, the vow which I have referred to. The period of keeping it had just expired, and his head was shorn before taking ship from the port of Corinth. It may be worth while further noticing, that Eastern travellers find similar customs, regarding vows, prevalent to this day. "An usage, similar to the vow of the Nazariteship, exists in Persia now. It frequently happens, after the birth of a son, that if the parent be in distress, or the child be sick, or any other cause of grief, the mother makes a vow that no razor shall come upon the child's head

* Josephus, book i, 2, 15.

for a certain portion of time, and sometimes for his whole life, as Samuel was (1 Sam. i. 11). If the child recovers, and the cause of grief be removed, then the mother shaves his head at the end of the time prescribed—makes a small entertainment—collects money and other things from her relations and friends, which are sent as *netzers* or offerings to the mosque at Kerbelah, and are there consecrated." *

We may imagine St Paul, with his two Corinthian friends, also Silas, Timothy, and a third apostle, Titus, here named for the first time, bidding adieu to the coast of Achaia—obtaining now and then, as they sail along, a glimpse of the Athenian Acropolis and the glittering statue of Minerva. Probably, instead of continuing a direct easterly course, he would have preferred sailing northwards again, between the island of Eubœa and the mainland, and coming ashore at the base of Olympus, to have visited his beloved church at Thessalonica. He tells us, indeed, how much he wished to do so; but something in God's good providence "hindered him" for the present, and many years were to elapse till they were to meet again face to face. Soon the voyagers are threading their way among the islands of the Archipelago,—the lovely "isles of Greece,"—and reach in safety the city of Ephesus, the great capital of Asia, as Corinth was of Achaia. Here the Apostle paused only for a day or two at this time; the ship in which they were sailing being destined for the coast of Syria. He had an opportunity, however, to hold a discussion with the Jews of Ephesus, in their synagogue, on Sabbath. It

* Morier's *Second Journey*, quoted by Horne in his *Introduction*, vol. ii. p. 329

was more encouraging than any recent meetings with his brethren; they even urged him to prolong his stay, which, however, he declined, as either the vessel which had brought him thither or another was about to sail, and he had a divine call to attend the approaching festival at Jerusalem—"I must by all means keep this feast;"* but he gave the promise of a speedy return, if God's will so ordered it. Again embarking, and leaving Aquila and Priscilla at Ephesus, we may follow him and his three companions in thought past the Island of Rhodes and Cyprus, till they land at the military port of Cesarea, with which we are already familiar.

The sacred oracles are silent about Paul's visit at this time to Jerusalem. It has been supposed his purpose of being present at the feast was by delay frustrated, as he merely speaks of "saluting the church," and then departing. He would doubtless repair to the temple, offering there the accustomed sacrifices in fulfilment of his vow, and anew tell with a joyous heart to his fellow-Christians and brethren all that the Lord had done in distant heathen lands. He bends his steps once more (probably along the coast road) to the Syrian Antioch, to which town the present was in all probability his last and closing visit. You, doubtless, have not forgotten that this was the church which first sent him out on his missionary work. He must have had towards it the feeling of a child to a parent. He had gone forth from them but a few years before, "bearing precious seed," and he had now come again "with rejoicing," bringing the tidings of sheaves with him, reaped in the great mission Harvest.

* Acts xviii. 21.

Is he here now to rest? is the "good soldier" to repose on the laurels he has won, and, ungirding his missionary armour, to spend the remainder of his days in inglorious ease on the banks of the Orontes? Having done so much himself, may he not now leave the work to others? He has borne "the burden and heat of the day,"—who could wonder if he wished to spend the evening of his life in quiet and peace, and send out younger and hardier warriors to fight the battles of the faith? This great standard-bearer in "the glorious company of apostles" had no such thought; he only comes to Antioch to gird on his armour for fresh conquests. "Not as though I had already attained," was the motto of his public as well as his private life. He prepares to set out from this city on his *Third Missionary Journey.**

He begins his new pilgrimage by fulfilling the promise we have just found him making to the church at Ephesus, going direct thither across the interior of Asia Minor. With the exception of Titus, we cannot exactly say who were his travelling companions. Silas he seems to have left behind him at Jerusalem; perhaps Erastus, Gaius, and Aristarchus, accompanied him.† We have every reason to believe Timothy still continued at his side. Travelling through Cilicia, the Great Apostle might possibly once more visit his native Tarsus, and have the fond memories of his boyhood again revived. Similar, too, must have been the feelings of Timothy as he passed with his "father in the faith" through the place of *his* birth and childhood. Paul must have, on this journey, also "saluted" his Galatian churches. You cannot have forgotten the kind-

* See now the *vermilion* line on the map.

† Acts xix. 29.

ness he received, on his first visit, from this singular people. I fear, however, by this time, judging from what he says afterwards in his "letter" to them, that they had been corrupted from the purity of the Gospel, and that "strifes, seditions, heresies," had taken the place of unity and brotherly love. One of the objects the Apostle had in this new missionary tour, was to gather collections in behalf of the poor saints and brethren in Judea, and his old friends in Galatia were not behind in their liberality. After visiting the churches in Phrygia, and getting from them similar contributions, he and his companions probably pursued the great highway in the direction of Colosse. Though we have no means of determining the precise route they adopted, we have little doubt that they travelled now the region he was "forbidden of the Holy Ghost" to visit before, and that he passed through some of those seven cities which were afterwards made famous as the sites of the seven churches mentioned in Revelation. We shall not, however, pause to describe their journey, but at once take our readers to the town of Ephesus; or rather we shall leave for a little the newly-arrived missionaries there, until we speak of a new character who presents himself to our notice in connexion with the same place.

CHAPTER XIV.

Paul at Ephesus.

"In the proud land of palaces wert thou
   Alone and matchless, as thine own fair queen
Shines 'midst the gems of night's star-crowned brow,
   Veiling their dim rays with superior sheen.
Thy countless columns gleam'd in rich array—
   The gifts of monarchs, and the work of men—
Whose nobler names, when regal thrones decay,
   Shall boast the meed of Fame's recording pen."

"Great is Diana of the Ephesians!"—Acts xix. 28.

ONE day, while the Jews of Ephesus were assembled in their synagogue, a stranger rose up to address them. They were at once struck with his fervour, learning, and eloquence. He was deeply read in their Old Testament Scriptures, and ably argued from them. Who can this be? It is a name that occurs now for the first time in our narrative.

Apollos was a native of Egypt. He had recently come to Ephesus, and, along with twelve others, was "a disciple of John the Baptist." "He knew only of the baptism of John,"—that is to say, all the knowledge he had of the true Messiah was derived from the preaching of the Baptist on the banks of the Jordan. He and his associates were ignorant of the fact, that Jesus Christ had really come into the world—had died, and risen again. Their minds, however, were in a state of "preparation;" they knew that "the kingdom of heaven was at hand," and now they were ready to receive, from the lips of the Great Apostle, the joyful intelligence that the Messiah *had* indeed suffered, and had "entered into His glory." *

Apollos, born and educated at Alexandria, had his mind stored with the learning of its celebrated university. To this he added a powerful eloquence. "He was mighty in the Scriptures;" he had studied and pondered with great care the Old Testament prophecies relating to the Messiah, and, being convinced himself, he zealously tried to convince others that the Saviour must soon come. With holy ardour, he seems to have travelled about from place to place, and, in the spirit of Elias, preached "the baptism of repentance,"—calling on all to forsake their sins, and to prepare their minds for the coming of the Lord.

Already in the Ephesian synagogue an interest had been excited about the Lord Jesus Christ. Paul had very lately been addressing his Jewish brethren there. Aquila and Priscilla had done so since his departure, doubtless instructing their fellow-countrymen in those great truths which they themselves had heard often and again from the lips of the Great Apostle of Tarsus, as he sat with them on the same floor at their tent-making. Upon the day to which I have referred, after listening to the eloquence and earnestness of this Alexandrian Jew, Aquila and Priscilla, at the end of the service, made themselves known to him. They invited him to their house, where they "taught him the way of the Lord more perfectly," showing him that "the

* See Olshausen *On Acts, in loc.*

mystery of godliness" had already been revealed—that God had been "manifest in the flesh."

The disciple of John, now a devoted servant of John's Great Master, went forth to proclaim in Achaia "the unsearchable riches" of a dying, and now ever-living Saviour. Receiving "letters of commendation" from the Christians at Ephesus, he took ship and sailed direct to Corinth; there, with his wonted eloquence, he argued with those Jews who had rejected Paul, showing that Jesus was indeed the Christ. They were totally unable to resist the force of his appeals. Paul himself alludes to this in one of his letters to them—"I have planted; Apollos watered."* His coming to Corinth produced one unfortunate result, which he, doubtless, greatly regretted. The Christians there, forgetful that both he and Paul were only lowly instruments in God's hand, separated themselves into two parties,—thereby causing those earnest and devoted brethren in a common Lord, to appear as if they were rivals, and opposed to one another. Some were "of Paul," and others "of Apollos." Our Apostle was also greatly grieved at this spirit. In words of holy rebuke, he writes to them, "Who, then, is Paul, and who is Apollos, but ministers by whom ye believed?" "Is Christ divided? was Paul crucified for you? or were ye baptized in the name of Paul?" †

We shall leave Apollos in his devoted work at Corinth, and once more return to Ephesus. Its importance in the life of Paul, and in the early Christian Church, entitles it to special notice. If you look at the picture we have given of it, it may help to give an idea of the city as it was when he now entered its

* 1 Cor. iii. 6. † 1 Cor. iii. 5; i. 13.

gates, and was about to gather in some more "first-fruits" of the great Gospel harvest. The city itself was at this time the largest and most renowned in Asia Minor. It was built near where the rivers Hermus and Mæander empty their waters into the Ægean Sea; and, from its situation, became the residence of many classes from all parts of the East. It was called by Pliny one of the "Eyes of Asia," Smyrna being the other. A Roman proconsul governed it in great splendour. He was clothed in purple, attended by twelve lictors with their fasces; and, like our judges in England and Scotland, made his circuit once a year to all the smaller towns in Asia, and held a court of justice.* The original city was built on the side of the hill Coressus, the base of which is nearest you to the left of the picture, sloping gradually into the plain. Mount Pactyas (from which the view is supposed to be taken) bounded it on the east, Mount Gallesius on the north, with a lake at its base; while the waters of the ocean were on the west (represented in the distance of the picture). All these hills were precipitous, enclosing, like so many ramparts, the plain on which Ephesus stood, except at the north-east, where the river Cayster, which you will observe on the right, wound its way through the plain to the sea. The prominent hill rising in front of Mount Coressus, is Mount Prion, famous for its quarries. In the valley between these two hills, may still be traced the remains of one of the celebrated "gymnasia." Mount Prion itself is overrun at this day with tangled thickets, but we may imagine what it must have been in the days of Paul, when covered with mason-work from its own

* Lewin.

quarries. Looking down from its summit, what is now a swamp, was then a spacious harbour, or inland basin, called Panormus, or "All-haven," where the ships of the European seas rode at anchor. It was at this harbour that Aquila, Priscilla, and Paul must have landed. From the same height might be seen the Stadium, or place where those engaged in the games contended, with its tiers of stone seats cut out of the natural rock (see the nearest part of the picture on the left). Also, midway between the Stadium and Mount Prion, the enormous Theatre, of which we shall by and by speak, where the Ephesian mob were addressed by the town-clerk.*

But the crowning glory of Ephesus was its wonderful temple to the goddess Diana, which I shall leave my young readers to find out for themselves. This was considered one of the wonders of the Old World; and well it might be called so. It was said that the sun, in all his course through the heavens, looked down on nothing so glorious.† It was composed of all that was magnificent in Asiatic art. The states round about had shared the cost of its erection. It was built of marble, found in the quarries of Mount Prion, and was said to be so pure and bright as to dazzle the eyes of mariners at a distance.

The story is worth giving as to how these marble quarries were discovered. A shepherd, named Pixodorus, was feeding his flock on the hill; two of his

* Chandler mentions, that among the pile of ruins which the Theatre has now become, he discovered an arch, next to the Stadium, on which was an inscription inviting the reader, if he did not join in the sports and festive scenes, at all events to be pleased with the architect's device. What a lesson would be read to him if he gazed on the triumph of his genius now!

† Chandler, p. 139.

rams began to fight with one another; the one of these, in making a rush at his enemy, missed his mark and struck his horn through the turf, goring some white substance with it. The shepherd dug up a specimen of the rock, and ran into the city with his prize. It was just what the Ephesians were in search of—marble for the building of their temple! The lucky shepherd was amply rewarded, and even got divine honours paid him at his death.*

The temple stood at the eastern end of the noble harbour of which we have just spoken. You may imagine what a pile it was when you hear that it was 220 years in building, 425 feet in length, by 220 in breadth. The shrine of the goddess was surrounded by a colonnade open to the sky, of 127 columns of Parian marble, each weighing 150 tons, 60 feet high, and each the gift of a king. It was decorated and beautified inside with cedar, cypress, gold, jewels, and precious stones; the roof was supported with columns of green jasper. Eight of these still remain entire in the great mosque of St. Sophia, in Constantinople, to which they were removed, along with other remains of its glory, in the reign of Justinian. Art must have attained great perfection in Ephesus. Apelles and Parrhasius, the two greatest painters that ever lived, were natives of the city. One picture of Apelles, which represented Alexander the Great grasping a thunderbolt, was hung in the temple of Diana, purchased at a cost of twenty talents of gold,—a sum which Chandler estimates at £38,750.† The magnificent altar was from the chisel of Praxiteles; the staircase was made of a single vine from the island of Cyprus;

* See Chandler, p. 126.

† See Mr. Lewin, p. 358.

the noblest pictures were hung on the walls; and, among many other statues, one of pure gold was erected to Antemidorus.* Besides these, much of the wealth of Asia was deposited for safety within this sacred shrine.

You may easily suppose how imposing the temple must have appeared, approaching from the sea—looking down on the ships which crowded the wharves of Panormus, and how justly proud every Ephesian must have been of this world-renowned edifice! It stood untouched for many ages. At last, like many other splendid relics of antiquity, it fell into the hands of the invading Goths, in A. D. 260, and was pillaged by them. Modern travellers have visited its remains, and, by means of torches, have threaded their way under the dark vaulted chambers on which it was built. Bats of large size struck against them, roused from the darkness and desolation which reigns within.† All combine in the testimony, that Ephesus is at this day a total wreck. "Its streets," says Dr Chandler, whose visit was in 1764, "are obscured and overgrown. A herd of goats was driven to it for shelter from the sun at noon, and a noisy flight of crows, from the quarries, seemed to insult its silence. We heard the partridge call in the area of the Theatre and the Stadium." "Nothing is seen, in its dripping marble quarries, but the marks of the tools of former days."‡ Alas for Ephesus! it did not listen to the warning voice—"Re-

* This full description of Ephesus is given by the historians Strabo and Pliny. See also Pocoke's *Travels*, Anacharsis' *Travels*, and the interesting narrative of Dr Chandler, who was sent out by the Dilettanti Society for the express purpose of exploring the remains of antiquity in Asia Minor, pp. 109–137.

† Ibid.

‡ Howson.

member, therefore, from whence thou art fallen, and repent, and do the first works; or else I will come into thee quickly and remove thy candlestick out of his place, except thou repent." That light, which burned for a while so brightly, is now quenched in total darkness—a "chaos of noble ruins!" "Even the sea has retired from the scene of desolation, and a pestilential morass, covered with mud and rushes, has succeeded to the waters which brought up the ships laden with merchandise from every country." *

On arriving, eighteen hundred years ago, at this city, the Apostle met those twelve disciples of John we have already alluded to. Not only were they, as I have told you, altogether ignorant of Christ; they were also ignorant of the Holy Spirit, the third person in the blessed Trinity, and of His outpouring on the day of Pentecost. "Have ye received," he asked them, "the Holy Ghost since ye believed?" They answered, "We have not so much as heard whether there be any Holy Ghost." † Paul expounded to them the glorious "truth as it is in Jesus." They received his testimony; were baptized; and by the laying-on of his hands, they prophesied and spake with various tongues. The Apostle, we have every reason to think, took up his abode again with Aquila and Priscilla. With them, too, he probably resumed his work at the tents; at all events, we know, from one of his own letters, ‡ that, during the three years he lived at Ephesus, he earned his bread by the "labour of his own hands." And he could at an after period extend these hands, rough with daily labour, before the elders

* Arundell's *Visit to the Seven Churches*.

† Acts xix. 2.

‡ 1 Cor. vi. 11, 12.

of Ephesus, and make the appeal, "Ye yourselves know that these have ministered to my necessities." * "For three months" he continued to speak boldly in their synagogue, till at last the old Jewish enmity manifested itself. His brethren falsely accused and derided him in the presence of the people. This led him openly to leave their synagogue; and for two years he preached in a separate place of meeting, in the "school" (or lecture-room) "of Tyrannus,"—probably a teacher or doctor, who had been by his means converted to Christianity. We have no certain information as to Paul's success during this long period of residence; but in the same address to the elders of Ephesus at Miletus, we see the more than tender affection borne for those he was now teaching, and among whom he had gone about from house to house, instructing and warning them "night and day with tears." We know that, before he left, a large and flourishing church was formed at Ephesus, not only in the city, but numbering many converts throughout the province. "The Word of God mightily grew and prevailed." † As was to be expected, however, he encountered still the envy of the Jews. This seems to have been great, if we may judge from the manner he refers to "the many tears and temptations which befell him by the lying in wait of the Jews." His preservation was itself a miracle. It was only the good and gracious hand of his God which could have protected him. His own short history of himself and his perils at this time, when he writes from Ephesus to the Corinthians, is this—"I die daily." ‡ Death every day seemed to stare him in the face.

* Acts xx. 34 † Acts xix. 20. ‡ 1 Cor. xv. 31.

There is a striking occurrence at this time mentioned in the Acts of the Apostles, which we cannot pass over in silence. I have already told you that the patron goddess of the city of Ephesus was Diana.* Her image was supposed to have fallen from the sky. An unshapely block it was; not like the beautiful forms we have been accustomed to think of among the statues of Athens, but a figure more like what is seen at this day in the pagodas of India.† To prevent its tottering, a bar of metal—some say of gold, others of iron—was placed under each hand. A veil, hanging from the roof of the temple, concealed it, unless on the great occasion of the festival, when it was exposed to public view. "Mutianus, a noble Roman, affirmed that the figure was made of vine, and had many holes, filled with nard, to nourish and moisten it, and to preserve the cement."‡ This hideous goddess was, however, gorgeously apparelled. She had a crown on her head, and a girdle round her waist; on the crown, girdle, and feet, there were engraven sundry curious letters, on which the Ephesians looked with superstitious awe. Copied and written out on rolls of parchment, these "letters" used to be carried about on the persons of many of the people, who foolishly considered that they would prove a sort of *charm*, protecting them from all kinds of evil. Many large books or scrolls were to be had, describing these same "Ephesian Letters," pretending to explain their secrets, and, as such, sold for

* It was a matter of policy often to keep up in the minds of the people the idea of such protectors over their city. The Trojans imagined their city's safety depended on the Palladium, an image of Pallas-Minerva, also believed to have fallen from heaven. The same with the Ancilia, or Sacred Shields; Ceres, in Sicily, &c.—See Barnes, *in loc.*

† See picture, Chap. xv.

‡ Chandler, p. 134.

enormous prices. There is a story told of an Ephesian and Milesian wrestling with one another at the Olympic games. The Ephesian got the better of his opponent, but the cause was soon discovered, the former having some of these magic letters bound round his heel! As soon as the other found out the reason, he insisted on their removal, and he was said to be instantly victorious! So says a grave old writer.* Indeed, there was no city in all the East where sorcery and magic were practised to such an extent as at Ephesus; and those, too, who believed in these, were not among the lowest of the people, but men and women of birth and reputation. God seems to have given his apostolic servant at this time a special power to work miracles, and that in the way best calculated to confound the arts of the sorcerers. For multitudes, we are told, brought "handkerchiefs and aprons" with which to touch the Apostle's person, and then they applied these to the bodies of their sick or diseased friends, and they were immediately healed.

Paul, like Aaron and Moses of old before the magicians of Egypt, met the magicians and sorcerers of Ephesus face to face. Among them were some Jewish *exorcists*, or pretended sorcerers, who professed to have the power of casting out devils by the use of certain words or incantations, many of which were believed to have been composed and used by King Solomon. Josephus, the historian, seems himself to have been carried away with these delusions. He gives a curious account of one Eleazar, a Jew, in the presence of the Emperor Vespasian and the officers of his army, curing a demoniac by holding a ring under his nose, in which

* Eustathius.

was placed a small portion of a plant prescribed by Solomon. At the smell of the plant, he solemnly tells us the demon took to flight, and overturned a full cup of water as he left the room where the feat was performed! * These Ephesian exorcists, when they saw that Paul, by the name of "*Jesus*," performed many miracles, impiously tried, by the use of the same holy name, to perform arts and wonders themselves. There were seven sons of a Jew named Sceva particularly mentioned, who attempted, by pronouncing the name of the Lord Jesus, to expel some demons from one who was possessed, saying, "We adjure you by Jesus, whom Paul preacheth." † The evil spirit in a loud voice rebuked their presumption. "Jesus I know, and Paul I know; but who are ye?" The man, goaded on to frenzy by the power of the demon within him, sprang upon the profane sorcerers, and made them in terror fly out of the house, "naked and wounded." Soon the tidings of what had taken place spread through the city; the dark heathen art fell immediately into discredit. Many of the sorcerers and magicians, trembling and astonished, came to the Apostle, mourning over their delusions. They sought repentance, and began to honour the name they and their fellows had so daringly blasphemed.

Their conduct is worthy of all mention and praise; not only did they give up and abandon their magical arts, but fearful lest they might be tempted at some future time to return to them, they resolved to put out of their reach anything likely to become a temptation, or to remind them of their former method of obtaining unlawful gain. What did they do? They brought

* Jos. Ant. viii. 2, quoted by Lewin.

† Acts xix. 13.

together all their magical books and burnt them! We know how valuable and expensive such written scrolls were in those days; perhaps in destroying them many parted with the most costly and valuable part of their property. Indeed, the estimated value was about £1800 or £2000 of our money—some even say £7000! But they had learned "to count all things, but loss for the excellency of the knowledge of Christ Jesus;" and now they showed how willing they were to "suffer the *loss* of all things, that they might win Him." Never would these strange "burnings" be forgotten in Ephesus. The Word of God quickly spread. The name of Jesus was magnified. Paul thus "out of weakness was made strong, waxed valiant in fight," and not only "turned to flight," but by God's grace turned to repentance and faith, and true conversion, "the army of the aliens."

CHAPTER XV.

The Tumult.

"Oft with the Spirit's force
His arm hath quell'd the foe,
And laid resistless in his course
The alien armies low.

Bent on such glorious toils,
The world to him was loss;
Yet all his trophies—all his spoils,
He hung upon the Cross."

"Behold us at Ephesus in the year 65! . . . Twenty years later, and an event, both insignificant and mighty, takes place in this city. A Christian Church has been born, separated from the bosom of Paganism like an isle in the midst of the sea."—MONOD.

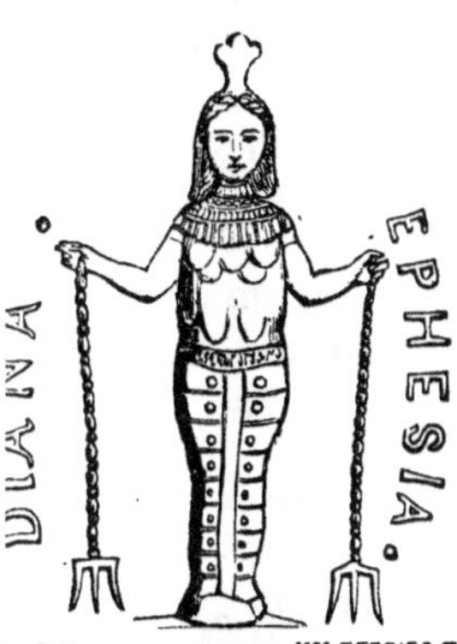

ALTHOUGH Luke makes no mention in the Acts of the Apostles, we gather, from a few expressions in the course of the Epistles, that Paul, some time during his residence at Ephesus, paid a visit to the city of Corinth. "Of all the churches which he planted," it has been well said, "in none was there so much evil mixed up with so much good; and the training of so wayward a child, required the utmost care of the watchful parent."*

Apollos had now come back from that Greek city, and doubtless would have much to tell the Apostle about the state of his converts there—much that would cause him joy; but, we fear, more that made him sad and sorrowful. Corinth, we have found, was a very wicked place; and even after many of its heathen citizens had been baptized into the Christian name, they continued to live in the indulgence of their

* Lewin, p. 378.

former awful sins. Paul, deeply grieved at the stain their conduct affixed on the character of the religion they professed, himself sailed across from Ephesus to make personal inquiries on the matter. Alas! he found the report of Apollos too true! It was even worse than he expected. It would not appear that he tarried long among them on this occasion—perhaps not more than a few days or weeks. He had hoped, doubtless, by this visit, to check the growth of these crimes for the future. Not long after his return to Ephesus, however, he learnt that the offenders were increasing in their daring guilt. He resolved to adopt harsher measures, and wrote a severe letter of rebuke, which is now lost.

Nor was it one description of sin alone of which the Corinthians were guilty. Some members of a Corinthian family—"the house of Chloe"—had at this time come to reside at Ephesus. They informed the Apostle that a sad party-spirit was continuing among his converts in the capital of Achaia. Some Jewish Christians from Palestine, who bitterly disliked Paul, had been successful in stirring up the church there against him. They induced some to look up to Peter (Cephas) as their head; others, to St James; others, who boasted of their learning and wisdom, to Apollos. "It hath been declared unto me of you, my brethren," he writes, "by them which are of the house of Chloe, that there are contentions among you. Now this I say, that every one of you saith, I am of Paul, and I of Apollos, and I of Cephas, and I of Christ."* Add to this, instead of settling their disputes and differences, as they ought to have done, with one an-

* 1 Cor. i. 11, 12.

other, they had been going to the courts of law, and that, too, publicly before the heathen citizens of Corinth. Even in their own meetings for religious worship, there had been much vanity and show; they seemed to be loving and courting the praise of man more than the praise of God. The very hour of communion was profaned with their sins. In that age, it would seem that the celebration of the Lord's Supper generally took place after the *agape*, or concluding meal of the day. The Corinthians had impiously got into the habit of partaking of it just as a common feast,—the rich bringing their dainties, and the poor often not having enough to eat.

In the mean time, Paul selected Timothy and Erastus to go to Corinth, and wait there his own arrival,—endeavouring, in the interval, to bring the church to a sense of its many sins, and to heal its party-divisions. Timothy you already well know. Erastus seems to have been a citizen of Corinth, converted to the faith of Jesus, and one of some standing there. We find him, the following year, chamberlain of the city. Though it was a circuitous way of reaching Corinth, Paul asked these two faithful men to visit, in going thither, the churches of Macedonia—to acquaint them of his own intended coming, and to request them to be ready with their money-collection for the poor Christians in Judea. Other messengers from Corinth—Stephanas, Fortunatus, and Achaicus—had by this time arrived, bearing a reply to the Apostle's letter, and also bringing from their church a number of questions on difficult points of conduct, duty, and doctrine, upon which they wished his judgment. Paul set himself immediately to answer these. His answer consists of what is known to us by the name of "*The First Epistle to the Corinthians.*" It was written, probably, some time or other in March, or April, and during the third year of his residence at Ephesus. This letter is full of sharp rebukes for the many and grievous sins which disgraced that much-loved church. It does not seem to bear his wonted tender affection for them, but threatens them with "the rod" if they still continue in their guilt. He afterwards, however, lets us into the true state of his feelings while writing it,—"Out of much affliction and anguish of heart I wrote unto you with many tears."* It contains much important and precious truth. Its beautiful 15th chapter especially, has afforded joy and consolation to millions—opening up to them hopes which are "full of immortality." We gather, from the close of the letter, that the Apostle was planning the journey to which we have referred, through the churches of Macedonia to Corinth, and from thence he purposed to go to Jerusalem; indeed, he even looked farther before him, intending to proceed, were it his Lord's will, to visit the world's distant capital itself—imperial Rome.

Meanwhile he sent Titus, and probably Trophimus, with the answer to the Corinthian letter, requesting the former to use all his influence in putting matters to rights in that erring church. Titus was himself a native of Corinth. He seemed to have shrunk from this difficult mission, knowing too well the sad repute of the city; but Paul encouraged him to go, and he seems to have had no cause to regret having obeyed; for we thus find the Great Apostle, in an after Corinthian epistle, referring to the way they had received

* 2 Cor. ii. 14

Titus:—"Therefore we were comforted in your comfort: yea, and exceedingly the more joyed we for the joy of Titus, because his spirit was refreshed by you all. For if I have boasted any thing to him of you, I am not ashamed; but as we spake all things to you in truth, even so our boasting, which I made before Titus, is found a truth. And his inward affection is more abundant toward you, whilst he remembereth the obedience of you all, how with fear and trembling ye received him. I rejoice therefore that I have confidence in you in all things."*

Meanwhile the Apostle himself lingered a little while behind at Ephesus, hopeful that Timothy and Titus, meeting together at Corinth, and using their joint exertions, would prepare the minds of the professing converts there for his coming to them "in peace." Aquila and Priscilla, Apollos, Gaius, and Aristarchus, remained with him at Ephesus, and perhaps also Luke. The latter we have for some time lost sight of. It has been thought that he had been busy meanwhile in writing his Gospel, which he soon after published in Macedonia.†

It was at this period that a new event took place in the city of Ephesus, which at the moment threatened to bring the Apostle into great danger, but which, in the end, turned out "rather for the furtherance of the Gospel." A large and lucrative trade seems to have been carried on there in the manufacture of copies or models of the shrine of the goddess Diana. At one season of the year, in particular,—the month of May,—multitudes from all parts of Asia, and even of Europe, crowded to the great annual festival in honour of the

* 2 Cor. vii. 13-16.

† Lewin.

deity. If you look at Paul's first letter to the Corinthians, of which I have just been speaking, you will find one reason he gives for not leaving Ephesus at present was, "that a great door and effectual was opened unto him, and there were many enemies." * Might he not—or rather, *does* he not—in this, allude to the glorious opportunity afforded him of preaching the Gospel when "all the world" were collected together at these memorable games?—just as the honoured Whitfield more than once erected his tent on the race-course, to proclaim in the ears of those who were "minding earthly things," the better and more enduring substance. A whole month, called "*Artemisius*," or the "month of Diana," was allotted every year to this great festival-gathering. What a concourse it must have been! You can look at the picture of the city, and imagine the hundreds of vessels crowding the harbour—gaily-painted boats flitting up and down the basin of Panormus—crowds of pilgrims looking from the heights of Mount Prion—pleasure-hunters in all directions—the Theatre, with its shows—the Hippodrome, with its horse-racing—the wrestling and beast-fighting in the huge Stadium to the left—individuals dressed up in fancy costume—mock gods and mock goddesses—Jupiters, with their glittering crowns, bolts of war, and white sandals—Apollo, with his wreath of laurel and white robes—and Mercury, with dress appropriate to the swift-footed messenger of the deities of Olympus.† To complete the picture, you may imagine thousands of eyes, old and young, entranced with wonder as they gazed on the Ionic columns of the

* 1 Cor. xvi. 9.
† Domninus. See the quotation in full by Mr Lewin, vol. i. p. 441.

great temple, or as they followed thither the bleating sacrifices, crowned with garlands. Goats'-hair tents, too, would be dotted over the plain outside the city walls for the accommodation of the vast number of strangers. Who can tell but some of these may have been the handiwork of the Great Apostle, who was still night and day "labouring that he might be chargeable to no man"?

You can imagine, too, how the shops and bazaars would be filled with everything attractive for the visitors. Parents, who had left their children behind, were in the habit of buying for them little memorials of their visit. Among these *souvenirs* there was one that commanded a more especial sale—few pilgrims returned home without carrying along with them one of the copies or models of the famous shrine. They were made either of gold, silver, or wood, as the purchaser could afford, and were called *Aphidrumata.** There was one maker of these who had many workmen under him—his name was Demetrius. He was beginning to find that the influence and preaching of Paul in town and round about was seriously interfering with the sale of his images. The Apostle had been pointing the people, not to Diana, but to Jesus Christ as their only Saviour; doubtless telling them, as he had done the Athenians, that "the Godhead was not like to wood or stone, or brass, graven with man's device," and that there was but "one name given under heaven among men by which sinners could be saved." Demetrius resolved to do what he could to crush those who were so ruining his trade. The month of May had by this time returned. The Ionians were already crowding again with their

* Dionysius ii. 22.

wives and children to the city to take part in the games and other festivities of the season. Demetrius called his own and other workmen together, and addressed them on the subject. It was an easy matter to get the crowd increased in such a place as Ephesus. He began by telling of the serious loss incurred in their lawful trade; pointing, as we may suppose him, with his finger, to the vast temple in their view, he sought to rouse their vengeance against Paul, whom he represented as "causing the great goddess Diana to be despised, and her magnificence destroyed." The speech had the desired effect; they were filled with wrath, and one long and loud shout arose, "Great is Diana of the Ephesians!" * The whole city was filled with confusion; the crowd was still increasing, and with one accord they cry out, "To the Theatre! to the Theatre!" dragging along with them Paul's two companions, Gaius and Aristarchus. The theatre was the place where great assemblages on political matters generally convened. It was surrounded with stone-seats, rising one above the other all around. You may imagine the rush which now took place to it, each anxious to get the seat most advantageous for hearing. But where was Paul all this time? When he heard of the commotion, how his Master's name was assailed, and the truth he himself proclaimed, we need not say he would be the first in desiring to answer publicly the charges brought against him. How joyfully would he have availed himself of the opportunity of preaching the glorious Gospel before that vast concourse! But his wiser Christian converts, and the "chief of Asia" (or the Asiarchs, men of high rank and

* Acts xix. 27, 28.

standing in the kingdom),* prevented him exposing himself to certain danger and death. The mob had rushed to the house of Aquila, expecting to find him there, but they had secured his escape. It is to be feared his faithful friends Aquila and Priscilla must have been rudely handled on this occasion. Paul tells us that they had "for his life laid down their own necks."† He talked afterwards of having "fought with wild beasts at Ephesus." If he had gone now to the Theatre, he would have been obliged to encounter wild beasts in a human form; his kind friends, however, knowing better than he did the fury of an Ephesian mob, would not allow him to hazard himself. It has been supposed, indeed, if he had ventured to the Theatre, the base passions of some of the crowd, and the love of cruel sport among others, would have urged that the Apostle be given up to one of those terrible conflicts with wild animals, with which many of the early martyrs were so sadly familiar. Often, we know, were the Christians in an after age accustomed to hear the shout of the enraged populace, "Ad bestias! ad leonem!" May it not be to this Paul refers in the verse I have just quoted: "After the manner of men," or rather, "according to the intention of men,"—the intention of this Ephesus mob,—"I have fought with wild beasts"—I had all the fearful prospect of such a death! Fortunately for the Apostle, the "Asiarchs" interfered for his safety. With them rested the power of entertaining the people with such savage sport. Old Polycarp was brought into the Theatre at

* "The Asiarchs had the oversight of the sacred places of the city, and were required to manage the sacred games at their own expense."—Olshausen, *in loc.*

† Rom. xvi. 4.

Smyrna to be torn thus by lions; but the *Asiarch*, or governor there (Philip), would not consent to let the animals loose on the aged man.* Be this as it may, however, we may well imagine Paul's agony of mind when he heard the distant tumult, and thought of his two devoted friends, Gaius and Aristarchus, about perhaps to be cruelly martyred, while *he* had escaped. Indeed, we know, for many weeks he did not recover the effects of this agitation. For him, however, to have ventured, would only have added fuel to the fire, and been certain destruction to all. When the people were assembled in their seats, the Jews, who wished to show that they hated Paul as much as the heathen, put forward one of their own number, Alexander the coppersmith, a man of fluent speech, and bearing a stern hatred to the Apostle. Whenever the mob saw he was a Jew, his voice was drowned with their clamour. They would not hear him speak, and for two hours the air was rent with the cry, "*Great is Diana of the Ephesians!*" When they could cry no longer, and their spirits and voice began to flag, the town-clerk, or "recorder," next presented himself in the midst of the excited assembly. He was an individual of great official influence, and had the charge of the vast sums of money and other treasures which were kept in the temple. In his speech, he shows great prudence and tact in dealing with those he addressed. He began by telling them of the greatness and glory of their temple and goddess; that its fame filled the world, and that one or two poor Jewish strangers would never for a moment be able to inflict upon it any injury; moreover, that Paul had not, as was alleged, sought in any way

* See Fleetwood's *Lives of the Apostles*.

to profane the shrine, or blaspheme the patron deity. He closes his address by reminding them of the danger of such tumultuary meetings as the present. His powerful words had the desired effect. The voices of the dense crowd were stilled. The Theatre gradually emptied, and they dispersed to their several homes.

We have no further notice after this of Paul's doings at Ephesus. It continued for long an important city in infant Christendom. The Apostle John is believed here to have closed his mission of love in peace, and his dust was said to repose, along with that of Timothy,* among the thickets and ruins of Mount Prion. To this day, a little mound nearly opposite Mount Prion has a small village on its crest, bearing the name of *Aiasaluk*, a corruption of *Agios Theologos* (the Holy Divine).† In Ephesus, probably, he wrote his Gospel and Epistles. Here it was, looking down on the noblest temple ever made with human hands, that he "remembered the words of the Lord Jesus, how he said," "God is a Spirit: and they that worship him must worship him in spirit and in truth." Tradition adds, that Mary the mother of Jesus closed her honoured life in the same city, the disciple of love being faithful to the last in the sacred trust committed to him by his Lord on the cross:—"Son, behold thy mother; and from that hour, that disciple took her unto his own home."

* "The body of Timothy was afterwards translated to Constantinople by the founder of that city, or his son Constantius, and placed with St Luke and St Andrew in the Church of the Apostles."—So says Chandler, p. 126.

† Stanley's *Sermons on the Apostolic Age.*

CHAPTER XVI.

The Faithful Pastor.

"I'm not ashamed to own my Lord,
Or to defend His cause,
Maintain the glory of His cross,
And honour all His laws."

"'*Benjamin shall raven as a wolf. In the morning he shall devour the prey, and at night he shall divide the spoil.*' This prophetical character, Tertullian, and others after him, will have to be accomplished in our apostle. As a ravening wolf *in the morning devouring the prey*—that is, as a persecutor of the churches—in the first part of his life destroying the flock of God. *In the evening dividing the spoil*—that is, in his declining and reduced age, as doctor of the nations, feeding and distributing to Christ's sheep."—*Life of St Paul*, by WILLIAM CAVE, D.D., Chaplain in Ordinary to his Majesty. London, 1676.

If you look at the twentieth chapter of the Acts of the Apostles, and first verse, you will find a very short account, given by St Luke, of the next nine or ten months of Paul's life:—"He departed for to go into Macedonia. And when he had gone over those parts, and had given them much exhortation, he came into Greece, and there abode three months." Although the evangelist, in his narrative, says little about this important period of the Apostle's history, we may gather, from Paul's own Epistles, much that is interesting regarding it. From these, we find that he went from Ephesus to Troas, probably by sea,—his two Ephesian converts, Tychicus and Trophimus, most likely accompanying him. Aquila and Priscilla had meanwhile returned to Rome,—the edict of Claudius, which banished them, being now removed.

You may remember his former hurried visit to Troas, when he was called so suddenly away elsewhere by the vision of the man of Macedonia. Now he remained a longer time; not so long, however, as he had intended, in consequence of Titus not making his appearance with tidings about the church at Corinth. Titus was sent thither by Paul from Ephesus, not only to make a collection for the poor Christians in Jerusalem, but also to discover what effect his own letter had produced upon them. The Apostle seems to have waited, week after week, in great anxiety for the return of his younger brother. Days passed heavily away without any tidings of him. He was greatly disquieted because of the delay. "My spirit," he says, "had no rest because I found not Titus."* During his stay in Troas, he had much encouragement. "A door was opened to him of the Lord," and he very soon after came back again to carry on the good work which he had now commenced.

Meanwhile he set sail for Macedonia, expecting to meet Titus the sooner, who was coming to Troas by that route. Landing at Neapolis, he went thence to Philippi. From his Philippian converts he had received more kindness, and less cause of distress, than from any other church. He never uses towards them a word of censure. They were a poor people. He speaks of the "depths of their poverty;" and yet, three several times, when he was at Thessalonica, Corinth, and Rome, they forced him to take money

* 2 Cor. ii. 13.

they had collected for his support. "The Philippians are in the Epistles what that poor woman is in the Gospels, who placed two mites in the treasury. They gave much, because they gave of their poverty; and wherever the Gospel is preached throughout the world, there shall this liberality be told for a memorial of them."* Their example proves that it is not the wealthiest church which is always the most liberal in the cause of God; but that wherever there is a willing and bounteous heart, there will be a generous and giving hand.

We may imagine Paul's feelings when once more among his much-loved, I was going to say, his *most*-loved church. Six years had passed since he was last there. The remembrance of the shameful treatment he had then experienced—the lictors' rods—the cruel stocks—the dark dungeon,—must all have come vividly to his mind; but his sorrow was now turned into joy, in finding himself among homes and hearts so cherished. The load, however, was still on his spirit; Titus had not arrived, and he could not help feeling great uneasiness about the state of the church at Corinth. He knew, indeed, at this time, that not the Corinthian church alone, but all the others, were in no small peril. This was principally on account of those Jewish teachers who were jealous of their old national privileges, and who wished Christianity not to be the great religion of the world, but a mere branch and offshoot of Judaism. We can understand, therefore, how the "care of all the churches" was no slight matter to a mind like that of Paul; and with what anxiety he waited to hear how his remonstrances had been received

* See Conybeare and Howson, vol. ii. pp. 89, 124.

by a body so influential as that of the believers at Corinth.

At last, his time of painful suspense terminates,—Titus arrives. "God, who comforteth them that are cast down, comforted me by the coming of Titus."* He brings much more joyful intelligence than the Apostle expected. The far greater number of the Corinthians had submitted with meekness to his rebukes, and had cast out from their communion the offender who had been special cause of trouble. They longed for the Apostle's presence among them again, and were deeply affected at the thought of having cost him so much pain. Still there remained, however, a small party of these Judaising Christians, who were doing what they could to sow the seeds of dissension. They had ranged themselves under some designing ringleader, who had probably been sent by the sect in Jerusalem. He had come in as a wolf into the fold, doing what he could to undermine the Apostle's authority, and even turn his outward appearance and impaired eyesight into ridicule.† It is needful that we keep in mind these two parties into which the church at Corinth was now divided, in order to understand aright the Second Epistle to the Corinthians, which the Apostle now wrote. This was sent back to them by the hands of Titus, accompanied by two other deputies, who were proceeding, at any rate, to renew the collection for the Jerusalem Christians.

You remember, I daresay, how unwilling Titus was, on a former occasion, to go to so wicked a place as Corinth; it is different, however, with him now. The Apostle thus expresses his happiness at the change of

* 2 Cor. vii. 6. † See 2 Cor. x. 1, 2, 10, 11.

feeling in his young brother's mind,—"But thanks be to God, which put the same earnest care into the heart of Titus for you. For indeed he accepted the exhortation; but, being more forward, of his own accord he went unto you."* In reading the epistle for yourselves, you will find Paul addresses both parties. To the one, in the first half of the letter, he speaks in language of kindness and consolation; to the other, in words of stern remonstrance and rebuke.

After Titus left, the Apostle proceeded to visit some of the churches in the northern part of Greece. While making this circuit, he fulfilled his promise to the poor saints at Jerusalem regarding the "collection." He seems, as you must have noted, to have been very zealous in this matter. He felt that, since the apostles of Christianity were Jews, and had ministered to the Gentiles in spiritual things, they ought to minister in return to them in "carnal things."† The method he seems to have enforced on his converts was to lay by a sum of money every Sabbath morning (the first day of the week). The Corinthians, who were the most able to give of all the churches, had been thus gathering their contributions for a whole year, and their readiness was held up to the Macedonians for imitation—"For I know the forwardness of your mind, for which I boast of you to them of Macedonia, that Achaia was ready a year ago; and your zeal hath provoked very many."‡ The zeal of the Macedonians, however, poorer though they were, so exceeded that of the Achaians, that we find the Apostle afterwards making the less opulent churches read a lesson of liberality to the wealthy one:—

* 2 Cor. viii. 16, 17. † Rom. xv. 27. ‡ 2 Cor. ix. 2.

"Moreover, brethren, we do you to wit of the grace of God bestowed on the churches of Macedonia; how that in a great trial of affliction, the abundance of their joy, and their deep poverty, abounded unto the riches of their liberality. For to their power, (I bear record,) yea, and beyond their power, they were willing of themselves; praying us with much entreaty that we would receive the gift, and take upon us the fellowship of the ministering to the saints. And this they did, not as we hoped; but first gave their own selves to the Lord, and unto us by the will of God. . . . Therefore, as ye abound in every thing, in faith, and utterance, and knowledge, and in all diligence, and in your love to us, see that ye abound in this grace also. I speak not by commandment, but by occasion of the forwardness of others, and to prove the sincerity of your love."* We find soon afterwards, when the money was all collected, that Luke, and probably Trophimus, were to be the bearers of it to Jerusalem. They are spoken of as "the messengers of the churches."†

Paul seems at present to have travelled farther west than on any of his former journeys. It is possible he may even have gone to the shores of the Adriatic Sea; for we read "that he fully preached the Gospel of Christ round about unto Illyricum."‡ What the particular towns were he visited, we are not informed as Luke was no longer with him as an eye-witness. Pursuing, in a westerly direction, the *Via Egnatia,* from Berea (from which town, you will remember, he was formerly obliged to take flight), he would probably come to Pella, the birth-place of Alexander the Great, and Pela-

* 2 Cor. viii. 1–8. † 2 Cor. viii. 23. ‡ Rom. xv. 19.

gonia, the capital of that district of Macedonia. He turned his steps, probably about the beginning of winter, towards Corinth. How he journeyed thither it is also impossible to determine; whether he would take the high-road from Berea to the Isthmus, or, what is perhaps more probable, return to Thessalonica, and take vessel from that sea-port. On the Isthmian city his fondest thoughts—his hopes and fears—had been long, as you have seen, centred. We may imagine with what emotions he now approached it, as its spacious harbour opened to his view, and the rocky citadel which rose above it. His feelings, in many respects, must have been of a saddening kind as he once more trod its busy streets; and yet how much cause, too, for gratitude had he since his first visit! *Then* he was all alone—solitary and friendless. He had come from a disheartening visit to Athens, where a mere handful and no more had listened to his teaching. *Now*, he was no longer a stranger—he was on his way with some faithful companions to a house which his former visit had opened to him,—that of Gaius,—a kind and good Christian, whom, as you already know, the Apostle had baptized with his own hand, and whose many charities were known to all the churches. Though greatly grieved to think of the sins which had crept in among his converts, and the violent opposition raised by others against himself, still Paul must have rejoiced in knowing that within these walls were many warm Christian hearts—many true sons of the faith. It is, besides, a deeply-interesting circumstance, that so noble a band of faithful *ministers*—standard-bearers of the Cross*—were now assembled at Corinth, who had to-

* See Lewin vol. ii. p. 530.

gether, there and elsewhere, proved mighty through God to the pulling down of Satan's strongholds. There was Luke, the polished physician; there was the gentle and pious Timothy; there was Titus, the calm and discreet adviser; there was Jason, who had risked his life for the Apostle at Thessalonica; there was Tychicus, a faithful brother to the last, when others grew faithless; there was Erastus and Sosthenes, miracles of grace from Corinth itself; and not to make mention of others, there was the Great Apostle, a befitting chief, at the head of this noble army. How different when he approached Damascus, many years before, at the head of *another* band!—the haughty young Pharisee, burning with false zeal—proud of his sect and of his national descent. Now, he is poor, weary, weighed down "with the care of all the churches," but "the peace of God," which he himself speaks of as "passing all understanding," is "garrisoning his heart;" though he walks in the midst of trouble, "the Lord revives him," and a bright crown of joy and rejoicing is waiting him on "*that* day!"

There were, however, tidings of sorrow of another kind, waiting him on his arrival, which he did not expect. The Church of Galatia, which had promised so well at first, was beginning to be sorely affected by the doctrines and influences of these same Judaisers. They were doing all in their power to weaken the hold which Paul had over his affectionate "Gauls." They had tried to persuade them that he was not "an apostle," in the true sense of the word,—not one of the twelve who were appointed by the Lord Jesus, but a mere teacher, not worthy of the credit due to the others. The influence of these "false brethren" was great;

they got many of the "fickle Galatians" to turn from the "simplicity of the truth." Several underwent the rite of circumcision, imagining that it was necessary to their salvation. It was a proof of what we described them to be—a strangely fitful people! A few years before, they would gladly, if they could, have "torn out their own eyes," and given them to Paul as a token of their attachment, and worshipped him as an angel; but now they had listened to artful seducers, who had "troubled them and perverted the Gospel of Christ." How different to the steady, fixed Christian principle of the Great Apostle himself! *They* were like the waves of the sea, driven by the wind and tossed,—*he*, like the rock which nothing could shake. What is he to do? will he take vessel, once more, and go personally to rebuke them? The distance is, for the present, too great; and, besides, he has other work in hand in the disorders at Corinth; but the *pen* must do what the human *voice* cannot. He writes, from Corinth, his "*Epistle to the Galatians.*" In sharp and severe terms he therein reproves his converts "for being removed so far unto another gospel." It must have been under the influence of deep feeling he could pen such words as these,—"O foolish Galatians, who hath bewitched you, that ye should not obey the truth?" "But though we, or an angel from heaven, preach any other gospel unto you than that which we have preached unto you, let him be accursed. As we said before, so say I now again, If any man preach any other gospel unto you than that ye have received, let him be accursed."*

After the messengers were sent to Ephesus with this

* Gal. i. 8, 9.

letter of reproof, Paul proceeded to expel from the church at Corinth those individuals who had been the cause of so much evil in it. The "signs of an apostle" were wrought before them, in order to show the Divine authority by which he taught. He exhibited his Divine mission by the working of miracles; and by this means many who had before questioned his authority must have been silenced. But he must make an example of those who had not only so deeply distressed himself, but who had wrought such mischief in the Church of God. A solemn assembly is convened —the wicked and unholy members are cast out, no longer permitted to hold communion with their brethren. Whether they ever sincerely repented, and were again restored to the privilege of church-fellowship, we cannot tell. There is no more mention made after this of "the church at Corinth." We have reason to hope that Paul's present visit had been much blest to many, and that the casting out of this "unholy leaven" had not only saved, but purified the remaining lump. We have a letter remaining still, written by the same Clement whom Paul calls his "fellow-labourer," in which he refers to the consistency, for many years at least, of their walk and conduct. "Who that visited you," says this good man, whose name Paul tells us is in "the Book of Life," "did not admire your sober and gentle piety in Christ? For ye did all things without respect of persons, and walked in the laws of God, obeying those who were set over you, and ye were all humble-minded, subjecting yourselves rather than subjecting others."

The Great Apostle seems in this closing visit to have spent about three months in Corinth and Achaia.

"watering the churches," and collecting money for that great object so near his heart, to which we have so often referred.

There was one never-to-be-forgotten occupation which at this time engaged his spare moments. A wealthy lady of the neighbourhood, a widow, and deaconess of the church, whose house was at Cenchrea, was about to go to Rome. A rising and promising church of Christians, chiefly Gentiles, was already formed in the world's great capital. Paul had long meditated a visit thither, on his way to Spain, after accomplishing his journey to Jerusalem; but being a comparative stranger personally to the members of the Roman church, he thought it would be well to send them by her a *letter* beforehand, to assure them of his affection, touching also on the points in which he knew they needed most direction. It was dictated to Tertius the scribe, with the exception of the closing benediction, which, as usual, was written by Paul in his own hand. We have had again and again occasion to speak of the evil influence the Judaising teachers were exercising in the different churches the Apostle had founded. He seemed anxious to have some written treatise that would be serviceable in putting down their false doctrines, and which would be regarded as a rule of faith for all his churches. The Spirit of God wisely guided him in composing that wondrous "body of divinity," contained in the "*Epistle to the Romans*," where the grand central doctrine of the Gospel, what Luther called "the doctrine of a standing or a falling Church," is brought so beautifully out—viz., Justification by Faith. It forms, indeed, a noble manual on the great peculiar truths of Christianity. Chrysostom may well call it "the golden key of Scripture;" and the older my readers become, the more they will value and admire it. It sometimes interests us to know where a great General penned his despatches, or a great poet his immortal strains; we read these with greater zest by connecting them with the spots where they were written. You may in future think of the Great Apostle, during his present residence at Corinth, seated in some quiet chamber in the house of Gaius; his window, it may be, looking out on the heights of Acrocorinthus, or on the blue waves of the Ionian sea, and with Tertius seated, pen in hand, at a table by his side, dictating to him his most precious EPISTLE TO THE ROMANS. It is evident from the close of the epistle that, although he himself had never been in Rome, he was acquainted with several Christian families there. The reason of this may probably be, that many, like Aquila and Priscilla, who had been expelled by the edict of Claudius, had met with the Apostle at Corinth, Ephesus, and elsewhere, and contracted a valued friendship with him. You will observe, in the messages or salutations in the concluding chapter, that he mentions two whole families, and twenty-six individuals, with some distinct allusion to their individual characters.* Although, therefore, he had never "seen their face in the flesh," he seems to have felt no common interest in their welfare—"he made mention of them always in his prayers."†

The time had now come when St Paul had to bid farewell to the church and converts at Corinth. His first purpose seems to have been to take ship, like Phœbe, and sail direct to Jerusalem; but his plans

* Lewin, vol. i. p. 536.

† Rom i. 9.

were changed on discovering a new plot for his destruction, secretly concocted by the Jews, who had been greatly irritated against him ever since the decision of Gallio. What the precise nature of the plot they had laid was, we cannot tell: possibly they had hired an assassin to despatch him on the road to Cenchrea; or, perhaps, they had contrived some plan to seize him after he had embarked, and plundering him of his collection-money, to make the Ægean Sea his grave. To escape from their fury, he resolved to go round for safety by the north of Greece; this would enable him also to visit all his churches by the way—Thessalonica, Apollonia, and Amphipolis. He must have painfully felt the continual peril to which he was exposed. He could not look without fear to the future; for if the enmity of distant Jews was so great, what might he expect on reaching Jerusalem itself? He thus refers to his danger in his letter just written to Rome:—"Now I beseech you, brethren, for the Lord Jesus Christ's sake, and for the love of the Spirit, that ye strive together with me in your prayers to God for me; that I may be delivered from them that do not believe in Judea; and that my service which I have for Jerusalem may be accepted of the saints."* The companions of this journey, we are told (in the 20th chapter of Acts, ver. 4), were Sopater, the Berean; Aristarchus and Secundus, of Thessalonica; Gaius, of Derbe, and Timotheus; also Tychicus and Trophimus, of the province of Asia. These, however, the better to effect the escape of St Paul, took ship direct to Troas, while he and Luke proceeded in haste by land to the north of Greece. When they reached his favourite city and

* Rom. xv. 30, 31.

church of Philippi, it was the time of the Jewish passover, which lasted eight days. Here the Apostle and his historian lingered, during the celebration of the old Jewish rite, now fulfilled in the great Antitype, "Christ our passover, sacrificed for us." They then hasten to follow the steps of their friends; this more especially as Paul was desirous of reaching Jerusalem before the feast of Pentecost. Coming down, therefore, to Neapolis, they embarked on board some ship bound for Troas,—a voyage which, under favourable circumstances, ought not to have taken two days, but which, in the present instance, either by reason of adverse winds or a calm, was lengthened to five.* The Apostle's previous visit to Troas, you will remember, was a hurried one; his anxious spirit could get no rest or comfort from Titus not being there to meet him as he expected. Now he hopes to be able to add to the church, whose foundation he had formerly laid. He seems to have arrived at an early part of the week. How he occupied it, we are not informed; we may well believe he was actively engaged in proclaiming his great message, and all the more so as his time was precious. In order to attend the feast at Jerusalem, he required to be in Palestine by the 9th of May. He evidently remained at Troas longer than he intended. His detention probably was caused by being obliged to wait the sailing of the ship, which might have taken all that time to unload her cargo and get in a fresh one; possibly he may have been retarded in sailing by adverse winds. We have an interesting account, however, left us of his *Sabbath* duties in this old city. The little church at Troas were convened together in a

* See Howson, vol. ii. p. 210.

small and confined upper chamber on the evening of that day. The place was intensely hot, from the dense crowd collected and the many lights burning in the chamber. The Apostle, feeling that, as he was to leave on the morrow, this might possibly be the last opportunity he would ever have of speaking to them about their souls, continued his address until midnight. Midnight arrived; but still the earnest man of God, taking no note of time, proceeded to urge his high lessons on a breathless audience. There was a young hearer seated at one of the open windows or balconies, which are common in the houses of the East, overhanging the court below. He had ventured too near the ledge; and being overcome, partly with the heat and partly with sleep, he fell down to the pavement, and was "taken up dead." Paul immediately ceased speaking. He descended to the anxious crowd, who were now gathered round the youth; and in the spirit and power of his Master, he brought him back to life. You may imagine the joy, not only of the friends and relatives of Eutychus, but of all the other converts; for, be assured, if it had been known that a violent death had taken place in this meeting of "the Christian sect," it would have been too good an opportunity for the enemies of the Cross to call in the authorities of the place to put a stop to all such assemblages in future. But the sorrow of the disciples was turned into joy. It was a new testimony that God was with His servant of a truth. They returned to their chamber; and after the excitement was allayed, they partook together, as was often the case with the early Christians before they parted, of the Lord's Supper, or *Eucharist*, as it was called,—a word which means "joy," or "thanksgiving;"—and their hearts at present were doubtless full of gratitude and thankfulness for the miraculous restoration of this life. All the scene in that Troas chamber beautifully accords with the description given us of the Sabbath meetings of the early Christians, in a letter written by the younger Pliny to the Emperor Trajan, from a place not far from Troas, a century later. He says—"The Christians were wont to meet together on a stated day, before it was light, to sing among themselves alternately a hymn to Christ and God, and bind themselves by an oath not to be guilty of the commission of any wickedness; . . . . and when these things were ended, it was their custom to separate, and then to come together again to a meal, which they ate in common without any disorder." * The other friends and companions of the Apostle early in the morning went on board their vessel, sailing round by Cape Lectum to Assos. Paul, however, waited behind them, remaining as long as he could with his converts, imparting to them instruction and comfort. He then set out alone on the Roman road, which skirted the base of Mount Ida on the one hand and the sea-shore on the other, on his way to Assos.† It forms a striking and pleasing incident in the history of the Great Apostle. We have him generally brought before us amid the bustle of cities, or reasoning and disputing in schools and synagogues; but here we

* See Pliny's *Letters*, where a remarkable account is given of the rapid spread of Christianity in Asia Minor.

† If what we have elsewhere supposed about the Apostle's eyesight be correct, we have here at least one instance in which he seems to have been so far recovered as to allow of his travelling alone. We have no grounds, however, for supposing that the disorder in his eyes made him at all times so helpless as to be unable to take such a journey as the present without the guidance of others.

have a glimpse of "Paul in solitude." The scene recalls the lines of a favourite poet—

> "There was a dell,
> Whose woven shades shut out the eye of day,
> While, towering near, the rugged mountains made
> Dark back-ground 'gainst the sky.
> Thither I went,
> And bade my spirit taste that lonely fount,
> For which it long had thirsted 'mid the strife
> And fever of the world."

We see a lone figure walking slowly along amid the oak-copse of Ida.* It is an early day in spring; the groves are filled with singing-birds; the trees are feathered with green leaves; the ocean is murmuring at his right hand; the rocky heights of the sacred mountain rise on his left, glittering with a hundred joyous streams. May we not imagine him, as the sun had just risen, pausing at times at some opening by the pebbly beach, and gazing across that great and wide sea, whose waters were washing ten thousand unseen and unknown shores,—perhaps thinking of it as an emblem of that glorious Gospel which, under the rising of a "Better Sun," was yet to send its ripples of love and peace on every spot where the trace of human footstep could be found? He walked on, a distance of twenty miles. It was a season of quiet communion with his God in the temple of nature, which, we may believe, he would often recall with pleasure. These shady woods, on that spring afternoon, doubtless listened to earnest prayers, which the last eighteen hundred years have been answering.

* See the picture at the beginning of the Chapter. See also Fellow's *Asia Minor*, and the description by Howson, p. 214.

CHAPTER XVII.

The Sea-Voyage.

"The warring winds have died away,
And clouds, beneath the glancing ray,
Melt off, and leave the lands and sea
Sleeping in bright tranquillity.
  Instead of one unchanging breeze,
There blow a thousand gentle airs,
And each a different perfume bears—
  As if the loveliest plants and trees
Had vassal breezes of their own
To watch and wait on them alone,
And waft no other breath than theirs."

"Food and raiment was his bill of fare; and more than this he never cared for,—accounting, that the less he was clogged with these things, the lighter he should march to heaven—especially travelling through a world overrun with troubles and persecutions."—CAVE's *Life of St Paul*, 1676.

We may imagine our Great Apostle reaching now the old arched gate at the northern entrance of Assos, and hastening to the harbour to see if the ship, which had his companions on board, had arrived. He would have to descend through abrupt and steep streets before reaching the sea-shore; so precipitous, indeed, was the way from the town to the port, that it was a common proverb—"Go to Assos and break your neck."* Probably he may have stood for a while on the shore watching the vessel gradually approaching. If it had already reached, no time was to be lost in getting on board. Probably, towards the evening of Monday, he once more found himself and his companions surrounded with the voices of Grecian sailors, spreading their sails to the breeze.

We may imagine the beauty of the scene as they

* See Lewin.

retired from the harbour of Assos,—its own long line of buildings; its striking citadel, perched on a rock; and, higher still, melted among the tints of the evening sky, was beautiful Ida, with her crags, and groves, and waterfalls. For some time the course of the vessel was not in the open sea; their voyage lay among creeks and islands where the navigation was difficult, and where safety required that they should cast anchor for the night. Modern travellers unite in describing the extreme beauty of the scenery through which, for several successive days, St Paul must have passed. The first place at which they paused was Mitylene, the chief city of the beautiful island of Lesbos, the largest in the Ægean Sea. The town was built on a narrow neck of land, with a port on the east and west side of it, and still remains, under the modern name of *Castro*. Here they waited over night, as there was at present no moonlight, and the intricate passage between the island and the mainland rendered it only safe to venture by day.

The next morning (Tuesday) they directed their course to Chios, where the straits between the island and the coast become narrower still. On the left, lofty precipices towered in terror over their heads—to the right, the lovely gardens of the island were bright with blossom.

Passing through similar scenery as they skirted the eastern shores of Samos, they reached Trogyllium, where they again cast anchor. On approaching the latter, Paul could not fail to cast an affectionate and longing look towards a spot much endeared to him, and which could not have been above a few miles distant. It was Ephesus, where, a brief year before, he had witnessed the terrors of a fanatical mob, and yet experienced the faithfulness of Christian friendship. His imminent danger had compelled him to hurry away in haste, without a word of benediction or farewell, and he could willingly now have landed, and gone direct to its gates to "salute" his attached friends there. Doubtless he could discern its site, at least, from the prow of his vessel; but it was either impossible for him to divert the ship from its course, or, what is equally probable, he was unwilling to allow anything to interfere with his purpose of being in time for the feast of Pentecost at Jerusalem. He could not, however, pass this much-loved place, where so many brethren and sisters of the Lord were, without trying to hold some intercourse with them. He knew that his ship would be detained for a day or two at the port-town of Miletus. Could he not send a messenger to Ephesus (not more than thirty miles) to tell the presbyters of the church to come and see him? He would hear from their lips about his dear converts, and both he and they would have the privilege, at all events, of uniting in prayer, and getting a mutual blessing. He saw, moreover, that dangers and trials, more especially from the wiles of the Judaising Christians, were waiting them; and he was anxious to take the only opportunity he was likely ever to have on earth of uplifting his warning voice. He lived to see how needful the warning was; for, amorg the very last words he dictated, probably a few days before his death, he tells us, what was not the least of his closing trials,—"This thou knowest, that all *they which are in Asia* be turned away from me; of whom are Phygellus and Hermogenes."*

* 2 Tim. i. 15.

Meanwhile, however, we may imagine the joy of the Christians at Ephesus when they were told—"Our beloved Paul is at Miletus, and is waiting for our coming!" We may imagine their journey—their meeting! It is one of the most touching scenes in all the Apostle's life, or indeed throughout the Bible itself. They are gathered (probably from the time that had elapsed since leaving Troas) on the *Sabbath* day. It is in no house—no church; their place of assembling is on the solitary beach, within sound of the rippling sea. It was a little prayer-meeting like the one by the river-side at Philippi, beneath the canopy of nature; but never, we believe, did sermon tell with more touching power, or were hearts united in more fervent supplication. The sermon is still left to us.* It is short; but it is one of those beautiful passages of Scripture which no one, to this day, can read without being touched by its beauty and tenderness. They kneeled down at its close on the shore—tears fell fast—old and young flung their arms around Paul's neck, embracing and kissing him—"sorrowing most of all for the words which he spake to them, that they would see his face no more; and they accompanied him to the ship." There is no time for delay; the Great Apostle, with a bursting heart, is once more on the blue deep—his eye wistfully following his downcast friends, till distance has separated them for ever.

Before leaving the town of Miletus, we may just remark, that, when Paul knelt by its sea-shore, he must have gazed, close by, on a busy city—a forest of masts crowding its four ports. Already was it beginning to interfere with the trade of Ephesus. If he

* Acts xx. 18–36.

looked towards the sea, a cluster of islands would be right in view, well-known haunts of smugglers and pirates. Owing to the quantity of soil carried down by the stream of the Meander, these islands are now no longer washed by the ocean, but are little elevations rising in the midst of a fertile plain; and Miletus itself has shared in the altered face of nature.*

Chandler visited it, among other places, in his tour in Asia Minor, and was struck with its desolation, though still retaining, in its name (Palat, or *Palatia*, the *Palaces*), the remembrance of its ancient greatness. "Miletus," he says, "was once exceedingly powerful and illustrious. Its early navigators extended its commerce to remote regions; the whole Euxine Sea, the Propontis, Egypt, and other countries, were frequented by its ships and settled by its colonies. . . . . It afterwards fell so low as to furnish a proverbial saying—'The Milesians were once great.' . . . . The whole site of the town, to a great extent, is spread with rubbish and overrun with thickets. The vestiges of the heathen city are pieces of wall, broken arches, and a few scattered pedestals and inscriptions, a square marble urn, and many wells." †

The Greek sailors and their holy voyagers pursue their course towards the island of Cos, which has been called "the garden of the Ægean," celebrated for wine and silkworms. Among the groups of smaller islands which they passed, they may have got a glimpse of one we have already alluded to, unknown then in sacred story—the island of Patmos, from whose lonely rock there sounded forth the last messages of Deity to our world.

* Lewin, *in loc.*

† Chandler, pp. 148, 149.

Rhodes was the next place to which they sailed. Doubling its northern promontory, they came in sight of the beautiful town and harbour, rising in the midst of gardens and hills. It was celebrated for its roses, which gave the name to the island—its Temple of the Sun, and great Colossus. This last was said to stand across the harbour, and was so high that vessels passed under its legs. Every finger of the image was as big as a man. It was reckoned the greatest of the seven wonders of the world while it stood; but, in the time of Paul, it was a huge ruin—nothing remaining but the limbs; the vast monument of human labour, 105 feet high, which attracted from afar the eye of the mariner, had been overthrown by an earthquake. As the Apostle passed into the port, the brazen monster was lying prone on the beach, where it continued for ages, until the Saracens took possession of the island, when the brass of the Colossus was sold to a Jew, who carried it away on the backs of 900 camels.*

It is not said whether the ship landed at Rhodes. Most probably it only cast anchor for the night, and, at early dawn, proceeded along the Lycian coast, with a "knot of high and rugged mountains in view,"† which the writer we quote calls Mount Cragus, the haunt of the fabled Chimæra. A little way east of this, they come in sight of Patara, the port of the river Xanthus, ten miles from the city of the same name. The vessel in which they were now sailing seems not to have been bound for Syria; but, fortunately, on reaching Patara, they found one just about to start for Tyre. Without loss of time, the Apostle seized the favourable opportunity, and once more, under a bright

* Cedrenus. † Beaufort's *Karamania*.

full-moon and a favouring breeze, we may imagine him out on the broad ocean—no longer now any creeks or currents to render anchorage for the night necessary.

It is worse than vain and unprofitable, in Bible narrative, to imagine things that are not described; but it may be pardonable for us to picture, in the present voyage, the weather-beaten Apostle standing on the deck of his vessel, "in the great and wide sea,"—the clear moonbeams playing on its white sails, or on the rippling foam of its wake. Every traveller who has been on the Mediterranean by moonlight, has spoken with rapture of the scene. Paul had left his warm cloak behind him at Troas; and we shall afterwards find him wishing much that he had it to protect his shivering frame in the damps of a Roman dungeon. But he can dispense with it now, in a summer night in these genial climes, and under such a canopy. Nature, we know, in her intense repose, has a wonderful power on the human spirit. Those glittering stars above his head, looking down from their quiet heaven like so many ministering angels, may have whispered peace to his lonely spirit. If the rude heathen sailors around were beguiling the hours by their wonted songs, may not the Apostle-voyager and his companions have had also *their* "songs in the night?" One of these, we know, was often on the lips of pilgrims like himself going up to the Passover;—may it not now have soothed his spirit in that moonlit sea, and led him to cast his burden on a faithful God? "The Lord is thy keeper; the Lord is thy shade upon thy right hand. The sun shall not smite thee by day, nor the moon by night. The Lord shall preserve thee from all evil; he shall preserve thy soul. The Lord shall preserve thy going out, and thy coming in, from this time forth, and even for evermore." * Perhaps you may remember the first time he sailed along this same sea—it was while, a brave-hearted boy, he stood on the deck of some Phœnician trader, with his father or some other friend at his side, pointing out, one by one, the objects of interest in the land of promise. How different *this* voyage! That father had, for aught we know, long ere now sunk into his grave, reposing with his dead in the Jewish sepulchre in Tarsus;—perhaps gone down to the tomb in sadness because the child of high promise had become an apostate and a Nazarene! It may be so; but Paul felt that better than father or friend was with him. If his "father and mother had forsaken him," the Lord had "taken him up." A mother's smile may possibly have never fallen upon her boy; but amid the stillness of that midnight hour, a voice would break upon the ear of the orphaned Apostle, as he drew nigh, with a trembling heart, to the city of God. "As one whom his mother comforteth, so will *I* comfort you, and ye shall be comforted in *Jerusalem!*" A few days, as we shall see, fulfilled the promise.

The distance from Patara to Tyre was a considerable one,—about four hundred miles; but with a favouring north-west wind, the voyage might easily be made in forty-eight hours.† The first land he would descry would be the round-topped mountain of Cyprus, with its summit of snow; and, not long after, he would catch his first glimpse, in the hazy distance, of the peaks of Lebanon.

They have now reached Tyre, the once "*great* city,"

* Psalm cxxi 5–8. † Howson, vol. i. p. 238.

all that remains of which, at the present day, is a few rocks and miserable huts, on which the fishermen spread their nets. When Paul visited it, it was far past the height of its glory, though still large. It was originally situated on the mainland, but the conquering army of Nebuchadnezzar drove the Tyrians to an island close by. Here they fortified themselves, and built a new city, jutting into the sea a mile long. Alexander the Great was only able to take it by connecting, at great labour, the mainland with the island-town. Its port, into which the Apostle entered, was situated on the north of the peninsula.

Since the Phœnician territory, between the sea and the mountain range of Lebanon, was small, Tyre was still indebted to neighbouring countries for various commodities which she received in exchange for her manufactures; and it has been conjectured, with great probability, that this vessel from Patara, in which Paul now was, may have been laden with grain or wine from the rich provinces of Asia Minor or the islands of the Ægean.* She was bound for Ptolemais, but, before proceeding thither, had to unlade in the Tyrian harbour. This occupied several days; and as the Apostle found he was in ample time for the Jerusalem festival, he willingly spent the leisure thus afforded him with the "brethren at Tyre." A church seems to have already existed here, and among its members at present were some "*prophets*," to whom had been imparted a knowledge of coming events. These used their influence with Paul to try and prevent him from going to Jerusalem, as they had a foresight given them of his coming trials. Their efforts,

* See Howson, vol. i. p. 235.

however, were vain. I need not say if there had been any express divine *command* in the matter, Paul was not one who would be found "to fight against God." But it was only a prophetic warning on the part of these Christians, "that if he valued his own liberty and safety, he ought not to venture, since it would certainly expose him to very great hazard." * He had, however, like his Lord before him, "set his face steadfastly to go up to Jerusalem," and no danger would divert him from what he considered his path of duty, although he had frankly owned to the elders of Ephesus that his spirit was clouded with the many intimations he had received of coming "bonds and imprisonment." After spending seven days at Tyre, including a Sabbath, the master of the vessel availed himself of the first fair wind to proceed to Ptolemais. Paul was followed to the seaside, as at Miletus, by many affectionate friends, their wives and children mingling in the sorrowing group who had come to bid him farewell. After uniting in prayer on the shore, the canvas is again spread to the breeze, and in a few hours they are sailing up the spacious bay, at the bend of which is situated the modern *Acre*, the ancient Ptolemais. We need not stop to describe this illustrious town. It was famous in the time of the Crusades, when England's lion-hearted king fought under its walls. It defied the power of Napoleon. In more recent times, it was less successful in withstanding the might of our own gallant fleet. Mount Carmel casts its shadow on the south part of the bay, where the principal anchorage was, and here, we may conclude, St Paul ended his present sea-voyage. At Ptolemais,

* Doddridge.

he only remained a single day, visiting the disciples resident there, and then took the road which skirts the base of Mount Carmel to Cesarea,—a distance of thirty-five miles. There were in this latter city many endeared Christian disciples,—one especially, under whose roof he had taken "sweet counsel" before now. Philip the Evangelist and his four daughters dwelt in the town of Herod. These four females seem to have been devoted servants of Jesus, on whom also the gift of prophecy had descended, as in the case of Deborah and Miriam in Old Testament times, and also in accordance with the prediction of Joel. Here the same mournful intimations met the Apostle, of approaching trials and persecution if he ventured to go to Jerusalem. Agabus, a convert and a prophet, the same who had years before predicted the famine in Judea, hearing of Paul's arrival, had come down all the way from the Holy City to lift his voice of prophetical warning. His former prediction relative to the dearth had been so accurately fulfilled, that the disciples would naturally listen with anxiety to what he would say regarding the future destiny of their revered father. The prophets, in olden time, had a peculiar way of foretelling coming events by *acting* these in expressive signs or symbols before the eye. Thus Jeremiah foretold the coming Jewish captivity by burying his girdle on the banks of the Euphrates; and Isaiah walked naked and barefoot to proclaim the humbling bondage which awaited Egypt and Ethiopia by the King of Assyria. Agabus used the same striking method now of making known his prediction. He took off Paul's girdle, binding his own hands and feet with it, and saying, "Thus saith the Holy Ghost, So shall the Jews at Jerusalem bind the man to whom this girdle belongs, and they shall deliver him into the hands of the Gentiles." Luke, Aristarchus, Trophimus, and his interested friends at Cesarea, implored the Great Apostle to listen to the voice of warning and abandon his purpose of proceeding to Jerusalem. But Paul's lofty spirit would allow no fears or threats to terrify him; he was bold in his Master's work. It pained him much to resist the advice of affectionate brethren, but he had been forewarned by a voice of *love* what "great things he must *suffer* for His sake." Is he to shrink from the cross? No! he acts up to his own advice to a younger believer—"Endure hardness as a good soldier of Jesus Christ." He had counted the cost, and found it worthy of martyrdom. "What mean ye to weep and to break mine heart? for I am ready not to be bound only, but also to die at Jerusalem for the name of the Lord Jesus." * When they saw they could not move him from his purpose, they submitted; and with hearts filled with gloom at all these manifold warnings, said, "The will of the Lord be done." There was much, indeed, that might well have filled the bold soul of our Apostle with dread; all throughout this journey we cannot fail to mark a dejection that was not usual to him. The Holy Ghost had witnessed in every city that bonds and afflictions were in store for him. He knew he could expect little justice at the hands of the worthless Governor of Judea, the abandoned Felix; and there were low assassins at this time in Jerusalem, who would be ready, for the basest bribe, to sacrifice the noblest life in the world.†

* Acts xxi. 13. † Neander.

But the baggage is put in order; his resolution is taken.

The distance to Jerusalem was seventy-five miles,—a three days' journey. As many of his personal friends, and Christians from Cesarea, were going up to the Pentecost feast, they must have formed together a goodly company or caravan.

We close this chapter by leaving the noble-minded servant of God in the house of Mnason, an old disciple of Cyprus, looking out on the same streets and scenes with which his eye had been formerly familiar, when, as the boy of Tarsus, he had day by day gone to sit at the feet of the learned Gamaliel.

CHAPTER XVIII.

Paul in Jerusalem.

"Jerusalem! Jerusalem!
  Enthroned once on high,
Thou favour'd home of God on earth—
  Thou heaven below the sky!
* * * * *
Till to the Saviou of mankind
  Thou humbly bow the knee,
Jerusalem! Jerusalem!
  Our tears shall flow for thee."

"And now, behold, I go bound in the spirit unto Jerusalem, not knowing the things that shall befall me there: save that the Holy Ghost witnesseth in every city, saying that bonds and afflictions abide me. But none of these things move me, neither count I my life dear unto myself, so that I might finish my course with joy, and the ministry which I have received of the Lord Jesus to testify the Gospel of the grace of God."—ACTS xx. 22-24.

IT was now the lovely month of May. The hills and valleys of old Palestine were clothed in their summer beauty. The husbandman saw the labours of early spring rewarded with fields of plenty. It was the time of year when good King David's pastoral song must have been on many lips—"Thou crownest the year with Thy goodness; and Thy paths drop fatness. . . . . The pastures are clothed with flocks; the valleys also are covered over with corn; they shout for joy, they also sing."* Thousands upon thousands from all parts of Judea, and Israelites from distant lands, were assembling at the feast of Pentecost, to offer to Jehovah thanksgiving for the bounties of harvest. Already, when the Apostle

* Psalm lxv. 11, 13.

arrived in Jerusalem, multitudes of stranger-Jews were crowding the streets; and the slopes of Mount Olivet, and the valley of the Kedron, as far as the eye could reach, were dotted over with the well-known goats'-hair tents. Many a young Hebrew youth, doubtless, had come up, for the first time, from his distant home, to see the city of the Great King—his heart bounding with joy. Many, too, unknown to themselves, had made their last pilgrimage to the place of ordinances. Among the latter, was the sojourner in the house of old Mnason, who was now, we have every reason to believe, spending his last Pentecost in the earthly Zion.

Let us think of him, then, once more in the "city of God," within sight of the splendid temple and the green Mount of Olives. Many changes had taken place since his last visit. Four years before, his old teacher, Gamaliel, had gone the way of all the earth, and been laid in the sepulchre of his fathers. His two sons still survived, Simon and Jesus. With them Paul doubtless had been acquainted in former years. They had probably been his companions during his school-days. Their path in life, however, from that time became very different. The sons of the Rabbi were afterwards exalted respectively to the chair of the Sanhedrim and the office of high priest, while their old Cilician friend and playmate arrives in their city a care-worn traveller, with no thought but that of bonds and imprisonment. Theophilus (the same to whom "Saul the persecutor" had applied for letters to seize the Damascus Christians) was still alive. Felix was residing in his gorgeous palace at Cesarea; and the Roman officer in command at Jerusalem, as we shall presently see, was Claudius Lysias. It was often the case then, as it is now when multitudes are gathered together in one place, that breaches of the peace were committed. Any such riots were best suppressed by the presence of military; and for this purpose, Claudius, during the feast of Pentecost, had, like his predecessors, soldiers ready armed to march, in case of disturbance, from the fort of Antonia.

The Apostle arrived (for even the date may with probability be given) on the 8th day of May, A. D. 56. He was kindly received, and seems to have spent the evening in company with the disciples. The next day was an anxious one to him; he was then to meet all the presbyters, in order to deliver the contributions he had brought for the relief of the poor Hebrews. He well knew that there were among them many "Judaisers," who regarded him with bitter dislike, as one who was doing all he could to destroy their national glory, and abolish their legal rites and ceremonies. One great purpose for which he came at present to Jerusalem was, to try and soothe their bitterness, and to convince them that he was but a single-minded disciple, who had no interest at heart but that of his dear Lord. However much, therefore, he dreaded the coming storm, he was resolved boldly, in the strength of his God, to meet it.

The venerable Apostle James at present presided over the assembly of presbyters. These met the next day, in order to receive Paul and the other brethren from a distance. They greeted one another with "the kiss of charity," common in these times as a symbol of brotherly affection. The strangers first laid down the money which had been collected in distant countries for the poor saints, and then Paul proceeded to address the meeting. He rehearsed all that had been done by himself and his companions, during the last four years, among the Gentiles. He would probably enlarge on the many promising churches he had founded—the perilous and trying scenes, more especially that at Ephesus, through which he had passed. Moreover, that he was not come now among them to seek an idle repose; but that, though his face was beginning to be deeply furrowed with wrinkles he was still resolved to "spend and be spent" in the service of his Master.

"How must his hearers have rejoiced to listen to every detail of those wonderful achievements, far more interesting than were ever told to admiring senates by the conquerors of the earth, and of the power of Divine grace, which, by the foolishness of preaching, had overcome the pride of the Areopagite, and subdued the rugged nature of the barbarous jailer, with as much facility as it had melted the heart of the tender Lydia! Surely few eyes were dry in that assembly."*

His address, indeed, seems to have been listened to with intense interest by the bulk of those present; for we are told, that the first thing they did, after hearing him speak, was to glorify God for the things He had wrought among the Gentiles by his ministry.

There were many deep prejudices, however, in the minds of "thousands of Jews which believed," which would not be so easily allayed. Many of those, as you remember in a former chapter, could not brook the thought of a gospel proclaimed to the heathen. They imagined that, as Israel had all along been the favoured and peculiar people of God, Christianity was only in-

* Blunt.

[illegible] them. *This* question had been finally disposed of and settled by the decree of the Jerusalem Council — copies of which, you will recollect, were carried by Paul, Barnabas, and Titus, to Antioch, and distributed through the different cities in Asia Minor. Another equally strong feeling, however, had now taken hold of their minds,—viz., a dread that the Jews, who had been converted to Christianity, might be induced or compelled to give up the observance of the Mosaic law. What were Paul's views on this subject? He distinctly held that the Jewish Christians might still, if they chose, observe their ancient rites; but these were in no respect to come in the place of the great work of Christ, by which alone both Jew and Gentile are "justified from all things, from which they could not be justified by the law of Moses." But the Jewish believers had accused him of going much farther, and of absolutely prohibiting the Hebrew converts among the heathen from having their children circumcised, and retaining any of the institutions of Moses. "Thou seest, brother," said the elders at this conference we refer to, "how many thousands of Jews there are which believe, and they are all zealous of the law; and they are informed of thee that thou teachest all the Jews which are among the Gentiles to forsake Moses, saying that they ought not to circumcise their children, neither to walk after their customs."

Paul's friends knew well that there would be many Asiatic Jews present at the feast from a far distance, whose feelings of national pride and glory would be roused by treading once more the city of their fathers. These friends of the Apostle considered it desirable if he could in some way give public proof that he was not the enemy of the Hebrew rites which he had been represented to be. The following was the device they fell upon. There were four Jewish Christians among themselves who had taken the "Nazarite vow." This, I have already explained, consisted in not cutting or shaving the hair or beard, nor taking wine for thirty days. I told you that at the end of that period, those who thus vowed were expected to repair to the temple, where they had their hair cut off and burnt on the altar. If they were poor, they generally got the assistance of some wealthy friend to pay the necessary expense; and nothing so raised a man in the estimation of the Jews as this act of charity towards a poor brother. Josephus tells us that King Agrippa, on returning to Jerusalem after having undergone many dangers and escapes, gave orders that the expense of shaving several Nazarites be paid out of his own private purse.*

These four Nazarites had fulfilled the "days of separation;" but they had not sufficient to pay the charge of the wonted sacrifices. The proposal of the Apostle's advisers was, that he should go in company with these four men to the courts of the temple, and defray the expense incurred according to the law. Being poor himself, his friends would likely furnish him with money sufficient for the purpose; and thus, in a way most gratifying to Jewish feeling, he would show his good-will to the Jewish Church.

Paul seems willingly to have complied with the suggestion. If he had thought it in any degree inconsistent with right principle, and the duty he owed to his Lord, we may be very sure he would never have agreed to it.

* Josephus, ant xix. 6, 1.

He viewed it, doubtless, as a mere outward compliance with a custom unimportant in itself, but which would tend to calm the feelings of those whom he was desirous of counting one with him in Christ Jesus. He ever sought, as he tells us elsewhere, to become "all things to all men, if by any means he might gain some." Circumcision in itself was nothing to him, neither was uncircumcision, "but faith, which worketh by love."

It is only fair, however, to mention, that many good men have considered the Apostle was, in this instance, guilty of an unwise compliance; and it is striking to observe, which we shall immediately do, that instead of soothing his enemies, his visit to the temple at this time threatened him with serious consequences. "He was brought," says John Knox, "into the most desperate danger that he ever sustained—God designing to show thereby that we must not do evil that good may come." We may picture to ourselves the Great Apostle, accompanied with his four friends, with their haggard looks and unshaven beards, ascending to the temple, entering by the Corinthian or Beautiful gate to the place allotted to the Nazarites to undergo their seven days' purification. It was customary, after each day's purification had taken place, for the Nazarite to remain in the temple. Paul in this way must have been daily in the court of the Gentiles, although he wisely abstained from entering into religious discussion with any of the worshippers. As I have said, multitudes of Jews from all parts of Asia, (and among these from Ephesus, to whom the Apostle's face was well known,) were mingling in the crowd around him. They had not forgotten his victory in their synagogue in the city of Diana, and they thought that now would be a befitting opportunity to have their revenge. They at once spread the intelligence that this false and traitor apostate was present, and had ventured to take Trophimus, his companion, a Greek, within the holy place. Probably they had seen Paul and Trophimus walking together on the streets, and had inferred that he had brought him also within the sacred courts. The introduction of any Gentile there, I need not tell you, was strictly forbidden. Josephus informs us that tablets were hung out in sight of all, with words upon them to caution those who might not be aware of the sacredness of the enclosure.* In a moment he is surrounded with an infuriated mob and frantic cries. The whole scene of Stephen's martyrdom must have flashed across him. They are almost within sight of the spot. Could a like terrible end be now in prospect for himself? They have laid fast hold of him, and are shouting aloud, "Men of Israel, help! this is the man that teacheth all men everywhere against the people and the law and this place."† We can readily imagine their fury. Soon their madness turns into blows. They drag him down the steps from the court of the women. The Levites within, afraid that murder might be committed, and their sanctuary thereby profaned, closed the weighty brazen gates, and left him to his fate. Fortunately the little time that elapsed in taking him from one court to the other saved his life. The Roman sentries, some of whom were pacing the colonnade of the temple, and others on the towers of Antonia, heard the noise of the tumult, and rushed with their arms to quell it. They saw it was no trifle, and therefore sent in haste to

* See Olshausen.

† Acts xxi 28.

Claudius Lysias, the governor of the castle, to acquaint him of the uproar. The Castle of Antonia was a strongly fortified place at the north-western side of the temple.* It contained large barracks for the Roman troops, in which a thousand were generally stationed. Its form was a vast square, described as having "the magnificence of a palace, and the conveniences of a city." A wall 300 cubits high and several fortifications were around it, and a tower at each corner to defend it. It was a sort of citadel of the temple.† One of these lofty turrets overlooked the temple courts, and Roman sentinels were always on watch to give intimation of any disturbance that might occur within the sacred precincts.

Claudius Lysias lost no time, after he received the message, in ordering out some officers and troops. He rushed down himself sword in hand. The sight of the Roman legion overawed the furious mob, and for the time they "left off beating Paul." Their object, however, was so far gained, for Lysias gave orders that his wrists be bound with two chains, these chains fastened to a soldier on either side. Hurried along, with a maddened crowd behind him, in the direction of the castle, he is taken to the barracks within the fortress. While led up the flight of stairs between the two places, so great was the pressure, he was literally carried off his feet, and borne upon the shoulders of the throng, who were crying out, "Away with him."

Lysias, in the confusion, could get no account of who his prisoner was. He imagined that he had cap-

* See the tower, in the picture of Jerusalem, at the farther extremity of the temple.

† Calmet.

tured a different victim. A violent impostor and false prophet—a native of Egypt—had, at the preceding Passover, come to Jerusalem, pretending that he had been sent by God to restore the kingdom to Israel. Four thousand deluded people had at first followed him; they had, ere long, increased to 30,000. These he led to the brow of Mount Olivet, and gave them to believe that they would see the walls of Jerusalem falling to the ground, and a way miraculously made for a triumphant entry into the city. Felix resolved to quell the tumult and disperse the fanatics. Putting himself at the head of the Roman troops, the motley crowd were scattered in every direction, and four hundred of them slain. The artful leader succeeded in escaping; but, at the very time when Paul was now in the temple, a rigid search was being made, and rewards offered for his apprehension. This explains the conversation which was now held between Claudius Lysias and his prisoner, as they were ascending, in the crush, the stairs of the castle.*

Paul, in calm composure, requests a word of the chief officer, "May I speak unto thee?" Lysias allows him. To the astonishment of the latter, he speaks not in Hebrew, but in Greek. The Governor then asked him if he was under a mistake in thinking him that Egyptian impostor who had led out into the wilderness a multitude of fanatics, to be slain by the troops of Felix? Paul assured him he was no Egyptian, but a citizen of Tarsus, and begged he might be permitted to address the people. We almost wonder that Lysias so readily complied with his request: but he

* See Lewin and Olshausen, with the references to the passage in Josephus.

seems to have been impressed by the whole bearing of his prisoner. At once silence appears to have been obtained We have seen Paul unfolding his great Gospel message to the crowd of philosophers on Mars Hill in Athens; and we feel that the scene must have been deeply impressive; but never, perhaps, did he address so vast and strange an audience as at present from the castle stairs at Fort Antonio—never was the power of his words more deeply felt. The storm was, in a moment, changed into a deep calm. Every voice was hushed into stillness as the gentle tones of the greatest of then living men broke over the turrets of the temple,—"Brethren and fathers, hear me!" What helped still more to lull the tumult and secure attention was, that he no longer spoke in Greek, but in their own much-loved Hebrew tongue. It was like oil thrown on a fretful sea! He commenced by telling them of his birth and education—his strong Jewish feelings and partialities—his wonderful conversion while in the very act of persecuting. He then passed to other events subsequent to that great turning-point in his history. They listen to him with patience and in silence, till he comes to speak of his special destination as the Apostle of the *Heathen;* but whenever the words were uttered which he tells them he had received as a special command from God, "Depart: for I will send thee far hence unto the Gentiles," there was no controlling their rage: "Away," they cried, "with such a fellow from the earth; for it is not fit that he should live." * They dared not at present attempt any violence, as the prisoner was in the hands of Roman soldiers; and the only way, therefore, of exhibiting

* Acts xxii 22.

their wrath was by threats and menaces. The Jews had their own peculiar way of expressing passionate anger or malice. You remember when King David was going along by the side of Mount Olivet, weeping and barefoot, and when Shimei came out to curse and revile him, he further showed the vehemence of his hatred by casting stones and *throwing dust.* The enraged and agitated Hebrew mob now thronging around the stairs of the castle do the same thing. They tore off their upper garments and cast dust into the air, as if really preparing for a repetition of the murderous scene which Paul had, many years before, "consented to" in the valley below. Lysias, not knowing, from the Hebrew language in which the speech was given, what the cause was of the renewed uproar, concluded that the speaker must have been guilty of some great crime. He commanded that he should be taken back again to the castle, and examined there by torture, so as to get a confession of his guilt. The command of the Roman is speedily obeyed; he is even stretched on the rack, ready to be scourged. A wooden post, slightly inclined, is driven into the ground, and the holy Apostle is bound tightly to it by his hands and feet. A centurion stands by him to see that the order is duly executed, when Paul, summoning up his wonted fortitude, demanded, "Is it lawful for you to scourge one who is a Roman uncondemned?" The centurion immediately informed Lysias of the prisoner's question. The governor felt he had placed himself in imminent peril by the act. "He was afraid after he knew that he was a Roman." We have found before now that, by the Sempronian law, those were liable to severe punishment who, however high their rank, presumed to beat a Roman citizen. He gave orders instantly that the cords which bound him be untied, but that he be kept in safe custody within the fortress. He was again secured by chains between two soldiers. His conscience, however, was void of offence; he had the fear of God, and no other fear; and he laid him down in that strange place "in peace and sleep," feeling that God enabled him "to dwell in safety."

Next day a new persecution awaited him. Lysias called together the Jewish Sanhedrim to try his case, in the same hall, Gazith, where Paul himself in former days had sat as one of the judges in condemning the martyr Stephen. There was only a short way between the steps that led down from the tower of Antonio to those which conducted up to the Jewish court.* Strange must have been the Apostle's feelings in entering this place! and stranger still the feelings of those who were now called together to sit in judgment on him! Ananias, though he had been deposed from the office of high priest by the Romans, presided on this occasion, as his successor, Jonathan, had been lately murdered by assassins. Simeon and Jesus, Paul's old schoolfellows, were also doubtless there, and Theophilus, the old high priest,—perhaps even some of those who had journeyed along with him to Damascus! What a change from that day!—the persecutor now the persecuted!—twenty full years he had been boldly "preaching that faith" which he had sought then "to destroy!"

The innocent Apostle looked steadfastly upon those seventy senators, in whose presence he now was, affirming with boldness that he had ever maintained "a

* Howson, vol. ii. p. 268.

good conscience before God." The rage of the presiding high priest vented itself in a base action. He commanded those that stood near Paul to smite him on the mouth. The Apostle, naturally of a quick temper, was roused to indignation, and exclaimed, "God shall smite thee, thou whited wall!" The saying was, ere long, fearfully fulfilled. At the commencement of the siege of Jerusalem, in after years, Ananias and his followers took refuge in the upper city from the fury of the opposing faction. His palace being burnt, he fled to the Pretorium, but *it* too had to yield to the enemies' assault. The wretched fugitive was discovered hiding in an aqueduct in the gardens, and fell by the daggers of the Sicarii. "Righteous art thou, O Lord!"

Paul, on this occasion, remarkably followed the injunction of his divine Master, "Be ye wise as serpents, and harmless as doves." He soon observed how hopeless his cause would be, argued before so prejudiced an assembly. With his usual tact and prudence, he turns the discussion on another point. He observed that the meeting around him was composed partly of Pharisees and partly of Sadducees; and as he knew there was a far more violent opposition existing between these sects than between either of them and the Christians, he started the great topic of their rivalry, declaring, "I am a Pharisee, and the son of a Pharisee: for the hope of the *resurrection from the dead* I am called in question."* The result proved as he had expected. He had cast a spark amid combustible materials, which set the whole in a blaze. The two factions turned their weapons against one another;

* Acts xxiii. 6.

and in the midst of the turmoil, Claudius Lysias, fearing it might end seriously, sent down his troops from the castle to bring back his prisoner in safety.

We may now think of the solitary Apostle, after the agitation of the few last days, left all alone to his solitary meditations in the cell of a Roman barrack. The future must have appeared painfully dark to him. The thought which had for long been near his heart, to "see Rome," and preach the Gospel in the world's capital, seemed now well-nigh hopeless. Could it be that his apostolic work was to be so soon terminated by a martyr's death? But God, when his favoured servants are in gloom and despondency, has always visited them with some special encouragement and comfort. He did so now. In the depth of midnight, when the weary prisoner was stretched on his bed of straw, the Lord appeared to him, and said, "Be of good cheer, Paul; for as thou hast testified of me in *Jerusalem*, so must thou bear witness also at *Rome*." *

Great need, truly, was there for such a welcome assurance, as fresh plots were concocted to effect his destruction. At break of day, forty Jews made a vow together, that "they would neither eat nor drink till they had killed Paul." They made known their infamous design to the chief priests and elders. It gives us an awful idea of the state of public morals, when these leaders of the people could become a party to so horrible a crime. Their plan was to get Claudius Lysias to request another meeting of the Sanhedrim, in order that a fresh trial might take place, and then they would murder him on his way from the castle of Antonio to the hall. The Apostle's life was in the great

* Acts xxiii. 11.

est danger; but God mercifully warded off the blow, by means of a new personage, whose name is brought before us here—the son of that sister of Paul's whom we have already spoken of at the commencement of this volume, as sharing the pleasures of infancy with him at Tarsus. Lysias had, in kind consideration, granted free admission to any of the prisoner's friends, and this nephew (whose name is not given) hastened to tell his uncle the fearful secret which had reached his ears. When Paul was seated in his lonely place of concealment, a footstep is heard; the door opens; his young nephew enters with an anxious look; when he ascertains that they are all alone, he informs him of the plot which had been devised against his life. What is to be done? The Great Apostle does not hesitate; he has confidence in the kindness and prudence of the commander of the garrison, and instantly asks a centurion to take the young man to the presence of Lysias, as he had something important to tell him. The meeting was a kind one on the part of the Roman soldier. He "took him by the hand," and leading him aside, asked him in private what he had to say. No sooner did Lysias receive the dangerous intelligence, than he dismissed the youth, with the injunction to tell no one of what had passed between them. And then, calling several of his officers, he told them to be ready at nine in the evening with two hundred soldiers, seventy cavalry, and two hundred lancers or spearmen, to take Paul down to the town of Cesarea, where Felix, the governor, was then residing. He further ordered them to have more than one horse for the prisoner, probably one for each of the soldiers who rode on either side of him, and to whom he was to be chained. The horses and horsemen were ready at the hour appointed at the gates of Fort Antonio. Bands of Jews may have been still lingering on the streets, talking about the success of the plot against a life they all hated, when the troops swept past them. They may have wondered at so large a detachment of soldiery at that hour of the night, but they would little dream that the central horseman was the victim of their fury, thus "escaping like a bird out of the snare of the fowler." We may imagine the journey of seventy-six miles.* The foot soldiers went no further than Antipatris, and then returned to Jerusalem. The rest, after two hard days, would be seen with tired and jaded horses entering the gates of the seaport town of the Cæsars.

The centurion in command took his prisoner at once to the Pretorium, or Palace of Herod, where Felix lived, and presented, along with him, the letter from Lysias. The letter was as follows:—"Claudius Lysias unto the most excellent governor Felix, sendeth greeting. This man was taken of the Jews, and should have been killed of them: then came I with an army, and rescued him, having understood that he was a Roman. And when I would have known the cause wherefore they accused him, I brought him forth into their council; whom I perceived to be accused of questions of their law, but to have nothing laid to his charge worthy of death or bonds. And when it was told me how that the Jews laid wait for the man, I sent straightway to thee, and gave commandment to his accusers also to say before thee what they had against him. Farewell." † It was a letter worthy of the generous-hearted writer. If Lysias had been actu

* See the picture. † Acts xxiii. 26-30.

ated by unworthy motives, if he had wished to please the Jews, and increase his popularity with them, he might have represented the prisoner as a "pestilent fellow," and worthy only of death. Had he done so, moreover, we can have little doubt as to the result. No mercy was to be expected from the hands of the abandoned Felix; but the letter expressly mentions that his crime was merely holding opinions contrary to the Jewish law; nothing was laid to his charge demanding a severe sentence. Felix having read it, looked at the prisoner who had been the cause of the disturbance, and put the question to him, "What province art thou from?" Being told it was Cilicia, he gave orders that he should be taken to Herod's judgment-hall, and kept there until, in accordance with law, his accusers made their appearance.

CHAPTER XIX.

Paul in Cesarea.

"These are the tones to brace and cheer
The lonely watcher of the fold,
When nights are dark and foemen near—
When visions fade, and hearts grow cold."

"And ye shall be brought before governors and kings for My sake, for a testimony against them and the Gentiles. But when they deliver you up, take no thought how or what ye shall speak; for it shall be given you in that same hour what ye shall speak. For it is not ye that speak, but the Spirit of your Father which speaketh in you." —MATTHEW x. 18–20.

"When I consider this Apostle as appearing either before the witty Athenians, or before a Roman court of judicature, in the presence of their great men and ladies, I see how handsomely he accommodateth himself to the apprehension and temper of those politer people."—LORD SHAFTESBURY'S *Characteristics*, vol. i. p. 30.

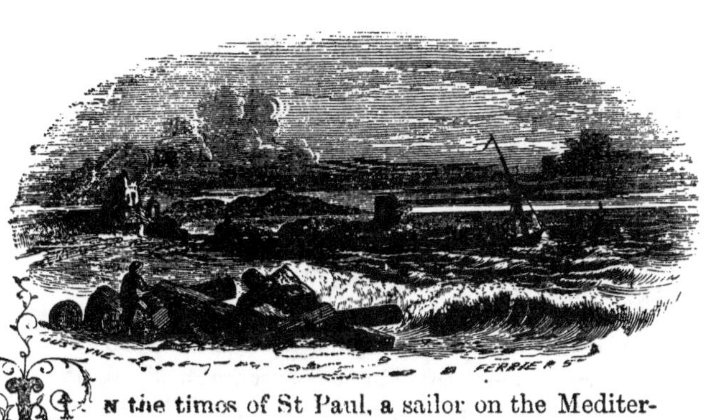

In the times of St Paul, a sailor on the Mediterranean, approaching the city of Cesarea, must have been struck with its greatness and grandeur. The first thing which caught the eye in sailing into its port, was the Temple of Sebasteum. It was perched on a lofty rock in front of the town, dedicated to Rome and her great emperor, and mainly intended as a sea-mark for mariners. The site of the city had evidently been selected owing to the spaciousness of the natural harbour. The coast was terribly swept by westerly winds, and there being no refuge for ships between Dora and Joppa, Herod the Great, at enormous labour, turned the natural advantages, of what was originally a little fishing-town, into a great capital. "He drew his model," says Josephus, "and set people to work, and, in twelve years' time, finished it. The buildings were all of marble, private houses as well as palaces; but his master-piece was the port, which he made as large as the Piræus of Athens—a safe station against all winds and weathers."* Immense blocks of stone, fifty feet long, were sunk to twenty fathoms, on the south and south-west, to form a breakwater, leaving a free passage only by the north.

Cesarea seems to have risen rapidly to importance, and as rapidly to have dwindled into insignificance. Not long after the period of which we write, it began to decline. It now lies, as you see in our picture, a pile of ruins sunk in the sands. It is far distant even from the common coast-road, and therefore comparatively little known or visited by travellers. At the time of St Paul, many heathens and foreigners mingled with the Jewish population. In a Roman-named town, where the Roman procurator lived, it was natural to suppose that there would be many habits, tastes, and customs, introduced from the great Roman capital.

In this city we left the Apostle, by the orders of Felix, in confinement in Herod's judgment-hall (the guard-room adjoining his magnificent palace), till his accusers arrived from Jerusalem. He had not to wait long. In five days, Ananias, his heart still burning with revenge, and other members of the Sanhedrim, made their appearance. They were accompanied by an advocate named Tertullus, or Tertius, whose name tells us he was of Latin origin—one versed in the usages of the Roman law, and also able to speak in the Latin tongue, both of which were necessary qualifications in cases similar to the present. Paul was sum-

* Josephus' *Antiquities*, book xv. chap. 13.

moned forthwith to appear before his accusers in the procurator's court, or place of judgment—the floor of which, if it were like others in the empire, was beautified with a tesselated pavement—square pieces of marble, or stones of various colours, disposed with art and elegance.*

Felix takes his place on his tribunal, and Tertullus delivers a speech, which, even in the brief outline we have of it, showed great power and dexterity. He begins by words of flattery to the judge, complimenting him on the only praiseworthy act of his government—the suppression of robbers and religious fanatics, who had recently, as in the case of the Egyptian impostor, disturbed the peace of Palestine.† Truly it required some ingenuity to say anything praiseworthy of a man like Felix, whom Josephus and Tacitus concur in denouncing as a monster of iniquity and injustice. "He exercised," says the latter, "the royal authority with the spirit of a slave, and indulged himself in every species of cruelty and lust." Tertullus then details in succession the charges brought against the Apostle. These were threefold:—1*st*, That he had been the means of creating disturbances among the Jews; 2*d*, That he was the ringleader of a sect called *Nazarenes;* and, 3*d*, That he was guilty of profaning the Jewish temple, which Roman law was bound to protect from insult. The object of his accusers evidently was, to get Felix to consent to deliver him up to be tried by their own Jewish courts—in which case they could, with the utmost ease, have effected his murder. The Jews pre-

* Horne's *Introduction*, vol. ii. p. 131.

† J sephus' *Antiquities*, book xx. chap. 8.

sent applauded violently the speech of their hired advocate, declaring that all he said was just.

If Felix had possessed the honourable feelings which we formerly found in Gallio, he would, on charges so false and frivolous, have driven the Jews from the judgment-seat, and dismissed the prisoner; but the Roman purple did not always cover true greatness of soul or rigid equity.

Paul was now called on to make his defence. He did so, answering the accusations of Tertullus one by one; and concluded by complaining, that the Asiatic Jews, who had first accused him, and with whom the uproar in the temple had begun, had not, according to the usage of law, come forward as witnesses against him. You may read for yourselves the brief account which St Luke gives of the Apostle's reply. You will find it in chapter xxiv. 10–22.

The speech of the Great Apostle seemed to make a decided impression on the mind of the governor; but, from all we can gather of the character of Felix, we need have no expectation on his part of leniency, or even fair dealing, if this were to interfere with his own private ends. As to the innocence of the Apostle, and the unfounded nature of the accusations brought against him, he could now, after having heard both sides, entertain little doubt; but Paul was a poor, persecuted, hated man. Felix would be no sufferer by oppressing *him;* but he might be so by offending the leaders of the Jewish people. He declined, therefore, at present giving any decision. He told them he would defer until "Lysias came down," who was shortly expected from Jerusalem. Till that time he gave orders that his prisoner be confined, enjoining, at the same time, that no severity, or harshness be shown towards him, but that any of his friends might have free liberty to go and visit him.

If Lysias came to Cesarea, we have no mention made of it. But a few days after the public trial, Felix and his wife Drusilla sent for Paul to come to the audience-chamber (or a private apartment in the palace), to have an interview with them. Drusilla was the sister of King Agrippa—herself a Jewess. She is spoken of as a young woman of great beauty, at this time only eighteen years of age. She had married Azizus, King of Emesa; but by the wicked influence of Simon Magus, the friend of Felix, she deserted her husband, and became the unlawful wife of the old profligate Felix. Paul's eloquence, power, and earnestness seem evidently to have arrested the attention of the governor; and Drusilla being a Jewess, and from her infancy having heard much of Paul, she was doubtless from curiosity anxious to see him. Behold, then, the Great Apostle called again to speak the word of his Master! Two wicked, hardened, selfish individuals were seated before him, probably on benches of Tyrian purple, and under a fretted ceiling. Remembering the manifold vices which lurked under all that outward grandeur, he directed the arrow of conviction to these seared consciences—reasoning of "righteousness, temperance, and the judgment to come." It was a bold thing for Paul to do; for the aged reprobate before him had his life in his hands—"he had power to crucify him, and power to release him," and to irritate his savage temper would be to bring down upon himself certain vengeance; but he felt that if he "pleased man, he was not the servant of Christ." It was no time to preach smooth things, by "the terrors of the Lord" he sought to persuade this ruler, revealing to him all the dread realities of that day of wrath, when small and great, mighty and mean, governor and apostle, would stand before God. "To penitent hearts he was in the habit of preaching the crucified Jesus as the Mediator; but to these worldly individuals, he displayed him as the Judge."*

> "No more he feels upon his high-raised arm
> The ponderous chain, than does the playful child
> The bracelet, form'd of many a flowery link.
> Heedless of self, forgetful that his life
> Is now to be defended by his words,
> He only thinks of doing good to them
> That seek his life." †

"Felix trembled!" conscience was aroused, and for the moment shook the iron frame of the debased Roman; but it was only for the moment. Conviction was suffered to pass away,—"Go thy way," said the procrastinator, "for this time, when I have a convenient season I will call for thee." Alas! we fear that *more* convenient season never came. Indeed, we find him, immediately after, guilty of the meanest and most dishonourable conduct towards the Apostle—conduct unworthy of his name and his office. He seems to have held many conversations and private conferences with Paul, to induce him to give a bribe in order to secure his release. He had heard, probably, that his relations were independent or perhaps he remembered that the prisoner in his defence had hinted at a collection he had brought from a distance to Jerusalem;‡ and from the known generosity of the Nazarene sect,

* Olshausen. † Graham's *Poems*. ‡ Cave, p. 96.

he knew there might be little difficulty in getting them to subscribe liberally to purchase the freedom of their champion. But the high-minded Christian principle of the Apostle scorned the base and impious attempt thus to evade the law. He would rather wear his chains than stoop to dishonour. The consequence, however, was a continuance of his imprisonment for two long years in the town of Cesarea. How he occupied himself during this lengthened interval in his life we know not. It must have been a precious season for turning his eye inwards on his own soul, and fostering the work of grace there. It was, as a writer has called it, "the school for his own personal improvement"*—the *Patmos* of his active life, where in silence and solitude he was permitted to hold communion with his God. We may imagine him seated in his prison or private house, chained by the right hand to the left arm of a Roman soldier, who was held responsible for the safety of his charge. Much of his time may probably have been spent in writing epistles to his various churches, which are now lost to us,—and also in receiving visits from Christians in Cesarea and Judea, who, as we have said, were allowed to come and cheer the hours of his solitude.

Little did the believers at Cesarea, who, a little while before, wept so touchingly at his going to Jerusalem, think that that very journey was to lead to a personal residence among them for two whole years. Among the friends who thus visited him, probably Timothy was, as formerly, a frequent and an always welcome guest. We know that Philip and his pious daughters were citizens of Cesarea, and more than likely Cornelius

* Olshausen.

the centurion was still stationed in the Roman barracks, rendering still to "Cæsar the things which were Cæsar's, and to God the things which were God's." Luke, too, we may believe, was much with him. It has even been supposed by many that the beloved physician occupied these years of leisure in writing his Gospel, with the inspired Apostle at his side, to guide him in the momentous task.

During this same period, Felix was recalled by the Emperor to Rome. His rapacity and violence had made him universally hated; and a cruel massacre of the Jews he had ordered in the streets of Cesarea, at the very time Paul was confined in the Pretorium, had added to the popular hatred which eight years of cruelty and selfishness had fostered. Before leaving, the selfishness of his character was still further displayed. He wished to appease and conciliate the Jews. He succeeded in doing so by an act which cost him nothing,—"*he left Paul bound*." "We are rather tempted to wonder, that to show them a still greater favour, he did not order Paul for execution. But here the providence of God interfered: God had said to Felix, as he said once before to Satan, 'Behold, he is in thine hand, but save his life.' The lion can only go the length of his chain; and thanks be to God, that chain is held by One, who, although he is almighty to destroy, is yet 'almightiest to redeem.'"* We know little more of this "bold, bad man." A number of Jews followed, at his departure, to accuse him before the Emperor at Rome; but by the powerful mediation of his brother Pallas, he escaped in this world the severe punishment his many crimes deserved.

* Blunt, vol. ii. p. 181.

Festus succeeded Felix in the Governor's house at Cesarea. He seems to have been a just and honourable man—a favourable contrast to his predecessor. At the outset of his official career, he was very properly anxious to get an insight into the character, customs, tastes, and feelings of those he had come to govern.* Accordingly, after he had been only three days in his new residence, he set out for Jerusalem. This, moreover, may probably have been a customary mark of respect on the part of a new imperial Prefect.

Ismael, the son of Fabei, had by this time been appointed to the vacant office of high priest,† inheriting all the bitter feelings of those who went before him towards the *Nazarenes.* No sooner did Festus arrive in the Jewish capital, than the chief priests and the leaders of the nation, along with many of the people, renewed in his ears the accusation against Paul. They were especially desirous that he would grant liberty to have him brought up for trial again at Jerusalem before the Sanhedrim—their real and covert purpose being to have hired assassins ready to despatch him on the road thither. Festus, however, in a spirit worthy of a noble-minded Roman, refused to give up his prisoner in this unlawful way; adding, if they had anything of which to accuse him, they must come down to Cesarea, and there meet him face to face. On the return of Festus, in a few days, to the seat of his government, the accusers of the Apostle followed him; the day after his arrival, we find Paul once more brought before the judgment-seat, and his relentless foes preferring their old charges. Festus, with a number of assessors or jury at his side, heard the

* Howson, vol. ii. p. 297. † Jos. book xx. chap. viii.

pleadings. He at once saw that they had reference, not to any political offences, but to differences in religious matters, which, he felt, lay beyond his province; moreover, that in all their accusations there was nothing that made the prisoner worthy of death. However, with a desire probably to gratify the accusers, and alleging the difficulty he had in settling the question, he proposed to Paul to go up under his protection to Jerusalem, and be tried there before the Sanhedrim. He promised that he would himself take part in the proceedings, and secure that these should be impartial. The Apostle saw the certain destruction awaiting him if this were determined upon. There was only one way left by which he could save himself from the "lion's mouth." But his clear judgment does not permit him for a moment to hesitate. *He claims his privilege as a Roman citizen.* He pronounces one little sentence which changes his whole history: he must have felt, while uttering it, that it involved the issues of life or death:—"I APPEAL UNTO CÆSAR."

These words, I repeat, not only changed in a moment the whole case, but gave a new character to the Apostle's future. It was not the first time we have found him availing himself of his right of *citizenship.* It was a privilege peculiarly valuable at the present crisis, protecting him, as it did, from the abuse of authority. His suit now *must* be tried before the Emperor himself, and in the Roman capital. Festus was doubtless astonished at the new turn which events had taken; perhaps, too, affronted at the great boldness of the prisoner. He consulted those around him if the plea were a sound one, and in every way admissible. Discovering that he had no power to set it aside, he declared, as the decision of the court, and as if he seemed right glad to get rid of the entire matter, "Hast thou appealed unto Cæsar? unto Cæsar shalt thou go." *

It only further remained for Festus to send to the supreme tribunal in Rome the necessary official documents about the case that was thus appealed, and to keep the person of the accused in safety before an opportunity occurred to forward him for his final trial. He was, however, in difficulty as to what charges he could specify against Paul, and which he could send along with him to the Emperor. In his perplexity, a thought occurred to him: Agrippa II., King of Chalcis, with his sister Bernice (sister also to Drusilla), had just come from Cesarea Philippi to offer their respects to Festus on his accession to the supreme power in the other Cesarea. As Agrippa had, from his earliest years, been familiar with Jewish customs and laws, Festus resolved to consult with him on this matter. He mentioned to him the opinions the prisoner was charged with holding, and especially "concerning one Jesus, who had died and was alive again." † Agrippa had often before heard of the fame of St Paul; curiosity made him desirous of seeing him personally, and next day Festus resolved to gratify his

* Among other testimonies, "a passage in Pliny's Epistle to Trajan confirms this right and privilege which Roman freemen enjoyed, of appealing from provincial courts to Rome. He thus writes:—'The method I have observed towards those who have been brought before me as Christians is this: I interrogated them whether they were Christians. If they confessed, I repeated the question twice again, adding threats at the same time, when, if they still persevered, I ordered them to be immediately punished. There were others also brought before me, possessed with the same infatuation, *but being citizens of Rome, I directed them to be carried thither.*'"—Horne's *Introduction*, vol. ii. p. 129.

† Acts xxv. 19.

wish. The Apostle, chained to the soldier who guarded him, was ushered into the audience-chamber in the Pretorium, where Agrippa, Bernice, and Festus were waiting in pomp to receive him. Roman officers quartered in the barracks and some leading people of the city were also invited to be present. Paul must have remembered the words of his Lord, which were now strikingly fulfilled as he stood in bonds before this royal audience—"Ye shall be brought before kings and rulers for my name's sake." * Festus began by making a formal speech, stating the case of the prisoner, and his perplexity in knowing how to represent it to the Emperor. Agrippa then asked Paul to speak for himself. The Apostle willingly complied. He went minutely over the circumstances of his own conversion, declaring that the faithful performance of his Divine mission to preach to the Gentiles had drawn down upon him the hatred and revenge of the Jews; that all his teaching and preaching was not contrary to, but in accordance with, Moses and the prophets, who had testified "that Messiah should suffer, and that He should be the first to rise from the dead, and should show light to the house of Israel, and also to the Gentiles." †

Festus had listened with silent attention. He could not have failed to admire the simple but impressive way in which the accused had stated his case—the grace of his manner, and the sincerity of his views. But when he heard about the bright light on the road to Damascus, the voice from heaven, and worse than all, his reference to the resurrection, he at once put the prisoner down for a fanatic or enthusiast, who had

* Matt. x. 18 † Acts xxvi. 1–23.

overworked his brain with severe study; and, interrupting him, said, "Paul, thou art beside thyself; much learning doth make thee mad." He was evidently surprised that a man so well educated and talented, and more than all, a Roman citizen, could give heed to such "cunningly devised fables"—submitting to evil, poverty, scourging, imprisonment, and all without hope of reward. To a selfish man of the world, there was nothing but insanity in all this. The Apostle calmly replied, "I am not mad, most noble Festus, but speak forth the words of truth and soberness." Then turning to Agrippa he made the appeal—"King Agrippa, believest thou the prophets? I know that thou believest;" I know that thou believest the testimony of those holy men who have told that Christ must needs suffer. The reply of Agrippa showed how deeply moved he was—"Almost thou persuadest me to be a Christian." What a confession for a monarch to make to one standing before him in chains! In answer, Paul held up his hands, clanking with these fetters, and made the noble and bold reply, "I would to God, that not only thou, but also all that hear me this day, were both almost, and altogether such as I am, except these bonds." Never was there a finer protestation—never a more glorious testimony to the happiness of the soul at peace with God. With all his chains, and the dark prospect of trial before him, the Apostle not only felt, but boldly avowed in the presence of a king, that he was the happier of the two!

But, alas! Agrippa was not "*altogether* persuaded." The name of Jesus, which was the boast of Paul, was hated by Agrippa's proud countrymen. He would not make up his mind to part with a corruptible crown, and thus, we fear, he lost the incorruptible.

The meeting thus ended. As the listeners talked the case over, they came to the conclusion that the accused had committed no crime worthy of death or of imprisonment,—indeed, Agrippa gave it as his opinion that he might have been released at once, if he had not already appealed unto Cæsar. That appeal, however, having been made by law, it could not be departed from; the first opportunity that occurs, the prisoner must be sent to Rome. His own ardent wish was thus at last to be fulfilled—not that he had ever doubted that, in some way or other, the hand of God would bring it about; for in the Castle of Antonio, you remember, two years before, his Saviour had appeared to him, and told him, that as he had witnessed for him at Jerusalem, so also was he to witness in the great city of the empire. In his voyage to the world's mighty capital, therefore, we must trace in the next chapter "the footsteps of St Paul."

CHAPTER XX.

The Shipwreck.

"Borne upon the Ocean's foam,
Far from native land and home,
Midnight's curtain, dense with wrath,
Brooding o'er our venturous path,
While the mountain wave is rolling,
And the ship's bell faintly tolling—
Saviour! on the boisterous sea
Bid us rest secure in Thee.

Blast and surge conflicting hoarse,
Sweep us on with headlong force;
And the bark, which tempests urge,
Moans and trembles at their scourge:
Yet should wildest tempests swell,
Be Thou near, and all is well—
Saviour! on the stormy sea
Let us find repose in Thee."

"If I take the wings of the morning, and dwell in the uttermost parts of the sea, even there shall Thy hand lead me, and Thy right hand shall hold me."—Ps. cxxxix. 9, 10.

IT was probably about the end of summer that Paul and his two companions, Luke and Aristarchus of Macedonia, set sail for Rome from the port of Cesarea. They embarked in a coasting vessel, bound for Adramyttium, a place in the north-west of the province of Asia Minor. We have no means of ascertaining what the crew consisted of, whether many or few. Julius, a centurion of the Augustan cohort, was the officer in charge of the prisoners; and he had a number of soldiers under him to guard them. It is not improbable there were several others on board, being conveyed, like these Christian missionaries, for trial to the capital. They coasted along the shores of Palestine and Phenicia till they arrived at Sidon. This was a distance of eighty miles, which, however, could be easily accomplished in twenty-four hours. Here, while the vessel was at anchor, Paul received permission to go on shore and visit any Christian friends or brethren. It is probable the officer had received orders, before leaving, to treat the Apostle with respect and kindness; at all events, we read "that he treated him courteously, and gave him liberty to go to his friends and refresh himself."* It is more than probable, also, that Julius had become intimately acquainted with Paul during his two years' residence at Cesarea, and had then formed that deep regard for his character which is manifested throughout tne eventful voyage on which they have just entered.†

No sooner had they set sail again from Sidon, than the wind became unfavourable, blowing from the westward. Their direct route to Asia Minor was by the southern side of Cyprus (keeping it on their right), and taking a straight course, as had been done two years before by the Apostle; but, in consequence of the wind being right against them, they had to coast along the shore, taking a circuit by the north of the Island. They must at many points have been within sight of land. Paul, for the last time, may have caught a glimpse of the lofty tops of Mount Taurus, as he sailed along the bold headlands of his native Cilicia. By the influence of some favouring breezes, which prevail at that season of the year, they made rapid progress along the Cilician and Pamphylian coasts. The first place they anchored at was *Myra*, a town in the south of the province of Lycia. Its situation was a

* Acts xxvii. 3.

† The reader is now requested to follow the line marked in ***black*** on the Map.

remarkable one—at the mouth of a narrow and precipitous valley which formed the outlet from a vast pile of mountains beyond. The town was built on a height about two and a half miles up the river, whose broad channel was guarded by a heavy chain which stretched across from shore to shore. Though now an utter ruin, Myra seems to have been, in Paul's time, a well-known and favourite port for merchant-vessels of the Mediterranean. It is not at all to be wondered at, that here our voyagers found a corn-ship of Alexandria on its way to Italy, as the Alexandrian vessels often put into its port from stress of weather.

We may wonder how these ships would take such a round-about way as this, in going to Italy. Why not skirt along the coast of Africa, and then direct northwards? The reason was, that at that season of the year a strong north-west wind always blew along the coast; and, therefore, although increasing the distance, they generally preferred going first northwards to the shores of Asia Minor, thence westwards among the Ægean islands. These islands, moreover, in the absence of the modern compass, served as landmarks to enable them to shape their course.

It would seem that the original intention had been to take the prisoners the whole way to Adramyttium, then to conduct them by land through the Via Egnatia to the port of Dyrrachium, and thence across the Adriatic to Rome. This was the route by which, in after years, one who bore the martyr-spirit of the Great Apostle, (Polycarp,) was taken from Antioch to the city of the Tiber.* But the centurion now decided on a different plan; he abandons all idea of the land-

* See Lewin, p. 713.

journey, and places his prisoners in the Alexandrian corn-ship.

It is probable that this new vessel was considerably larger than the one which brought them from Cesarea. The Egyptian ships of commerce were the largest in the Mediterranean. We must not, therefore, think of Paul in this voyage—as some of us, perhaps, have been accustomed to think of him—sailing in a rude bark, or small trading-vessel, with a handful of companions; he was within vast wooden walls, not unworthy of many of our own merchantmen.*

Lucian, who lived in the next century, gives an amusing description of one of these Alexandrian corn-ships coming into the port of Athens. It is lying at the Piræus, and the Athenians, with their well-known love of "seeing things new," come crowding down to inspect the floating monster. They are described as being greatly struck with its size—180 feet long, and 45 wide. Its masts, yards, cables, cabins, anchors, capstans, windlasses—all about it formed subject of comment and wonder; from the goddess on its prow, to the golden goose on its stern; and the corn in its store, which was enough to "keep all Attica for a year."†

They sail from the port of Myra, and they had good reason to calculate on a favourable voyage; for this being the beginning of September, the Etesian winds might be expected to cease. These, however, had continued longer than usual. He who holdeth the elements in His hands, had some wise reason for detaining the south wind, which would have brought them in due time to a quiet haven.

A distance of 130 miles, to Cnidus, is performed

* Howson. † See the passage given in full by Mr Lewin.

slowly—after "many days." Tossed about with contrary weather, they resolve to run down to the southern shores of Crete, where they would be protected from the fury of the north-west wind, and take refuge, if needed, in some of its harbours. By tacking and beating about, they accomplished the voyage without difficulty till they came to Cape Matala; but, whenever they doubled that promontory, the full force of the westerly gale met them in the face, and no vessel could ride out the blast. They gladly ran into a place called Fair Havens, and anchored behind some bold rocks. It now became a question whether it would be advisable to winter there, or to proceed to another harbour, and a more secure one—the port of Phœnix, or Lutro, forty miles westward. A council seems to have been held on board the ship. It shows the confidence reposed already in the good judgment of Paul, that he was not only permitted to be present, but allowed to give his opinion as to what was best to be done in the present "perils of waters." He was clearly of opinion they should not proceed, but avail themselves of the roadstead in "Fair Havens." "Sirs," said he, "I perceive that this voyage will be with hurt and much damage, not only of the lading and ship, but also of our lives."* But the advice, which so soon turned out a wise one, was not assented to. The centurion naturally thought the captain and pilot were better judges, and he decided that they should proceed.

Towards the close of October, the wind all at once suddenly changed; the sky cleared, the sails were hoisted, and the crew, little aware of coming dangers,

* Acts xxvii. 10.

were proceeding round Cape Matala to this new anchorage. All at once, after rounding the Cape, another violent wind came sweeping down from the mountains of Crete. It was a peculiar hurricane, known to the sailors by the name of Euroclydon. So furious was it, that they were utterly unable either to retrace their steps or proceed. They were at the mercy of the storm. The helmsman lost all command over the vessel. They were involved in a sort of whirlwind, which lashed the sea into fury, and drove them in the direction of Clauda, now Gozzo, a small island to the southwest of Crete. There being, however, no anchorage there, there was nothing for it but to make every preparation for weathering the storm. Large ropes, which they had on board just to meet such an emergency as now occurred, were taken for "undergirding" the ship; that is to say, they were tied round and round the under-part of the vessel, meeting on the deck, the design being to prevent the consequences of springing a leak;* perhaps the storm had raged so violently, when her sails were up, as to have already strained her and started her timbers. They "lowered the gear," took down a number of sails, some of which were doubtless already shivered to pieces, and others which, by remaining up, added to their danger.

The vessel now drifted from Clauda west by north. They must beware, however, of scudding before the wind, else twenty-four hours will sweep them a wreck on the great sandbank of Africa. These sandbanks

* An instance of the same kind is mentioned in Lord Anson's *Voyage Round the World.* Speaking of a Spanish man-of-war in a storm, he says, 'They were obliged to throw overboard all their upper-deck guns, and take six turns of the cable round the ship to prevent her opening."—Quoted by Barnes.

were constantly shifting their position by the action of the sea, so that they could not be sure how near they might be to danger. The storm rages fiercely as ever. The second and third day pass, and no prospect of abatement. The day after Clauda was left, they took the precaution to lighten the ship by casting overboard what was least valuable. More than probably she had now "sprung a leak," water was fast getting in, and, on the third day, all hands on deck were employed in throwing whatever could be spared overboard. In this was included the tackling of the ship; and when Luke tells us, "we cast it out with our own hands," we may picture the Great Apostle and Evangelist lending their assistance in these awful moments. The vast main-yard would require every effort to plunge it into the roaring sea.

Days of suspense and hardship followed. The sky was quite dark; no observations could be made. My readers may picture the terrible scene. The creaking of the timbers—the howling of the storm—the passengers, with exhausted bodies, plying the pumps night and day, and all seemingly in vain. "Neither stars nor sun were seen for many days." Where they were, they could not tell; for the valuable compass, as I have a little ago said, was not discovered at that time, and they were wholly dependent on the observation of the heavenly bodies. The next moment they might strike on some rock, or be driven on some unknown shore. Add to all this, the provisions were so injured, that they began to suffer from want of food; and so fast was the water gaining ground, that the crew seem to have resigned themselves to hopeless despair.

Where was Paul all this while? Doubtless he bore his part nobly in all these sufferings and endurances; but there was one duty which he specially engaged in, in those hours of terror. As at Damascus, in the quiet chamber of the street called "Straight," so here, amid the moanings of the storm, "behold, he prayeth!"

"Behold the man of God!
His hallow'd voice of prayer
Rises above the stifled groan
Of that intense despair.

How precious are those tones
On that sad verge of life,
Amid the fierce and freezing storm,
And the mountain-billows' strife!"

His prayer is heard! He had been wrestling with that God who commandeth the winds and the sea, and they obey him. God, at midnight, gives his honoured servant another of those visions with which he had already more than once favoured him in his hour of trial. An angel wings his flight across these dark waters—visits that labouring vessel—and, amid the roar of the pitiless storm, whispers, "Fear not, Paul." The Apostle, at the dawn of the next day, calls the heathen passengers and crew around him; and, lifting up his own voice amid the din of the waters, told the glad news: "Sirs, ye should have hearkened unto me, and not have loosed from Crete, and to have gained this harm and loss. And now I exhort you to be of good cheer: for there shall be no loss of any man's life among you, but of the ship. For there stood by me this night the angel of God, whose I am, and whom I serve, saying, Fear not, Paul; thou must be brought before Cæsar: and lo, God hath given thee all them that sail with thee. Wherefore, sirs, be of good cheer. for I believe God, that it shall be even as it was told me. Howbeit we must be cast upon a certain island." *

There is something very sublime in this. To see a poor bound prisoner, on his way to the bar, a convict, in a convict ship, standing forth at this awful crisis, alone able to comfort and sustain a sinking crew. He had known in the past the faithfulness of God's word, and he believes it now. He looked around him on the mountain billows, but he rejoiced in the Psalmist's assurance, "The Lord sitteth on the floods, yea, the Lord sitteth King for ever." "Though the waters thereof roar and be troubled,—though the mountains shake with the swelling thereof,"—"the Lord on high is mightier than the noise of many waters, yea, than the mighty waves of the sea." The night before, "all hope that they should be saved was taken away." The next day no ray of light fringed these dark clouds; but, though the sea was still running mountains high, he was not afraid,—"his heart was fixed, trusting in the Lord."

His speech soothed the agitated spirits around. The crew were nerved by his words of encouragement, and set themselves with new vigour to weather the tempest. It was raging still with unabated violence. Fourteen days in succession they drifted along the trough of the ocean. At the close of the fourteenth day, about midnight, the well-known sound of "breakers" fell on the ear of the trembling mariners, and warned them that they must be drawing near to land. Through the hazy darkness they descried to the left a fringe of white foam. They let down the sounding-lead—the depth of the sea

* Acts xxvii. 21–26.

was twenty fathoms; they sounded shortly after, it was only fifteen! As they were so rapidly coming to shallow water, they saw that their only hope of safety was to get the ship anchored till day-dawn, and then to run in the best way they could to some creek or bay in this strange coast. Orders were given to cast out four anchors by the stern; but after this was done, as they had good ground to fear she might break from these and be driven on shore, every eye "looked anxiously for the day."

And what land was this they were now approaching? All the description we have of it in the Acts is, "a certain island." Able writers, who have turned their attention to the subject, have most satisfactorily proved that this could be none other than the island of *Malta*, which the youngest reader knows to be situated to the south of Sicily. You may picture to yourselves these terrible moments—land close at hand, but death and destruction between! The sea rolling mountains high, the vessel pitching all the more heavily by the strain from her anchors. The breakers were roaring ahead—the leak was increasing—the rain or sleet poured down from a black sky. The sailors, fearing that the ship would go to pieces before daylight, were making an unmanly attempt to save themselves and leave the others to the mercy of the storm. They lowered the small boat from the side of the vessel under a false pretence, saying that another anchor would require to be let down to steady the pitching ship, but that it would be needful, for this purpose, to convey it first of all in the boat to a little distance. Paul detected their cowardly purpose, and saw that, if they did not wait and assist, they would all perish. "Except these abide in the ship," said he, "ye cannot be saved." The Apostle directed his remonstrance, not to the sailors, but to the soldiers and the centurion. It showed the influence this great man had acquired. They instantly decided the matter by cutting the ropes by which the small boat was let down—it plunged into the sea, and was left to drift away in the dark, and become the sport of the breakers.

The dawn of day broke wildly in the eastern horizon. It was a gladsome sight, but only served to disclose to them more fearfully the reality of their peril. The clouds of spray still screened from view the adjoining shore. Of many shipwrecks, doubtless, we all have read; but there is something of terrible interest surely in the one before us. Imagine 276 individuals, wan with terror, and faint from want of food and rest, clustered together on the deck, which they expected to see every moment shivered under their feet. As the gray dawn of morning is lighting dimly up these countenances, one figure stands conspicuous in the midst of them. He began that voyage a prisoner—he is now their acknowledged director and counsellor; even the heathen sailors and crew have seen that a nobler spirit than that of earth animates him. He again raises his voice in the storm—he reminds them that for fourteen days they had gone without food; that it was a duty to suspend for a little their labour, and partake of the gifts which God had given them—adding, moreover, as a reason, that a hair of their head would not perish. He himself set the example, and in the dim light of that eventful morning, in presence of the crew, he said *grace*, asked the divine blessing on the food of which he partook, and, in accordance with his advice and example, they partook also.

Their next occupation was to unburden the vessel of the cargo of wheat, which not only added to the difficulty of running safely ashore, but probably it had also been so soaked with sea-water as to be rendered useless. This done, the lingering shades of night had all dispersed, and the land appeared.

On looking towards the shore, they observed a small creek, or bay, with a sandy beach; here they were anxious, if possible, to effect a landing. After making necessary preparations for the hazardous attempt (setting up the foresail, taking up the anchors, and loosing the rudder-bands), in a place where two seas meet, they ran the ship aground. A sand bank, a little in front of the shore, had been concealed by the waves; on this the forepart of the vessel stuck fast, but the hinder part was driven to pieces by the violence of the billows. It was quite evident now that nothing possibly could save the ship,— a few minutes more, and her shivered planks would be strewed over the waters. In this perilous moment the thought struck the soldiers, what shall we do with our prisoners, Paul among the number? If they escape from our hands, we shall be responsible for their safety. Their first proposal, under a stern sense of duty, was to kill them at once; and there seems little doubt this would have been carried into effect, had it not been for the influence the Apostle had gained over the centurion. It would indeed have been an unpardonable act to have dyed these raging waters with the blood of those who had struggled so bravely in behalf of the crew; and more especially to sacrifice the life of one whose presence and manly bearing had so greatly contributed hitherto to their safety. The centurion, therefore, "willing to save Paul," gave orders that all who could swim should plunge into the water, and make the best of their way to the shore. His advice was immediately obeyed—some swam, others on broken boards and pieces of the vessel surmounted the angry breakers, and they got all safe to land.*

"The name of the island was *Melita.*" Malta was then a thinly-peopled place, and its inhabitants were of Phœnician origin. The bay where they landed was a few miles to the north of the present capital, Valetta, and is screened on the north by the rocky island of Salmonetta. It is remarkable that the soundings at the eastern entrance of the bay at this day exactly correspond with those given in the Acts. A number of the islanders, who had witnessed the labouring of the Alexandrian corn ship, now crowded down to the creek where the faint and weary crew were huddled together, drawing breath, after so long a period of terrible torture. They are called "barbarians," but their natural kindness got the better of any baser passions. They sympathised with the shivering sufferers; and in some sheltered hollow they lighted a fire to restore warmth. We may imagine how grateful this would be, when we remember that most of them must have been soaked and dripping with sea-water. Some had no clothes at all; the rain was pelting from above; and all this under the chill and wintry winds of November. The Apostle himself had been assisting in collecting sticks to kindle the blaze, and was casting these into the

* See the picture

flames, when a viper came "out of the heat," and fastened on his hand. The natives, when they beheld this, immediately drew the conclusion that Paul must be a murderer—that, though he had escaped the sea, vengeance still pursued him, and would not suffer him to live. How remarkable, that even among barbarians there is a conviction of the certainty of vengeance overtaking the sinner,—nature confirming the Bible truth, that, "though hand join in hand, the wicked shall not escape unpunished!" The Apostle shook the reptile into the flames. They expected every moment to see his body swelling with the poisonous sting, and falling lifeless to the ground; but when they saw that he remained unharmed, they gazed with wonder, and pronounced him to be a god. An objection has been raised by some to the accuracy of the incident here recorded, that no poisonous vipers or snakes are now found in Malta. The answer, however, is quite satisfactory. At the time of St Luke, Malta was an uncultivated, unpeopled island; whereas, now, it is, without exception, for its size, the most densely crowded spot in Europe; and population and civilization always tend to rid an insular country of dangerous tribes of animals. We have seen the Highlanders on a Scottish loch point with pride to the hill on which the last wolf in Britain was killed. We cannot, at all events, receive the silly and superstitious explanation which tradition gives us, and which is believed in by some of the islanders to this day. They think that the same kind of vipers still exist, but that they ceased to be poisonous reptiles ever since the Apostle flung the one which fastened on him into the fire. They tell a story of an islander, from curiosity, carrying one of these vipers into Sicily, and that it immediately became poisonous, but on coming back again to the charmed land of Malta, its venom left it! *

But to return to the narrative. We are not told what further effect this miracle had upon the minds of the people. It was not the only exertion of miraculous power on the part of the Apostle. Near the spot where the vessel was wrecked, Publius, the governor of the island, had his residence and possessions. He received kindly the shipwrecked crew, and entertained them for three days. His humanity and pity did not go unrewarded. His aged father was, at the time, lying dangerously ill of fever. St Paul went and laid his hands on him, and prayed, and his recovery ensued. Others who had diseases heard of the marvellous cure, and came themselves to be healed. Before the strangers departed, they were laden with proofs of the gratitude of the islanders.

We cannot resist mentioning, in passing, that there is a name we have often had occasion to refer to in the notes at the foot of the page, which possesses some interest in connexion with Paul's voyage and shipwreck,—it is that of the Jewish historian *Josephus,* whose writings tend to throw so much valuable light on that period. There seems, at least, a *probability* that he formed one of the crew in the Alexandrian corn-ship; and, if so, that he met the Apostle, and was witness of the prisoner's noble bearing throughout the storm. Without offering any opinion on the subject, I shall quote to you the words of the young historian himself, who, at the age of twenty-five, made a voyage to Rome, and gives the following account of it:—"At the time when

* See note in Stackhouse's *History of the Bible,* vol. vi. p. 421.

Felix was procurator of Judea, there were certain priests of my acquaintance, good and worthy persons, whom, on a small and trifling occasion, he had put into bonds and sent to Rome to plead their cause before Cæsar. For these I was desirous to procure deliverance, and that especially because I was informed that they were not unmindful of piety towards God even under their affliction, but supported themselves with figs and nuts. Accordingly, I came to Rome, though it was often through great hazards by sea; for our ship being wrecked in the midst of the Adriatic Sea, we that were in it swam for our lives all the night, when, upon the first appearance of the day, a ship of Cyrene appearing to us by the providence of God, I and some others, eighty in all, going before the rest, were taken up into the ship. And when I had thus escaped and came to Puteoli, I became acquainted with Aliturus, an actor of plays, a Jew by birth, and much beloved by Nero, and, through his interest, became known to Poppæa, Cæsar's wife, and took care, as soon as possible, to entreat her to procure that the priests might be set at liberty." We shall immediately find this was the same direction Paul and his friends followed from Malta.

Three months had been spent on the hospitable shores of that island home, the Apostle doubtless taking every opportunity, in exchange for their temporal, to give its people of "spiritual things." It is unlikely that he who would not pass a night in a dungeon without preaching the gospel, could now continue twelve weeks with his lips silent regarding the truth. Tradition even says that Publius himself not only became a Christian, but died Bishop of Malta. We know that, ever since the shipwreck of Paul, the religion of Christ has had a footing in that island. My young readers may have heard that, in 1838, our former good Queen Adelaide visited Malta, and that, among the first objects which meet the eye of the voyager in landing, is a Christian church, a memorial of her piety and generosity.

The season of the year when our voyagers could, with favourable winds, prosecute their route, had now set in, and Julius was desirous, without delay, of reaching the capital. Here the Alexandrian ship, called the "Castor and Pollux," had wintered at Malta, and was again about to sail for Italy. Castor and Pollux, it is scarcely necessary to add, were two fabled twin brothers among the Roman deities. They were supposed to be sons of Jupiter, who, at their death, were translated to heaven, and formed into a constellation under the name of *Gemini* (or twins). Sailors were considered to be specially under their protection; hence it was a favourite name for Roman vessels, and their image was often placed on the ship's prow, as was possibly the case with the one in which the Apostle now embarks.

The voyage was completed in safety without any memorable occurrence. They put in for three days into the famous harbour of Syracuse in Sicily, one hundred miles distant from Malta. We are not told whether Paul landed; but it is more than probable that the permission granted him by Julius before, would not be refused him here,* and that he preached in this sea-port of the West "the unsearchable riches of Christ."

Syracuse was at that time, a great mercantile city.

* Howson, vol. ii. p. 358.

It was situated on a bold promontory, jutting out at the east of the island; and the bay, in which hundreds of ships rode at anchor, was screened on the south by the island of Ortygia. The Apostle must, at all events, have gazed on the beautiful buildings which lined the shore, "the fair walls of white marble" which surrounded the town; also the temples of Jupiter, Diana, and Minerva,—the latter towering high in the centre of Ortygia,—these testifying too plainly to its Pagan worship. It was, however, greatly shorn, by this time, of its ancient extent and splendour, although the loveliness of the surrounding scenery, both by sea and land, no changes could alter.

Again they set sail, and after beating about for some time, they reached, under less favourable weather, the town of Rhegium, situated on the extreme south of Italy, just before entering the Straits of Messina. After one day spent here, they availed themselves of a fair wind from the south, passed through the Straits, and the favourable breeze still continuing, they were at anchor "next day" in the harbour of Puteoli.

Puteoli, now Pozzuoli, was situated at the northern curve of that loveliest of all bays, the Bay of Naples, which extends from twenty-five to thirty miles across: the northern promontory being called the Promontory of Misenum; the southern, that of Minerva. As Paul and his fellow-passengers passed the latter, the rocky island of Capreæ, with its white cliffs and rugged outline, must have been close at their right. It seemed to have been placed by nature as a barrier to check the tempest, and protect the interior of the bay from its fury.* But it recalled sadder thoughts, as blackened

* Eustace

with the dreadful sins and crimes of the Emperor Tiberius. He was one of those of whom the Apostle speaks as "being past feeling, having given themselves over to licentiousness to work all uncleanness with greediness." Paul must have gazed with horror on the precipice from which the monster used to hurl, after fearful torture, the victims of his cruelty, while hired ruffians were waiting in boats at the foot of the rock to despatch them with oars and bludgeons.*

They have entered the lovely Bay of Naples. No wonder the Romans selected Venus, the fabled goddess of love and beauty, to preside over the baths, fountains, and groves of this delicious shore. "A sky for ever serene—seas never ruffled—perpetual spring and eternal verdure, may be supposed to have allured the goddess to her new abode." † The most prominent object in the landscape was Vesuvius,—not, as now, the angry guardian of the scene, but a soft and beautiful mountain with vine-clad sides. Herculaneum and Pompeii, now dug from their bed of lava and ashes, were then sleeping in quiet grandeur at the foot of the mountain. But a short time after Paul gazed on them from the "Castor and Pollux," they were entombed in their lava sepulchre; and the historian Josephus mentions that, among others who were buried in this living grave were Drusilla and her little one, before whom and her husband Felix the Apostle had so recently reasoned of a still more terrible "judgment to come." ‡

We may imagine the scene as the Egyptian corn-vessel

* Suetonius's *Life of Tiberius*

† Eustace's *Classical Tour*, vol. i. p. 374.

‡ Howson and Conybeare, vol. ii. p 360

approached the harbour of Puteoli. Crowds of people would be loitering about the docks, watching its approach. This old seaport was situated on a smaller but scarce less beautiful bay of blue water, running five miles northward from the larger one, sheltered by the promontory of Misenum from the south wind. While Puteoli was built on the eastern side, the well-known Baiæ (the great resort for people of fashion at particular seasons from Rome) occupied the west. Puteoli looked across to the elegant villas of this "Roman Brighton,"—the marine palace of Nero rising conspicuously, among myrtle-trees and orange-groves, to the left.

Paul must have gazed upon those magnificent buildings, the remains of which the modern traveller sees in fine weather down in the clear water, which has now encroached upon the old shore; or rather, they are parts of those dwellings to which Horace humorously refers, when he speaks of the Romans as not being content with the space the land gives them, they must needs encroach on the territory of the sea :—

"And though the waves indignant roar,
Forward you urge the Baian shore;
While earth's too narrow bounds in vain
Your guilty progress would restrain." *

From Puteoli, an artificial mole jutted out far into the sea, worthy, from its dimensions, of belonging to the port of the world's capital. Puteoli indeed was the great "sea-gateway" to the imperial city. The grain-waggons, that fed the many thousands within the walls of Rome, passed through its streets ; others were filled with the finer sorts of wood, brought by vessels from

* See Eustace's *Classical Tour*, p. 373.

Africa to make furniture for the Roman houses; others with blocks of marble and granite, from African and Asiatic quarries, to be fashioned into baths or statuary for the adornment of Roman palaces. There are still seventeen piers of the ancient mole remaining, within which the merchant-vessels rode at anchor, and on which stood the lighthouse.

We are told by Seneca, that when an Alexandrian corn-ship hove in sight, they were, unlike other vessels, privileged to enter the bay in full sail; all others were compelled to lower their topsail. When the "Castor and Pollux," therefore, was seen entering with her sails fully spread to the breeze, we may imagine the crowd at the pier assembling to receive her, and see her cargo and crew disembarked. We may picture to ourselves the Great Apostle standing on the deck of the vessel, as the shores of illustrious Italy first opened to him! In entering the Piræus at Athens, he had felt himself going among the world's sages and philosophers; here, it was amid the lavish opulence and splendour of the Mistress of Kingdoms. The power and wealth of Rome glittered around that beautiful bay. The first object probably his eye rested on, after passing the promontory of Misenum, was the Roman navy riding at anchor,—next, the palace of Baulos, which we have just mentioned,—then villa on villa at Baiæ. If the day was calm, hundreds of pleasure-boats and yachts would be studding the bay, with their white sails and gaily-coloured pennons. At last, entering the harbour of Puteoli, amid the clattering of ship-hammers and the heavy roll of laden waggons. the busy hum of ten thousand voices in the Latin tongue intimated that they were nearing one of the two "*Liverpools* of Italy," of which Ostia, at the mouth of the Tiber, was the other. Of the two, however, Puteoli was the more important; it admitted to its port vessels of dimensions of which Ostia could not boast.*

Josephus informs us, that from the connexion of its trade with Alexandria and the surrounding eastern countries, there were many Jews residing at Puteoli. The Great Apostle found also Christian disciples. They had been long anxiously expecting to see his face; now their fondest wishes were gratified. He came, indeed, "bearing in his body the marks of the Lord Jesus." He was not then the bold and vigorous Roman citizen who had stood, a few years before, on Mars' Hill among Grecian sages; he was now a prisoner chained to a soldier's arm, wan and weary after a voyage chequered with so many disasters; but he was still "strong" as ever "in the Lord, and in the power of His might;" and though moral storms, more fearful far than what he had undergone in the Sea of Adria, might be in reserve for him, he could look calm and undismayed, amid them all, towards the better haven above, and feel that that God, who had made good His promise in the one, would be equally faithful regarding the other.

It was indeed a memorable day, in the annals of the infant Church, which brought its great ambassador to the shores of imperial Italy—to the very bay, also, which was fresh with the footprints of Augustus and Cicero, Horace, Virgil, and Mæcenas. The harbour of Puteoli had, 250 years before the time of Paul, witnessed an imposing spectacle in the landing of the embassy from Carthage at the close of the second Punic

* See Howson, Lewin, and Olshausen.

war, to sue for peace at the gates of the capital; but there was a truer moral grandeur in the arrival of this poor Voyager, whose errand, from a mightier than earthly court, was, not to sue for peace, but to proclaim, in the name of the King of kings, the only true peace for men and for nations—"peace through the blood of the Cross."

No sooner did he arrive, than tidings were sent of the event to the brethren in Rome. The Puteoli Christians requested that he might be allowed to remain a few days with them. Julius, who owed, in common with all the crew, such a debt of gratitude to the prisoner, consented.

We shall close this chapter, leaving the Apostle to enjoy this short while of quiet in this bustling city, before setting out on the last stage of his journey to the world's great capital.

CHAPTER XXI.

Paul in Rome.

"Jesus! avenger of our fall,
Thou faithful lover above all
The cross has ever borne!
O tell me—life is in Thy voice—
How much afflictions were Thy choice,
And sloth and ease Thy scorn?

Thy choice and mine shall be the same,
Inspirer of that holy flame,
Which must for ever blaze!
To take the cross and follow Thee,
Where love and duty lead, shall be
My portion and my praise."

COWPER.

"The Apostle prisoner; but, though a prisoner, an Apostle. . . . A spiritual Atlas—Paul carries the whole heathen world upon his shoulders. That Roman empire, the most powerful on the face of the earth, which required seven ages to be established, this man takes only a quarter of an age to regenerate."—MONOD.

What a change of scene now waited the Apostle! All at once, from the dreary experiences of his sea-voyage, he found himself travelling, under the escort of soldiers, along one of the great public highways leading to the capital.

We have no means of knowing what particular road was selected. There was one that led in a northern direction by Capua; but it is more probable they adopted the route along the coast, as the most direct, by Vulturnum and Sinuessa to Minturnæ. In either case, however, the little band would be treading the famous *Appian Way*, which still remains, like other monuments of antiquity. It is from 13 to 14 feet broad, having a hewn foundation, with regularly-formed stones above, smooth and square, fitting in to one another, and many of which, after 2000 years, are comparatively little worn.* As in our modern turnpikes, milestones were set up on this great highway every twenty miles, where were erected also inns or taverns for the baiting of horses and mules, and the accommodation of travellers.† Many objects of interest must have passed before the Apostle's eye. The vine-clad plains of fertile Campania; the villas and terraces of beautiful Formiæ, where the illustrious Cicero had his favourite retreat; the walls, now seen scattered over the fields, and half covered with vines, olives, and hedges, must then have been entire, and full of the memory of the great orator. The road continued thence through the narrow passes of the Cœcuban hills, touching once more the sea, where the splendid villas and palaces of the ancient Auxur crowned the cliffs which towered above. Paul must have observed, conspicuous above the rest of the buildings, the Temple of Jupiter, standing on the summit of the rock, and looking over the vast country, on every side of which he was regarded as the protector and guardian. Crossing the mountains immediately above Auxur, the travellers would find themselves again in an extensive level, stretching miles on miles in the far distance, with patches here and there of luxuriant pasture, grazed on by numerous herds of cattle and horses. Here were the celebated Pomptine marshes, through which, in the time of the Apostle, a canal (still remaining, and called Cavata) had been formed by Augustus, mainly with the view of draining the morass. At its commencement, a few paces from the road, there was a fountain in the midst of a grove, with a temple, sacred to Feronia, the goddess of freedom. One soli-

* Eustace's *Classical Tour*. † See Lewin.

tary ilex, hanging over the fountain, is all the modern traveller can discover of the old thicket. The temple has sunk into the dust, and not even a stone remains. Slaves who were about to obtain their freedom were brought to this shrine; they were seated within on a sacred chair, and on rising were declared free. Such was the form of religious rite in obtaining *earthly* freedom. Some may have been at the moment kneeling or coming forth rejoicing in the assurance that they were slaves no more, when the Apostle of a nobler *spiritual* freedom was passing by. That chained prisoner could have told them of a nobler and purer *fountain*, washing in which they could be made "free indeed," rejoicing in "the glorious liberty of the sons of God."

We are not informed whether Julius and his band continued their journey on the paved road, or in track-boats dragged by mules. It is probable they would use the latter, which were most commonly employed; and if so, the *time* of travelling would be the same as that spoken of by other wayfarers. Horace, in his *Satires*, gives a vivid description of a night journey along the canal. He complains of the buzzing of gnats, the croaking of frogs, and the still more vexatious tardiness of the muleteer, who took sixteen hours to a distance of twenty-seven miles. Night was the time, as Strabo relates, when passengers were in the habit of commencing their journey, because the vapours, continually arising from the swamps, are less noxious then than during the heat of the day.* At the end of the canal, eighteen miles from Terracina, and fifty-one miles from Rome, was a place called *Appii Forum*, filled with low taverns, where the mules were unyoked after

* Eustace's *Tour*, p. 321.

a long stage. It was called, probably, after the consul Appius Claudius, who had constructed this famous Appian Way, and to whose memory a statue had been erected in the busy town which bore his name.* It was a well-known place of refreshment for travellers passing north or south, and enjoyed no very favourable reputation. It was the noted resort, in that age, of what we may call the "swell mob" of the Italian London. Thieves, pickpockets, and pedlars had always a promising trade amid its bustle and confusion.†

In the dense and busy crowd of idlers and traffickers there, we are led to wonder if Paul would meet one friend to cheer his drooping spirit? Strange to say, in that unlikeliest of places, Christian friends discover him, and amid the rude voices and jostling of the multitude, the disciples of a crucified Jesus embrace one another! The Christians from Rome had heard from their brethren at Puteoli of the Apostle's arrival. They had come down to this meeting-place, fifty-one miles from the capital, to welcome him. They might probably have gone even further; but not knowing whether he would travel by the road or the canal, they waited at the common terminus of both, *Appii Forum.*

Ten miles farther on, at a place called "The Three Taverns," ‡ a second band of Christian friends met him —perhaps the older and more infirm, who had tarried behind their more robust and younger brethren. The spirit of the Aged Apostle revived. He had for long

* Calmet. † See Horace *Sat.*, v. 3.

‡ In the time of Constantine we find that the Three Taverns had become the seat of a bishop. That emperor appointed nineteen bishops throughout his dominions, to settle the controversy between Donatus and Cæcilianus, and among these we find the name of *Felix a Tribus Tabernis* (Felix from "The Three Taverns").—Hammond's *Annotations.*

been accustomed to nothing but a prison life; for two years frowns more than smiles had been familiar to him; but prisoner though still he was, he had much of the aspect of a hero returning in triumph. Never did a nobler champion tread the Appian Way, nor one more truly entitled to the term of "Great." There is a world of touching meaning in Luke's short statement, "When Paul saw the brethren, he thanked God, and took courage." His sensitive heart was deeply touched by the kindness of those who, in a strange land, thus welcomed him. He was doubtless cheered also by seeing the liberty they appeared to enjoy. Seventeen miles farther brought him to the base of the Alban hills. These separated the plains we have just spoken of from the Campagna of Rome. Here he would pass through the lovely valley of Aricia, and see probably the same dark background spoken of by modern travellers, "formed by the groves and evergreen forests that clothe the higher regions of the mountains." * Gay equipages would be increasing on his view, and crowded villas and gardens studding the slopes of the Alban mount. After two other gentle elevations, he would get his first glimpse of the Great Capital of the world, with its two millions of human beings! Perhaps he saw it first at the hour the poet describes—

"'Tis sunset on the Palatine. A flood
Of living glory wraps the Sabine hills,
And o'er the rough and serrate Apennines
Floats like a burning mantle."

What his impressions were when its domes and columns rose before him, we cannot say. His feelings regarding it must, at least, have been very different

* Eustace.

from those recorded of the St Paul of the sixteenth century, whom we have more than once already compared with our Apostle. To the former, with all its glory and grandeur, as mistress of the nations, Rome was a *heathen* city in the saddest sense, full of dreadful vice, her boasted virtues only what an old writer calls "splendid sins." When the Saxon monk, on the other hand, first saw the city of the Tiber, the chains of superstition were still binding him. He was yet a devoted son of the Papal Church, his eyes closed to those enormous evils which he was yet to expose before Christendom. Rome, therefore, was still to him what Jerusalem was to the child of Abraham. It was the mother of all Churches—the Zion of the gospel age —the "city of God." The historian of the German Reformer thus describes Luther's first approach to it:— "After a painful journey in the beginning of summer, under the burning sun of Italy, he approached the seven-hilled city; his heart was stirred, his eyes sought the Queen of the World and of the Church. As soon as he caught sight in the distance of the eternal city —the city of St Peter and St Paul—the metropolis of Catholicity—he prostrated himself on the ground, exclaiming, 'Holy Rome, I salute thee!'" Paul's exclamation, if he had any, must have been very different. We may well suppose it would rather have been this, "*Unhappy* Rome! I *pity* thee! but, in the name of my divine Lord and Master, I come proclaiming to thee a freedom which all thy boasted glory knows nothing of!"

Soon they were in the vast suburbs, among villas, gardens, and tombs. The houses became denser, the streets narrower. At last they come to the Porta

Capena, the great arch through which often and again triumphant legions had marched. Continuing their way through the streets, they reached the *Forum,* the great centre of interest, where the golden milestone stood, at which the various roads, leading to different parts of Italy, met.* Gigantic buildings rose all around it—arches, colonnades, temples, and statues. Porticoes lined either side; under one stood, in bronze, the Latin and Roman kings, from Æneas down to Tarquinius Superbus; on the other were ranged the Roman heroes, all in triumphal robes. In the centre rose a colossal statue of Augustus.† How striking a contrast is the description of the same scene by a traveller eighteen hundred years later, who, in describing its "colonnades encumbering the pavements buried under their ruins"—"shattered porticoes, broken shafts, and vast fragments of marble capitals, and cornices heaped together," concludes by saying, "A herdsman seated on a pedestal, while his oxen were drinking at the fountain, and a few passengers moving at a distance in different directions, were the only living beings that disturbed the silence and solitude which reigned around!"‡ The Capitoline hill terminated the other end of the Forum; and if we are correct in describing the Apostle's route, it must have now risen straight before him. It had on its summit the parent temple of the imperial city. A hundred steps led up to the shrine of Jupiter Tonans. It is described as having been "adorned with all the refinements of art, and blazing with the plunder of the world. In the centre of the temple, with Juno on his left, and Minerva on his right side, the Thunderer

* See Eustace's *Tour,* vol. ii. p. 83. † Eustace, vol. ii. p. 88.
‡ See our picture of the Forum as it now is, in ruins.

sat on a throne of gold, grasping the lightning in one hand, and in the other wielding the sceptre of the universe." On the Apostle's left rose the palace of the Cæsars on the Palatine; where was preserved, in the midst of the gorgeous buildings, the lowly cottage of Romulus thatched with reeds. The dominion of the founder of Rome extended no further than the seven hills. But in the time of Paul, this Palatine hill alone was found too small for the imperial palace; and no wonder! when we read of its avenues, triple porticoes, and thousand columns, extending for a mile in length. A flight of steps led up from the Forum to the royal residence. Sentries paced in front of the gates, and the palisades were crowned with laurel, in token of victory. A temple of Apollo stood within the royal precincts, and spacious gardens stretched down towards the circus behind.

It is more than probable that the place to which Paul was conducted was the camp or barrack of the Pretorians,—a large square with buildings all round, erected during the reign of Tiberius, outside the city walls. The Pretorian troops were the picked favourites in the Roman army. There were ten thousand of them in all. They were in receipt of double pay, besides other privileges not possessed by the rest of the soldiers. We may imagine, then, the Great Apostle conducted outside the gate of the city, and entering through strong fortifications into these imperial barracks. He and his guard would cross a deep ditch, or *vallum*, which enclosed the camp, and then by a gateway they would reach the interior of the barracks. His eye would probably rest on a large field immediately in front for military exercise and where, a few years before, the Britian king Caractacus had been led in triumph. Many prisoners from distant parts of the empire were within these same walls. He might hear the clank of the chain by which they were fastened to the attendant soldier, giving him intimation of what might be waiting himself! God, however, had in his mercy ordered for his servant a kindlier treatment. Afranius Burrus was at this time the Pretorian Prefect.* He was a hardy, but noble-minded Roman, whom Tacitus describes as having his one hand maimed with honourable wounds. To him Paul was surrendered by Julius. The latter, it is evident, had mentioned favourably to the Roman Prefect the character and heroic spirit of his prisoner, and peculiarly commended him to his clemency. Burrus was convinced that he had been guilty of no crime worthy of bonds. But as it was needful for him to undergo the form of a trial, the Prefect could not with safety grant him his liberty. He so far relaxed, however, the severity of imprisonment by allowing him to live in his own hired lodging in the city, with the usual precaution of having a soldier by him, to whom he was chained. These soldiers probably relieved one another. Who can tell but that under the instructions of their prisoner, their hardened spirits may have learned to "fight the good fight of faith, and to lay hold of eternal life"? What sort of an apartment Paul occupied, of course we can form no conjecture. As silver and gold he had none, most probably the expense of it was defrayed by the "devout brethren" who had come to welcome him at *Appii Forum.* If so, they would probably secure a room of sufficient dimensions to form "a church in the house," where they might

* Tacit. *Ann.* xii. 42. 1.

meet often, and listen to his heart-stirring words. Here he was left in custody, to be tried in due time before the emperor.

Nero was now sovereign of the Roman world. He was still but a youth of twenty-one, but his life of guilt and infamy had already begun. His beauty, among other things, had proved a snare to him. He delighted to deck himself out in finery, and his light glossy hair hung in ringlets, like a woman's, over his shoulders. His whole education gives us a painful specimen of the follies of what was thought a brilliant age. His early guardians and instructors were his aunt Lepida, a dancing master, and a barber! and when, as a mere youth, he was exalted to the throne of the world, the frivolity of his early training showed itself in public exhibitions in the theatre, where the emperor played on the harp, sang, and recited verses of his own, amid thunders of applause. Upon one of these rehearsals, a solemn thanksgiving to the gods was decreed, and still further to flatter his vanity, it was resolved to dedicate a part of the verses in letters of gold to Jupiter Capitolinus;—a folly trifling in comparison with his own; on the day of the athletic games, he shaved his beard, put the hair into a box of pure gold, enchased with precious stones, and consecrated it to the same "Father of gods and men!" * Miserable as all this was, it would have been well for himself and the world if his puerilities had never gone further. There is scarce the crime, however, that can be named, into which this wicked emperor did not plunge. He had murdered many courtiers in cold blood; and when the Great Apostle arrived in Rome, Octavia, his beauti-

* Suetonius's *Life of Nero*, pp. 347, 349.

ful and noble-minded queen, was living in cruel exile. The infamous Poppæa was residing with him as his unlawful wife, in his splendid Palatine Palace. Shortly after, he not only gave orders for Octavia's murder, but had her head brought to Rome, savagely to witness it! A few weeks later, he committed the most enormous of his many fearful crimes, in the assassination of his own mother. His first purpose was to loosen the rafters of her bed-chamber, and to bury her as she was asleep under the ruins of the ceiling. This failing, he next arranged to drown her on her way to her villa on the Lucrine Lake, when on board an ornamental yacht, so contrived as, on a given signal, to fall to pieces. This also having failed, she was despatched the same night with daggers! "The freedman, Anicetus, undertook the mission; and on entering the chamber where Agrippina reclined with a single female slave, and solitary lamp, she said to him, 'If you bring a message from my son, to inquire after my health, tell him I am better; if your purpose be murder, do it quickly;' then baring her bosom, with a design of shortening her sufferings, or reproaching the parricide, she exclaimed, 'Strike here,' and was despatched with repeated wounds." *

It gives a mournful picture of his hardened levity, that a short time after, he was seen singing to the guitar, and acting in presence of crowds of Romans, the nobler of whom shed tears when they saw the imperial honour so tarnished. When the tidings of revolt among his subjects on one occasion came to his ears, he threatened to poison the whole senate, consume the city by fire, and let loose wild beasts among the people in the streets. No

* Lempriere's *Dictionary*.

wonder Paul afterwards speaks of him as a "*Lion*," and thanks his God who had rescued him from his jaws.*

Perhaps never in the history of our race did there live at one time two such opposite specimens of humanity as now in the city of Rome—Nero and Paul. The one, the nominal master of the world, but an awful mixture of the beast and the fiend; the other, a "persecuted tent-maker," but possessing a nature with all that was lofty, pure, lovely, and of good report.

It was then under the reign of this "bold, bad man," and while some of the scenes we have described were transacting in the palace, that our Great Apostle lived for two years in the capital.†

There were many Jews resident in Rome then as now. They were confined, however, as at this day, to a "Jewish Quarter." This was situated on the other side of the Tiber. Here they were allowed to have their own synagogues, and to collect their annual tribute of two drachmæ on each head, for the support of the temple treasury in Jerusalem. There were also, as we have seen, at present in the imperial city not a few Christians. Many of the latter, like Aquila and Priscilla, had been driven from Rome to cities bordering on the Mediterranean, in consequence of the edict of Claudius. While sojourning in these eastern countries, as I before observed, some of them had seen Paul personally. Their faith and devotedness had been deepened. They had returned to the great capital with their minds much impressed by the holy teaching they had received from his lips. The long list of names in the closing chapter of his Roman epistle informs us how many devoted believers were in the city

* 2 Tim. iv. 17. † Lempriere. See also Mr Lewin, vol. ii. p. 764.

of the Tiber, waiting to welcome their spiritual father and friend.

As was the Apostle's custom in other cities, he preached in Rome to the "Jews first." After occupying for three days his solitary room, he sent for the principal people among the Israelites to have a conversation with them. Probably he was anxious to explain his conduct, and get their feelings enlisted on his side before they were prejudiced against him by communications from their brethren at a distance. We perhaps could not have wondered if they had been unprepared to meet the Apostle in a kindly spirit. The very fact of his having come thither, appealing to the Roman Emperor against their own Sanhedrim, was, in itself, enough to rouse their suspicions and prejudices. When "the heads of the nation"—the leading Jewish citizens—therefore, arrived at his lodging, he endeavoured at first to remove from their minds any unjust and unfounded impressions. He showed that it was they, his own countrymen at Jerusalem, who had in the first instance done him the cruel injustice of handing over one of their own nation to the Roman power. Even the Roman Governor had been ready to let him go, but his Jewish enemies had refused. In these circumstances, he could do no otherwise than appeal unto Cæsar. He concludes by telling them that his only crime had been preaching the great expectation given to his fathers of a coming Messiah. "For the hope of Israel, I am bound with this chain."

They assured him, in reply, that they had got no tidings regarding him from their countrymen in the East, nor had they ever heard any evil concerning him. His vessel, wrecked as it was, had evidently brought its crew more speedily to Rome than other ships which had embarked at the same time from Syria, and which had been kept back by stress of weather during that stormy winter

Although, however, the Jewish brethren at Rome had no charge of a personal kind to bring against Paul, it was different about the cause he was pleading, as they added, that the sect to which he belonged, called "Christians," was "everywhere spoken against." * There was nothing in their reply to discourage the Apostle; if anything, he might conclude they were disposed to hear him in a more candid spirit than he could have expected. A day, therefore, was fixed for a meeting at his own lodging, where, to all willing to come, he would unfold the great doctrines for which he had been called in question.

A large body of Jews assembled at the time specified. From morning to evening the Apostle continued his argument, trying to convince them from their own Scriptures that Jesus was the Christ. There was a division among the hearers; some (the honest portion, open to conviction) believed; but others, as is ever the case, continued in their bigotry and prejudice, and went away unbelieving as they came. Paul could not suffer them to depart without a word of awful warning—the doom pronounced against obstinate and wilful unbelievers by the Prophet Isaiah. "Go unto this people, and say, Hearing ye shall hear, and shall not understand; and seeing ye shall see, and not perceive: for the heart of this people is waxed gross, and their ears are dull of hearing, and their eyes have they closed; lest they should see with their eyes, and hear

* Acts xxviii. 22.

with their ears, and understand with their heart, and should be converted, and I should heal them. Be it known therefore unto you, that the salvation of God is sent unto the Gentiles, and that they will hear it." *

As the Apostle now commenced unfolding that gospel to the Gentiles which his own countrymen in Rome rejected, the unbelieving Jews began among themselves an active opposition. He, however, remained for two years in his own hired house, proclaiming faithfully to all who would hear regarding the kingdom of his Lord. The kindness of Burrus, which he experienced when he first came, was still continued. He was spared the ignominy and discomfort of being shut up with other prisoners in the Pretorian barracks, but was allowed to remain in his own lodging, and to see there what friends he chose. It was necessary, however, that the Roman law should be enforced in his being strictly guarded; day and night he was chained by the arm to a Roman soldier, but this was his consolation and joy, that "the Word of God was not bound." The effects of his preaching appear first among the Pretorian guards;—probably the soldiers who had the charge of him, carried back day after day to the camp the tidings of the truth he proclaimed. Though his weapons were not like theirs, carnal, they proved to be "mighty through God to the pulling down of strongholds." When he writes to his old Philippian friends, he tells them, with a joyful heart, that his "bonds in Christ are manifest in all the palace and in all other places." †

It is worthy of remark, in passing, that probably to Paul's intercourse with Roman soldiers at this time,

* Acts xxviii. 26–28. † Phil. i. 13

we may trace the references in his letters written from Rome, to *armour*, and *battle*, and *military* life. Both the Epistle to the Ephesians and the Epistles to Timothy were composed during his Roman captivity. They are just what we might naturally expect from a man living daily chained by the wrist to a soldier of the Imperial Guard—listening to the clank of their heavy armour, and hearing the sound of their bugles in the Pretorian tent. He tells Timothy to "act the part of the good soldier of Jesus Christ;" and the Ephesians have every part of the Roman armour spiritualised:—the "breastplate"—the "helmet"—the "sandals"—the "shield"—the "sword"—that they might be able "to stand in the evil day." *

But to return. The tidings of the gospel reached not merely the military camp, but the imperial palace. Though wicked Nero's heart remained untouched, Paul sends Christian greetings from the "saints in Cæsar's household." Even before the Apostle reached Rome, some noble women among the higher ranks had taken up the cross of Jesus, amid the frowns and ridicule of the "great and mighty." The wife of the conqueror of Britain, Pomponia Græcina, was only one of several who had embraced "the truth as it is in Jesus;" and now that Paul had himself come among them, we need not wonder that the good seed should spread. Among other converts, the Roman martyrology mentions Torpes, an officer of note; and Chrysostom speaks of one of Nero's cupbearers.† It is even said, although we have only tradition for it, that the aged philosopher Seneca, the tutor of Nero, in his old age, laid aside "philosophy falsely so called," for the glorious simplicities of the

* Eph. vi. 11 to end.

† Cave, p. 102.

faith of Jesus Seneca was the intimate friend of Burrus; and it is by no means improbable that he would introduce him to one so like-minded, gifted, and learned as Paul of Tarsus.*

"The sacred historian tells us, that the door of Paul's lodging was open to every comer, and he tells us no more; but curiosity would fain ask many an interesting question as to the personages then at Rome. What was Gallio about, who had known Paul at Corinth? . . . Under the auspices of his brother Seneca, did he now investigate the truth? How did Felix demean himself? did he renew the intimacy he had begun at Cesarea? or had he not the hardihood to look in the face the man whom he knew to be innocent, and ought to have acquitted, but had left bound to serve his own selfish purposes? Where were Caractacus and his family—his wife, and daughter, and brothers, who had, a few years before, been prisoners in the Pretorium? Were they still detained at Rome as hostages? and if so, did a British king ever have an interview with one of the apostles? Questions such as these cannot be solved, and it is idle to pursue them."†

At this period of Paul's life, as detailed in the Acts of the Apostles, the curtain falls—the history of Luke comes abruptly to a close. It is from the Apostle's after-epistles that we are able to get some knowledge of his future career, now that his ardent wish was at last fulfilled—"to preach the gospel at Rome also."

* See Lewin, p. 760. † Ibid, vol. ii. p. 762.

CHAPTER XXII.

Prison-Life.

"Look in and see Christ's chosen saint
In triumph wear his Christ-like chain!
Nor fear lest he should swerve or faint,—
'His life is Christ—his death is gain.'"
KEBLE.

"Lord Jesus, I am weary *in* Thy work, but not *of* Thy work. Let me go and speak for Thee once more, . . . seal Thy truth, and then die."—WHITFIELD'S *Life*.

WHEN prisoners were brought to Rome, as Paul now was, a long period often elapsed before their cases were finally tried. It not only was necessary that the accusers be present, but time was given them to summon their witnesses; and as these, in the case of the Apostle, would require to be brought from such a distance, it might easily be shown that his trial could not well have been concluded before the end of two years. This is the period mentioned by Luke during which he remained a prisoner in his hired house. The legal documents and papers, which were forwarded by Festus from Cesarea, were probably destroyed at the time of the shipwreck. Add to this, there were always such numbers of cases of the same kind to be heard, that the delay was often very long; the judges had their frequent holidays; prisoners were left for weeks in their chains, when the fagged and wearied lawyers and prætors were down refreshing themselves at the baths and sea-breezes of Baiæ. Moreover, Paul's accusers had no object in hastening the trial, as, from the private judgment which Festus had already pronounced, they could have little expectation of success. If they desired anything, therefore, it would be delay, in the hope of being able to work on the feelings or passions of the emperor.

The Apostle's own imprisonment, as we have said, was not irksome or severe, and, doubtless, "the things which happened to him, had fallen out rather to the furtherance of the gospel." His house was evidently of considerable size, capable of containing the multitudes which flocked to hear him. The sympathies of many must have been called forth as they saw the old man, his face wrinkled with cares and sorrows, lifting the hand that was chained to a rude soldier, and proclaiming those truths for which he suffered, and of which, "nevertheless, he was not ashamed." *

But it was not his converts at Rome only to whom he was now of service; he was the spiritual father of many churches scattered in different parts of the empire; and the old and faithful friends who came to visit him in his imprisonment, were sent with letters of comfort to all round about. Luke, Timothy, Tychicus, Demas, and Mark, were the bearers, every now and then, to churches and individuals, of messages and epistles. It is pleasing to hear of Mark, whose unfaithfulness led to such unpleasant consequences in separating Paul from Barnabas, again the devoted friend and attendant of his great spiritual father. Many of the Roman converts, too, began to take an active part in proclaiming the gospel. "Many of the

* See Howson and Conybeare, vol. ii. pp. 386, 387.

brethren in the Lord," he writes to the Philippians, "waxing confident by my bonds, are much more bold to speak the Word without fear." *

There was another of Paul's many converts in the capital, whose history possesses peculiar interest, not from his wearing the livery of Cæsar's dependants or courtiers, but from his being one of those apparently hopeless castaways in the lowest scale of life, who are ever and anon made the monuments and miracles of grace:—I refer to Onesimus. He was a runaway slave from Asia; his master's name was Philemon, a rich Gentile, a Christian, and member of the church of Colosse. Onesimus had plundered him, and taken refuge at Rome. We can well imagine the debasing companions among whom this man's lot must have been cast in the lowest streets of the capital. "Profligate and unprincipled as we know even the highest and most educated society to have then been, what must have been its dregs and offal!" † But what cannot grace do? He was brought, we know not how, along with the crowd that went day after day to hear the Great Apostle. He may not unlikely have seen Paul previously, through whose ministry his master Philemon had been converted; at all events, as he listened now to the preaching of the Apostle, he was led to feel his guilt, and to embrace Jesus as his only Saviour. The rude and debased slave became possessor of a liberty he in vain sought by deserting an indulgent master. He saw Paul alone, told him of his behaviour to Philemon, and besought his intercession for pardon. The Apostle seems ardently to have loved this penitent stranger; he saw that he was fitted for

* Phil. i. 14 † Howson.

nobler duties than to return again as a slave to Colosse, and was desirous therefore of retaining him in the service of the gospel at Rome. He would not, however, do his lawful master injustice by keeping him there, without first of all receiving the sanction of the former; he resolved to send Onesimus immediately to Philemon, with a letter and "promissory note" for the sum of money of which he had been robbed by his slave. The letter contained the intimation of his earnest wish, that Onesimus might be allowed to leave his master's service for the good of the Church at large. The "note" referred to is in the concluding part of the letter (ver. 18), "If he hath wronged thee, or oweth thee ought, put that on my account. *I, Paul, have written it with mine own hand, I will repay it.*" The whole epistle itself is a beautiful one, and though well known to all our readers, it may be well for them here to peruse it, before proceeding further. It has been universally admired as a perfect specimen of kindness, courtesy, honourable and delicate feeling, and Christian love. "In it," says an old writer, "are some of the finest strokes of *true rhetoric*—it may be called the *polite epistle.* Such a genteel and admirable address appear in every sentence, that it alone might be sufficient to convince us that Paul was not that weak, visionary, enthusiastic man, which the minute philosophers and little critics among the Deists have sometimes represented him to be." * We may imagine the mingled feelings with which Onesimus, when he arrived at Colosse, went to the house of his old master. He might well have trembled if he had been going back to any other than a Christian. It is, indeed, a beautiful example of the confidence one

* Benson.

believer may place in the forgiving spirit of another; for ' all masters were looked upon, not only by the Roman laws, but by the laws of all nations, as having an unlimited power over slaves; so that, without asking the magistrates' leave, or any public or formal trial, they might adjudge them to any work or punishment, even to the loss of life itself." * What effect the Apostle's letter produced we cannot tell; we may reasonably hope, however, that the good Colossian not only pardoned his penitent slave, but granted him his liberty, and that he returned to Paul, in order to labour with him as (shall we call it?) the first "*city missionary*" among the degraded outcasts in Rome. We read, fifty years afterwards, of one *Onesimus* being bishop of Ephesus. It has been conjectured that the pardoned and liberated slave of Colosse may thus have become the head of the Christian church in the great city of Diana!

But it was not a single letter to a solitary Christian of Asia that found its way, at this time, from Paul's "hired house." Learned writers, from different references in these epistles themselves, have inferred that two others, at least, were written by him at this time.† Epaphras, the founder of the church of Colosse, where Philemon was, had come all the way to Rome to see Paul about the lamentable errors which were fast creeping in among his converts. It would appear that some Alexandrian Jew had taken up his abode among the Colossians, and had contrived to draw them sadly away from the simplicity of their first faith. The Apostle, on learning this, thought it right to address them without delay, warning them of their danger,

* Cave's *Lives of the Apostles*.

† Neander, p. 318.

entreating them to return to the purity of the true gospel, and not to be led away with "enticing words of philosophy and vain deceit."

The other letter to which I refer is perhaps the richest and tenderest of all his epistles: it is that which is called in our Bibles the "Epistle to the Ephesians." There seems strong reason to doubt whether this epistle was written expressly for the church at Ephesus. There are many reasons which we shall not now detail for concluding rather that it was intended for a number or cluster of churches, of which that of Ephesus was one. Tychicus was about to visit this district in Asia Minor; and in consequence of Epaphras having been made prisoner at Rome, along with Paul, he had been entrusted with the epistle to the Colossians. He and Onesimus more than probably travelled together. It would naturally occur to the Apostle that it might be subject of great joy and comfort to the many Christians in these regions, if he were to send by him also a *circular* letter. It has been supposed that a copy was written out for each church, and that each of these was subscribed in his own handwriting in the usual form, "The salutation of me Paul by my own hand." *

It is supposed that these last three letters were written by Paul after the first year of his imprisonment, or early the following spring. Tychicus had scarcely left, when the Philippian church sent a trusty messenger to inquire for the welfare of the Apostle, and present him with a gift of money. This, we have

* This supposition, we believe, was first suggested by Archbishop Usher, and has been very generally adopted. See the whole question discussed in *Cyclopædia of Biblical Literature*, art. "Epistle to the Ephesians."

seen, was not the first occasion that devoted people had shown their liberality. It must have been very welcome, doubtless, to the Apostle at this time. He could not conveniently now, as formerly, labour with his hands to minister to his wants. These hands were chained; perhaps we may add, that, though as willing, they were not so able for hard toil as when he held them up before the elders of Ephesus, and told them they were all he had or wished to trust to. Epaphroditus was the Philippian messenger's name. On reaching Rome, he was seized with a severe illness, probably brought on by the length and fatigues of the journey, or it may be from arriving at the sick and unhealthy season of the year, so well known to this day by those who have visited the "Eternal City." "He was sick," Paul wrote immediately afterwards, "nigh unto death; but God had mercy on him, and not on him only, but on me also, lest I should have sorrow upon sorrow."*

The devoted Apostle met daily fresh encouragement in the great capital. Multitudes were added to the Christian Church, and the once despised doctrines were cordially embraced. Strangest of all was it, as we have seen, that the royal palace itself should have become the dwelling-place of believers in Jesus—those who were slaves of the most hideous vice having their spiritual fetters broken, and exulting in the liberty wherewith Christ made them free. We have also supposed as more than likely, that not a few of those rude and barbarous soldiers, to whom Paul was chained, were among the number of his spiritual children. If their hearts were not as hard as the iron mail that

* Phil. ii. 27.

covered them, they could not help being struck with the holy and peaceful calm which reigned in the house and heart of the Jewish prisoner:—what a contrast to the guilt and brutality which, in the prætorian barrack, must have constantly met their eye!

Our Apostle now lost one heathen friend, whose clemency had made imprisonment easy—viz., Burrus. His successor was a vicious, profligate courtier of Nero's. He does not seem, however, to have subjected Paul to any additional cruelties. The Apostle-prisoner had more to dread from Nero and his wicked wife Poppæa, who, being herself a proselyte to Judaism, would doubtless have it in her power to crush, by a word, the man who was so hated by the house of Israel.

When Epaphroditus had recovered, and was able to return home again to Philippi, Paul entrusted him with a letter to the church there—*The Epistle to the Philippians.* Had the Apostle consulted his own feelings, he would doubtless have detained this good Philippian in Rome, to cheer his own hours of captivity; but he saw not only that it would be desirable for Epaphroditus to return to his post of duty, but that his shattered frame required a change from the unhealthy damps of a Roman climate. "I have deemed it necessary," he writes to them, "to send to you Epaphroditus, my brother and companion in labour, and fellow-soldier, but your messenger, and he that ministered to my wants." * From the whole epistle we obtain a very favourable idea of the character of the Macedonian believers. They had, as yet, escaped the errors that were creeping into other churches; and, with the exception of a few words of reproof, to some

* Phil. ii. 25, 26.

who were not cultivating humility and lowliness of mind as they ought, the epistle is full of joyful commendation, and written in the strain of a father to his affectionate children. When Epaphroditus had returned to Philippi, Tychicus to Colosse, and Mark had probably become the attendant of Peter in Asia Minor, the Apostle's immediate personal friends were diminished. He had probably still, however, Timothy his "own son," Luke, and Aristarchus. His own prospects seemed to look brighter—a gleam before the gathering storm! He seems even to hint at what his plans would be when set at liberty. His eyes were turned westwards to the original lands of the old "Galatians," but before accomplishing such a visit, he appears to intimate a desire, if it were God's will, of going first to Lesser Asia, and mentions to Philemon his purpose of making his house his home. He would, doubtless, often long for release. He might perhaps think with regret, "What two important years of my life I have spent in this hired house! Might I not have been all this time preaching the gospel, or building up my churches?" Nay, in addition to the fruits of his preaching, God had *other* work for him to do. But for these two years of quiet and seclusion, when his mind and Christian experience were most matured, we should not now have been in the possession of those precious epistles, which have been the treasure, not of one age, but of the Church till the end of time. This is the most likely period to fix the date of that valuable and noble epistle, the Epistle to the Hebrews, which, though considered by some writers not to have been the work of Paul, has by far the greatest amount of evidence in its favour, as proceeding from no hand but his.* As we read it, we may think of its author dictating its sublime words during the last of the quiet hours he passed in "the solitude of a great city." The period of repose is soon to be over. The crisis is at hand. Is it to issue in a new lease of life and call of duty? Is he yet, "as Paul the aged," to be again summoned to bear the cross? or is he at once to get his crown?

* See note to Stackhouse, vol. vi. p. [illegible].

CHAPTER XXIII.

The Closing Scene.

"Servant of God, well done!
Rest from thy loved employ;
The battle fought—the victory won,
Enter thy Master's joy."

"He stood upon the brink of the grave, calm and unmoved, like the conqueror in the Capitol, waiting for the crown to be placed upon his brow."—BLUNT'S *Lectures on St Paul*, vol. ii. p. 250.

WE have now come to the last chapter in the history of the Great Apostle. We could have wished that more particulars had been left to complete the account of so eventful and interesting a life; but these materials are very few. As Irenæus says, "Luke, at the close of his history, leaves us thirsting for more." Indeed, we are left very much to fill up in our own minds how he "finished his course with joy." Why his faithful friend and biographer records so little regarding these concluding years, we cannot say. We have no cause, however, to complain. We have rather reason for gratitude, that the Holy Spirit moved him to transcribe so fully and faithfully what throws so much light on the infant Church, and the doings of her brightest Luminary.

There is a question which has much divided learned men, as to whether Paul was only once or twice imprisoned in Rome. Some think that his condemnation and death took place immediately after the events recorded in last chapter; others, we think with better grounds, have supposed that he was acquitted at this his first trial; that, on being set at liberty, he travelled to the extreme *west* of the Roman empire, and preached the gospel in Spain; also that he visited Asia Minor, and other churches in the East; and after being imprisoned a second time in Rome, he was sentenced to death, probably in the last year of the reign of Nero.*

We are left to imagine the scene of Paul's first trial before the emperor. It has been supposed to have taken place about March, 61,—the same year when the Roman arms in Britain received a signal repulse under the brave Queen Boadicea, and our own London was burnt to ashes by the infuriated legions of Nero.† Although such causes as that of the Apostle were sometimes heard by the consular-legate, most frequently the emperor himself was in the habit of presiding at them in his imperial palace on the Palatine Hill. We may think, then, of Nero, the monarch of the civilised world, himself a brutalised heathen, seated at the end of a gorgeous hall, "lined with the precious marbles of Egypt, and of Lybia,"‡ in raiment of purple and gold, surrounded with his twelve lictors, courtiers, and assessors. His face at one time had been

* Much diversity of opinion exists about the probable direction of Paul's concluding journeyings, (and all must be conjecture where there is nothing but brief hints in his epistles to guide us.) We have adhered to the order adopted by Messrs Howson and Conybeare in their closing chapters.

† Lewin.

‡ Howson and Conybeare.

handsome, but it now bore the marks of youthful profligacy. Suetonius adds, that the size of his body was considerable, his neck thick, and his eyes grey and dull. Before him stood, calm and unmoved, confident in his own integrity, and in the grace and strength of his God, the Jewish prisoner. He was loaded with fetters; but, captive as he was, with the almost certainty of a cruel death before him, he would not for worlds change places with the miserable being before him, whose hands were already, at the age of twenty-five or thirty, so deeply stained with blood. Paul might well have trembled in his presence; but he knew that there was One at his side "mightier than the mightiest;" and even should the ravenous "lion" be permitted to tear him in pieces, it would only be the sooner to receive his heavenly crown.

The witnesses would be called. Doubtless many had by this time been gathered from all parts of the East where Paul had sought to proclaim the gospel. The Sanhedrim, also, would not be idle. It is remarkable that Josephus, in his *History*, mentions that the high priest at Jerusalem, Ishmael, and many of the leading Jews, were at this time in Rome. He speaks of the main object of their journey being with reference to the building of a wall in the temple. May it not have more likely been, that they had in view the ruin of St Paul?* These collected Jews would doubtless have some chosen Roman orator hired to plead their cause; nor would it have been difficult to make out a strong case against the Apostle. They might have urged before Nero, that the prisoner was not only a ringleader of a new sect, but a subverter of his own power; and

* Lewin. Josephus' *Antiq.* book xx. chap. 8.

that this *Jesus* whom he preached, aspired to the temporal sovereignty of Judea, and of the world.

We may imagine the Apostle rising calmly in the midst of the court to make his reply. Many of his judges would understand Greek, and in this language probably he would address them. What he said, we know not. There may have been solemn things spoken home to their consciences. Like Felix, some may have trembled; but we fear, at least, that the monarch, on whom he kept his eye, only despised, and perished! So far as we could judge, everything combined to make Paul's a hopeless case. His enemies were many and powerful, their pleas were strong in such an ear as Nero's, and, above all, the influence exercised by his base queen, over whom Ishmael had great power, must have combined to seal the Apostle's fate. Moreover, Nero did not require to abide, as in our courts of law, by the opinion of the jury; he could pronounce what sentence he chose. His partiality for cruelty was too well known to give such a prisoner much hope of mercy; more especially when we think how the holy life and holy words of the Apostle must have rebuked the crimes of the judge. But He who turns the hearts of kings, and queens, and rulers, "even as he turns the rivers of waters," *did*, by His overruling providence, avert the threatened stroke. Paul once more is liberated—he is dismissed from the bar, and is free to preach the gospel where he pleases!

New thoughts of missionary zeal begin to fill his aged bosom. His first desire is to go to the East, and revisit some of the churches there, which seemed to stand in need of his presence and counsel.

There were many of these which he had never yet

seen; and from the wish he expresses in his letter, both to Philemon and the Philippians, we may well believe he would turn his steps immediately towards Macedonia and the churches in Asia Minor. How joyful would be his meeting with his Philippian friends! But it must only have been a passing "salutation," as he was anxious to hasten to other places still farther east. What he *did* visit, we know not. Possibly he would direct his course for the first time to Colosse. We may picture his probable interview with the wealthy but Christian-hearted Philemon. Who can tell but Onesimus his old slave may have joined them, and, under the same roof, three, so different from one another, may have rejoiced now in being all "one in Christ Jesus!" From Colosse, on his way to Ephesus, it is more than likely he would pause at Laodicea and Hierapolis.

The year following his acquittal at Rome, he made out his long-thought-of journey to Spain. Clemens, his own contemporary and fellow-labourer, tells us that "he went to the utmost bounds of the west." In going thither, it is most probable he would avoid the "perils of false brethren," by committing himself again to the waters of the Mediterranean. The persecutions of Nero were at their height, and he would feel that it were "better to fall into the hands of God than into the hands of men." Many vessels were continually plying between the east and the modern Marseilles, and from thence he would easily find his way by ship to Spain. How long he remained in the Peninsula we cannot even guess; most probably two years were spent there preaching the gospel of his Lord.

Some, indeed, have thought that the Apostle went further west still, and that the shores of our own island, and even the streets of our own London, were trodden by the "footsteps of St Paul!" Early writers in the fourth and fifth centuries speak of such a visit. However pleasing it would be for us to think of this as the case, of course it is a mere matter of conjecture. Claudia, whose name is mentioned by the Apostle in 2 Tim. iv. 21, has been supposed by some to have been the daughter of Caractacus, King of Britain, who was brought prisoner to Rome in A. D. 51, and who, with her grandfather Bran, was converted to Christianity. We have already mentioned that Pomponia Græcina, the wife of Aulus Plautius, the first Roman governor of Britain, was accused of having become a convert to a "strange foreign superstition," in other words, of being a Christian, and probably through her instrumentality the daughter of the British king and others were led to receive the truth. It is also said that the aged Briton *Bran* afterwards returned to his native shores, along with other converts, and that by them the religion of Jesus was taught to the Pagan savages. There is much, however, in this of tradition, and which it becomes us to receive with caution.*

If the dates we have already given be at all correct, we may imagine it was in the year 66 that our Apostle again returned from the west, and sailed back to Ephesus. It was a journey, or rather visit of sorrow. He found (according to the fears he had many years before expressed to the elders who met him at Miletus), that wolves had entered among his sheep. False teachers, among whom were Hymeneus and Philetus, were

* See Cave; and *Apostles* (Tract Society).

scattering the seeds of deadly error, and multitudes of his converts had thereby been led astray.

The epistles to Timothy and Titus were written about this time. From them we gather that his present visit to the east was a short one. His spirit seems to have been greatly bowed down by the errors and heresies which had sprung up like noxious weeds in a garden which once promised so well. We may believe he had lost none of his ardour and zeal in his Heavenly Master's cause, but his strength was not so able, at the age of nearly seventy, to cope with the hardships he once could encounter. We may feel assured, had it been so, he would not have employed others to grapple with these errors, but would have been on the field himself with the same "sword of the Spirit" he had so often wielded in the battles of the Lord.

There is something touching in the message which he sends during these later years of his life to bring back "the cloak that he had left behind him at Troas."* It had been his companion, perhaps, amid the cutting winds of the Pisidian mountains, and now, again, in the prospect either of a new sea-voyage, or the sadder one of a damp cell, he felt his aged frame could not dispense so easily as once it might with these aids to artificial warmth. He had left it in summer at Troas, with the prospect of getting it again on a return, which he never accomplished. What the books and parchments were he speaks of along with the cloak, we are not told; probably copies of the Law and the Prophets, with, perhaps, the Gospels of Matthew and Luke, which were the only two now written. The parchments may have been copies of his own epistles,

* 2 Tim. iv. 13.

with, perhaps, "the diploma of his Roman citizenship."*

Leaving Timothy to contend with the errors of the false teachers I have spoken of at Ephesus, Paul seems to have gone first to Macedonia, and then to Crete. If he returned to Ephesus, it was to leave it finally for Rome, taking Corinth on his way. It was when at Macedonia he wrote his first Epistle to Timothy, in which he gives him various directions about the government of the church at Ephesus, denounces and opposes the heretical teachers and doctrines, and adds many faithful counsels to his "own son" individually, and to ministers of Christ in every age.

Soon after writing this epistle, we find the Apostle in the island of Crete. It is more than probable the gospel had been introduced there before Paul's visit. This we are given to infer from the Epistle to Titus. Moreover, you will remember, at the day of Pentecost, *Cretans* are spoken of among the number of those who received the gift of tongues, and heard Peter preach the gospel. It is not unlikely that some of these may have carried the glad tidings from Jerusalem to their own island. The Apostle visited them now along with Titus, probably remaining for some months, and leaving this companion of his missionary tour behind him on his departure. Paul wrote to him afterwards (as we have just found him doing to Timothy) a letter of directions about the government of the church in that island; also, in order to silence some opposition which had arisen to his teaching. He seems to have sent it from Ephesus just when about to leave that city for the west. In

* Lewin.

reading the epistle, you will see that Paul asks Titus to come and join him at *Nicopolis*, where he was to "spend the winter." This town in Epirus, in Greece, was built by Augustus in memory of the famous battle of Actium, which he gained over Mark Antony, on 2d September, B. C. 31. It was situated on a narrow isthmus; a temple to Apollo marked the spot where the tent of Augustus had been pitched, and every five years famous games were celebrated close by. It is notable to us, as the last scene of Paul's public labours before his final trial. It has been supposed, indeed, that it was here he was arrested, and sent again to imprisonment at Rome—arriving there very possibly at the beginning of the year.*

There is surely something touching about this journey! The old man—with furrowed brow and feeble steps—with few friends to cheer him, and some of those few deserting him in the hour of danger:—Demas left him; Crescens "departed to Galatia;" even Titus went (though this may have been at Paul's request) to Dalmatia. *One* at least, however, we know remained faithful to the last—Luke the evangelist, the writer of his history, followed with trusty fidelity his aged father in the faith, to comfort him in his coming sorrows, and share his cross. It was indeed an honorable office to accompany such a man, who had now for a quarter of a century been the bold ambassador of Christ. During all that period he had never grown weary in his Lord's service. What was said of John Knox, might with truth have been said of him, "he

* Neander and others have supposed that his visit to Spain was after his eastern journey; that there he was seized and taken prisoner to Rome.—Neander's Planting, 1 '45.

never feared the face of man." The thongs and the scourge, the stocks of the prison, the rude language and buffetings of soldiers, the rage of mobs, tedious journeys, four shipwrecks,—all he had endured with heroical equanimity, and, if it pleased God, he was willing to endure tenfold more.

He once more enters Rome! We shall presently note how changed the outward aspect of the city was since he last was there,—whole streets and buildings had been swept away and restored, and new palaces were looking down from the heights of the Palatine. Among these new buildings, conspicuous must have been the golden palace of Nero, with his statue in the vestibule, 120 feet in height, the golden stalls for his chariot horses, and the porticoes and columns extending a mile in length. "It was richly overlaid," says Suetonius, "with gold, and everywhere adorned with the dazzling glitter of precious stones, and mother-of-pearl. In the vaulted roofs of his banqueting rooms were several little tables of ivory, so contrived as to turn round and scatter flowers, and hollow pipes to shower down sweet-scented oils upon the guests. His principal dining-room was round, and in perpetual motion, day and night, like the celestial sphere. His baths continually flowing, either with sea-water, or else fed from the sulphureous springs of Tivoli." But why, after all, linger in the description of these? They were little to the man who, we are supposing, was passing near them, and who had in his view "a building of God, an house not made with hands, eternal in the heavens."

Imagine Paul, then, amid what Horace calls "the smoke, the riches, and the noise of Rome," passing on, as in former years, chained to a soldier by the wrist, to the place of confinement. We found that, during his previous imprisonment, he had received kind and considerate treatment. He was allowed then to live in his own hired lodging, and, though chained, was permitted to see what friends he chose. Now he was confined to a dungeon, and treated as a malefactor.

The Mamertine prison is still pointed out as the scene of his incarceration. Its position is not far from the large pillars which occupy the foreground in our picture of the "Roman Forum." It is considered the oldest relic and building in the city, deriving its name from Ancus Martius, the fourth king of ancient Rome. It is reached, in the present day, by a vault under the Church of St Giuseppe, where the visitor finds himself in two dismal cells; the lower is only six and a half feet in height, and the stones of which it is built are "strangely united by cramps of iron." * There was a circular opening or aperture above, through which prisoners, on their condemnation, were lowered, either to starve or be strangled to death. Jugurtha suffered the former of these cruelties within these terrible walls. No wonder Paul wrote, as we have seen, so anxiously for his winter cloak to protect him from the pestilential damps and cold of such a place! Friends are still allowed to see him, but his mouth is shut in preaching the gospel; and those who *do* go, seem to venture with fear and trembling, lest, by showing sympathy, they might be involved in the fate which seemed so surely hanging over their reverend father.

But we must pause for a moment to inquire into the cause of this renewed imprisonment.

On the night of the 19th of July, A. D. 64, a ter-

* Sir William Gell.

rible fire broke out in the Circus Maximus of Rome, between the Palatine and Aventine Mount. It raged fiercely for six days and seven nights, spreading with amazing rapidity,—the people being forced to seek for shelter among the monuments and tombs of the dead. No besieging army could have so effected the work of destruction. The citizens saw, with bitter sorrow, their homes and noble buildings becoming a prey to the furious element; and it must have added much to their indignation to find (what it is to be feared was too true) that the monster Nero was the cause of this fearful calamity. "He was offended," says Suetonius, "with the deformity of the ancient buildings and the narrow passages and turnings of the streets. . . . . Besides the vast number of ordinary houses, the palaces of the great captains of former ages, adorned with the spoils of foreign conquests—were all consumed to ashes, together with the temples of the gods, which the ancient kings of Rome had raised, and had afterwards been consecrated to the memory of the Roman victories." It is even said the unfeeling tyrant gazed down with a smile on his face, playing on his musical instrument, from the tower of Mæcenas, while his capital was consuming, and the shrieks of his people were borne to his ear!

He soon came to find that so wanton and cruel an outrage had roused, as it might justly have done, the anger of the Romans. What is he to do? The base expedient occurs to him to fasten the guilt of the burning on the innocent *Christians*, whose purity he hated, because it condemned his own unblushing vices. The plot answered too well. The tyrant succeeded, by this malicious lie, in rousing the popular feeling against the followers of Jesus; saving himself by involving the innocent. Cruelties beyond description followed. The suffering Christians were besmeared with pitch, and then set fire to at night to lighten the darkness. Others were sewed up in the skins of beasts, hunted down by dogs, and torn to pieces. Nero exulted also in this spectacle. He moved about, as Tacitus tells us, in a circus erected in his own gardens, "in the dress of a charioteer, sometimes on foot and sometimes viewing the spectacle from his car."

We may imagine what the feelings of the mob were likely to be, towards the great "ringleader" of the hated sect of Nazarenes. Indeed, this was probably the main charge laid against Paul now, that before he last left Rome he had put this foul deed of burning the city into the minds of his converts. How the Apostle would mourn over the loss of Burrus and Seneca! The Prefect of the Pretorium was now a very different man. Tigellinus, the sharer of Nero's crimes and cruelties, we may feel assured would speak no kindly word for the prisoner.

The storm is fast gathering over his devoted head. It is likely that no time would elapse before his new trial. In the former one, we have supposed that he was summoned before the emperor. This, however, as we saw, was often the cause of considerable delay. At present he was brought probably before the "Prefect of the city,"—an officer appointed by his imperial master with supreme authority over criminal cases. How touching the position of the Apostle when standing in this court! "At my first answer," says he to Timothy, "no man stood with me, but all men forsook me: I pray God that it may not be laid to their charge.

Notwithstanding *the Lord* stood with me, and strengthened me!"*

He could get no advocate to plead his cause, and challenge his accusers. The terrible flames in the gardens of the emperor had struck terror into many otherwise brave hearts. There was *One*, and *only One*, with him; but *that* ONE was better than all! It was "the Captain of the Lord's host:" "*who* could be against Him?"

It has been supposed that the place of his trial was one of those spacious halls or basilicas (a king's bench) in the Forum. They were of vast size, and admitted great multitudes to see and hear. A row of columns ran down each side of the interior, and they were so well adapted for a large congregation, that when Pagan Rome became Christian, and churches were needed, these basilicas were used for this purpose, and became patterns for others throughout Christendom. The presiding magistrate sat on his tribune (an elevated chair of ivory at one end of the hall), surrounded with assessors or jurors to give him advice in questions of law. Before him stood the prisoner, and the other parts of the building would be crowded with eager listeners, both below and in the galleries. The aged Apostle, with sixty-eight years on his head,† is now brought up from the temporary cell under the basilica. When he appears, a hum goes through the crowded court. Every breath is stilled, and none can tell in the dense mass who are friends and who are foes. The jurors one by one lay their hand on the adjoining altar before the tribune, and in an audible voice swear that they will pronounce a righteous decision.

Paul pled his own cause, and that of his injured

* 2 Tim. iv 16, 17.

† Chrysostom.

Lord, before these malicious foes. He preached to them (it was his last time) of JESUS! He defended himself against the charge of being accessory to the burning of the city, and thus escaped the lingering agonies that might otherwise have been his.

He was sent back to prison to await a second stage of his trial. We know well how he spent this time, and what his feelings were. He knew what was in prospect, but he was unmoved. He himself tells us how his soul was nerved for the coming day of martyrdom. "The shades of evening are beginning to slope; the gleam of a brighter sky is seen beyond; and with the assured conviction that the object of his life was fully accomplished," * he can say, "I am now ready to be offered, and the time of my departure is at hand. I have fought a good fight, I have finished my course, I have kept the faith: henceforth there is laid up for me a crown of righteousness, which the Lord, the righteous Judge, shall give me at that day; and not to me only, but unto all them also that love his appearing." †

Such were the triumphant feelings of the criminal shivering in his dark dungeon! An inner light, however, was there, which turned the shadow of death into the morning. Can we pause, just for a moment, to hear what the historian has to say of the mind of Nero? How affecting the contrast! "Not all the congratulations of the soldiers, the senate, and the people, could release him from the horrors of a guilty conscience, which, from that time forward (since the burning of the city), never would permit him to rest, either awake or sleeping. Full often he confessed that the furies lashed him with their whips, and some-

* Stanley's *Sermons and Essays.* † 2 Tim. iv. 6–8.

times seared his skin with their burning torches." His last hours are full of awful lessons. The senate, wearied of his crimes, at length rose up against him. They resolved to scourge him to death and hurl him over the Tarpeian rock. When the resolution came to his ears, he rushed for his golden box of poisons to put an end to himself, but his servants had hidden it. In an agony of rage and terror, he found himself friendless. Barefoot, and covering his face with a napkin, he flung himself at midnight on his horse, and galloped in the dark from his capital with only four attendants, a storm of thunder and lightning increasing his panic. On passing the Pretorian camp we know so well, he heard a noise among his soldiers cursing him. He took refuge in a vault, four miles from the city, and, on hearing the hoofs of his pursuers' horses, he plunged a dagger, with the help of an attendant, into his throat, and expired; ridding the world of the foulest of her tyrants, at the early age of thirty-two!*

But to return from so sad a contemplation. Few, very few, of Paul's friends were still left to cheer him. The beloved Luke, we have already mentioned, was faithful to the last. Onesiphorus, too, had come all the way from Asia—forgetful of danger—to see his venerated father, and cheer the gloom of the Mamertine prison. "He sought him out diligently, and found him." It was a dangerous mission of Christian friendship; for, if his creed had been known, he would have shared the Apostle's coming fate. We learn, also, from the greetings in the Second Epistle to Timothy, that Linus, Pudens, the son of a senator and his wife Claudia, whom we have already mentioned, had come to visit him in his dungeon. One, however,

* See Suetonius' *Life of Nero*, pp. 374–395.

more than all, he longed to see, to give him his parting blessing, and receive, in return, his presence and support at the hour of death. This was *Timothy*, his own dear son in the faith. They seem to have taken a parting farewell before this, under an impression that they would never meet again. The faithful "son" of such an affectionate father had wept bitterly at the thought of seeing his face no more. "I thank God, whom I serve from my forefathers with pure conscience, that without ceasing I have remembrance of thee in my prayers night and day; greatly desiring to see thee, being mindful of thy tears, that I may be filled with joy."* But God had still spared him. They may yet meet again. The spirit of the old man, like another Jacob, revives at the thought! He was far distant in Asia, but Paul earnestly urges that he would come to him with all speed; and, fearing lest even he might be deterred, from the many dangers around, from giving his dying sympathy, he exhorts him, in this most touching and beautiful letter, the "Second Epistle to Timothy," to boldness in the cause of Jesus. The words at the close—"*Grace be with thee. Amen*"—were probably the last words the Great Apostle's trembling hand penned!

Whether Timothy was able to comply with this earnest wish, we cannot pronounce. We have reason to suppose, however, that he *did* succeed in reaching his aged father in his cell, and was with him in his closing hours.

For the rest, we have only tradition and common history to trust to. We left the prisoner standing before the tribune in the crowded basilica; the jurors were speaking together, advising what was to be the

* 2 Tim. i. 3, 4.

sentence. Each writes his own verdict on a separate tablet, either A (*absolvo*, not guilty), or the letter C (*condemno*, or guilty). The Apostle can easily foresee the result; the tablets are given into the hands of the presiding judge, and the significant word, "CONDEMNO," rings through the pillared hall, and the breathless audience! He would be led back to his cell. His Roman citizenship ought to have saved him from the cruel custom of scourging the condemned before death, but this seems doubtful on the present occasion. "Baronius tells us, that in the church of St Mary, beyond the bridge in Rome, the pillars are yet extant to which Paul is said to have been bound and scourged." * What time elapsed between the condemnation and the last fatal blow, we can also only conjecture. It was the usual custom for ten days to intervene, in order that the emperor, if he chose, might alter or reverse the sentence. But it is equally well known that Nero often hurried his victims from the bar to the place of execution, within an hour after judgment was given. It is probable, therefore, that but a short breathing time would be permitted the Great Apostle, before he finally passed to a more righteous judgment-seat, from the trials and persecutions of a world he had so long and so meekly borne. Tradition has fixed the 29th of June, A. D. 66, as the memorable day when the Church in heaven was to receive the greatest of her "cloud of witnesses." Paul's citizenship now, however, saved him once more from the cruel and lingering death of crucifixion he at one time expected. He was led outside the city walls, tied to a stake, and then beheaded. It was at Aquæ Salviæ, on the road to Ostia, the port of Rome, that the blood of the Apostle was

* Cave, p. 106.

shed. If there be a hallowed spot on earth, it is surely here!

Let us imagine the scene! Crowds to and from Ostia were hurrying along, little knowing all that was connected with that band of soldiers, who, under a burning sun, were hurrying their unresisting prisoner to the place of execution. Of those who attended him and witnessed his last moments, we have no information. Many converts, doubtless, who had heard him years before in "his own hired house," and who had welcomed the shipwrecked prisoner at *Appii Forum*, were now following the steps of their spiritual father with weeping eyes, feeling that their next meeting would be with tearless ones in heaven. We may only think of the possibility of Luke and Timothy lingering in the crowd, and giving that sympathy by looks and silent expression, which they dared not do by words. We need not, however, dwell on the closing spectacle. Soon all is over! He has willingly, like his Lord, borne his cross "without the gate." One stroke of the fatal weapon, and the soul of the glorious Hero is carried up by angels to Paradise!

The Church on earth never had such cause to weep since her Lord himself had left. But tears are unavailing. They take up the dead body, and either bury it on the spot, or, as tradition says, place it in the catacombs of the Roman city.

There was something befitting and appropriate in the Great Apostle of the Gentiles thus dying in the Gentile capital; nor can we regret the uncertainty that exists in marking the place of his burial. His true mausoleum is in the souls of the millions on millions who have read, and prayed, and rejoiced over his words. In one of the noblest of human temples—one, too, which bears the name of the Apostle-martyr (our own St Paul's in London)—few have failed to note the inscription on the monument to its illustrious architect, placed immediately under the dome. The spot where the dust of PAUL reposes is under no temple made with hands, but under the blue vault of an Italian sky, in the centre of the civilised world;—that world which, in one sense, he has made "consecrated ground;" for its remotest shores *have* listened, or *are* listening, to the echoes of his undying voice, and receiving his apostolic benediction. The Church may well inscribe on his Roman tomb, as she looks to the nations he has thus Christianised—the wide realms which, under God, he has made happier—

"SI MONUMENTUM REQUIRIS, CIRCUMSPICE!"

His own humility was content with a lowlier motto—

"To me to live is Christ, and to die is gain!"

"The pains of death are past;
Labour and sorrow cease;
And, life's long warfare closed at last,
His soul is found in peace!

"Soldier of Christ, well done!
Praise be thy new employ;
And while eternal ages run,
Rest in thy Saviour's joy."

THE END

www.ingramcontent.com/pod-product-compliance
Lightning Source LLC
LaVergne TN
LVHW021139110826
845150LV00005B/1069